THE EROTIC MARGIN

The Erotic Margin

Sexuality and Spatiality in Alteritist Discourse

İRVİN CEMİL SCHICK

VERSO

London • New York

First published by Verso 1999
© İrvin Cemil Schick 1999
All rights reserved

The moral rights of the author have been asserted

Verso
UK: 6 Meard Street, London W1V 3HR
US: 180 Varick Street, New York, NY 10014–4606

Verso is the imprint of New Left Books

ISBN 1–85984–732–3

British Library Cataloguing in Publication Data
A catalogue record for this book is available from the British Library

Library of Congress Cataloging-in-Publication Data
Schick. İrvin C. (İrvin Cemil)
    The erotic margin : sexuality and spatiality in alteritist discourse
/ İrvin Cemil Schick.
        p.   cm.
    Includes bibliographical references (p.) and index.
    ISBN 1–85984–732–3
    1. Sex.   2. Gender identity.   3. Identity (Psychology).   I. Title.
HQ21.S315 1999
306.7—dc21   99–17439
                                                                CIP
Typeset by SetSystems Ltd, Saffron Walden, Essex
Printed by Biddles Ltd, Guildford and King's Lynn

Contents

Illustrations

Erotic print by Thomas Rowlandson (1756–1827). Courtesy of the Victoria and Albert Museum. An especially graphic example of the conflation of sexuality and spatiality in alteritist discourse. p. xii.

Frontispiece of Pétrus Durel's *La Femme dans les colonies françaises* (Paris, 1898). Author's collection. An imperial vision of bodies and artifacts. p. 18.

Title page of Michel Baudier's *Histoire générale de la religion des Turcs* (Paris, 1625). Courtesy of the Henry Charles Lea Library, Special Collections, Van Pelt-Dietrich Library, University of Pennsylvania. Sexuality as a technology of difference in the juxtaposition of Islam and Christianity. p. 42.

Illustration from Carl Heinrich Stratz's *Die Rassenschönheit des Weibes* (Stuttgart, 1911). Author's collection. Such charts purporting to depict the proportions of women of different races endow this book with a thin veneer of scientific authority. p. 76.

Frontispiece of Gustave Le Rouge's *Encyclopédie de l'amour: Turquie* (Paris, 1912). Author's collection. Somewhere between phobia and fantasy: white women in bondage. p. 104.

Frontispiece of *The Book of Exposition in the Science of Complete and Perfect Coition* (Paris, 1900), based on a work by Suyūṭī. Author's collection.

One of the many translations and imitations of "oriental" works that set the tone of the representation of harem women. p. 176.

Frontispiece of the German edition of the anonymous *L'Odalisque* ("Konstantinopel," 1797). Author's collection. A thoroughly western interior, with turban and veil as signifiers of extra-territoriality. p. 196.

Photograph by the C. & G. Zangaki brothers (active from the 1870s on). Collection of Mohammed B. Alwan. The broken glass negative provides a seductive metaphor for the necessity of shattering hegemonic conceptions of space to make room for new, emancipating ones. p. 228.

Acknowledgments

This study owes much to Carter Umbarger, who helped me think about self and place, and to Amila Buturović, who challenged me.

I am grateful to Şavkar Altınel, Zeynep Çelik, Carter V. Findley, Cemal Kafadar, E. Ann Kaplan, Nilüfer İsvan, Margaret Ševčenko, and Zeynep Yonsel Ergün for reading versions or parts of the manuscript and giving me the benefit of their comments and criticism.

For granting me access to sources or supplying me with material, I thank the Houghton, Schlesinger, and Widener Libraries, and the Libraries of the Gray Herbarium and Arnold Arboretum at Harvard University; the Hayden and Rotch Libraries at the Massachusetts Institute of Technology; the Clapp Library Special Collections at Wellesley College; the New York Public Library; the British Library; and the Bibliothèque Nationale de France; as well as Mohammed B. Alwan, András Riedlmayer, and Clifford J. Scheiner. For permission to reproduce illustrations, I thank the Victoria and Albert Museum; the Henry Charles Lea Library, Special Collections, Van Pelt-Dietrich Library, University of Pennsylvania; and Mohammed B. Alwan.

I also wish to acknowledge K. Pelin Başcı, Benjamin Braude, Stefano Casadei, Fatma Müge Göçek, Judith Feher Gurewich, Nimet Pamir Gündoğan, Güven Güzeldere, Barak Kalfuss, Hasan Kayalı, Roni Margulies, Hatice Örün Öztürk, Ginan Raouf, Geoffrey J. Roper, and Sara

Yontan for providing information, suggesting sources, or helping me reach or interpret them. Last but not least, I thank Michael Sprinker, and Gillian Beaumont and Colin Robinson of Verso, for making the publication of this book a smooth, indeed enjoyable, process.

The separation between east and west is as old as Europa's abduction by the bull.

George Allgrove
Love in the East

[I]dentity acquires its satisfying solidity because of the effervescence of the continuously sexualized border, because of the turbulent forces, sexual and spiritual, that the border not so much contains as emits.

Michael Taussig
Mimesis and Alterity

Outside and inside form a dialectic of division, the obvious geometry of which blinds us as soon as we bring it into play in metaphorical domains. . . . Unless one is careful, it is made into a basis of images that govern all thoughts of positive and negative.

Gaston Bachelard
The Poetics of Space

[O]ne must understand the cause of the humanly made world through some knowledge of what *making* involves, and compare the unconscious making of the civic world to the conscious making of humanistic and theoretical truths.

Donald Kunze
Thought and Place

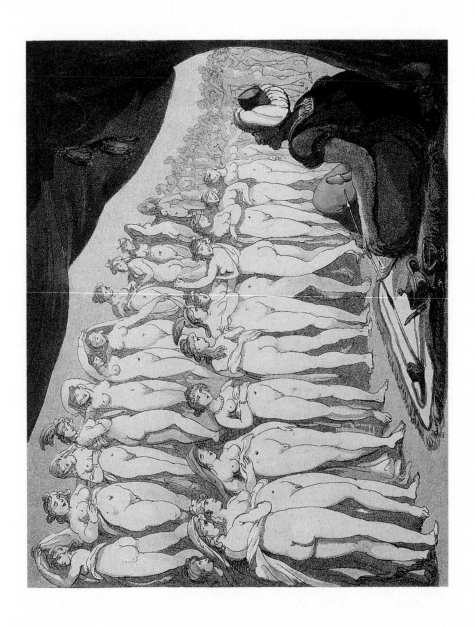

Introduction:
Spatiality and Sexuality

A whole history remains to be written of *spaces*—which would at the same time be the history of *powers* (both these terms in the plural)—from the great strategies of geo-politics to the little tactics of the habitat. (Foucault, 1980b: 149)

Sexuality is not the most intractable element in power relations, but rather one of those endowed with the greatest instrumentality: useful for the greatest number of maneuvers and capable of serving as a point of support, as a linchpin, for the most varied strategies. (Foucault, 1978–85, I: 103)

Stealing a figure of speech from Voltaire, it might perhaps be said that if harems and polygyny had not existed in parts of Asia and Africa, Europeans would have had to invent them. But exist they did, and Western attitudes towards Turkey, and Islam generally, have, for several centuries, been shaped by a combination of moral outrage and irrepressible concupiscence focused on the trope of "oriental sexuality."

Deploying an entire arsenal of fictionalized devices such as the harem, the public bath, the slave market, concubines, eunuchs, polygamy, and homosexuality, this theme gained a significant place in European visual and verbal artistic production beginning in the eighteenth century.[1] Although this phenomenon is frequently noted by

[1] These motifs are, of course, far too ubiquitous for my claim to require substantiation. Published surveys range from Huart and Tazi, 1980 and Croutier, 1989—the latter, an

present-day critics, it is explained only too often in rather unidimensional terms, primarily as a masculinist metonymic expression of the West's drive to possess the world. In fact, while it undoubtedly did serve that purpose as well, the sexuality of the "other" was a trope that played a much more central and much more polyvalent role in Western thought than is usually acknowledged. In failing to consider this variability, one runs the risk of reproducing both colonial and gender constructions of difference. In other words, positing a rigid correlation between male/female and colonizer/colonized not only perpetuates such gender stereotypes as active/passive or aggressor/victim, but furthermore leads, as Sara Suleri has argued, "to interpretive intransigence of a different order, through which an attempt to recognize marginality leads to an apposite replication of the uncrossable distance between margin and center." (Suleri, 1992: 15.)

The mirror image of the feminization of the colonized in feminist theory, namely the tendency to analyze patriarchal oppression through the paradigm of colonization, is likewise highly problematical. Once again, it takes too much for granted, and fails to recognize that both gender and colonialism are contested and contradictory. Indeed, their histories argue eloquently for the necessity—both political and theoretical—of abandoning the notion of gender identity as fixed and coherent, viewing it instead as "a site of conflicting subjective processes." (Donaldson, 1992: 6.) Thus, both feminist and post-colonial theories require a much more nuanced reading of the functions of gender and sexuality in the tropology of colonial discourse.

The last two decades have witnessed a shift away from the study of the mechanics of colonialism, towards a confrontation with the mental and significational structures that animated it. This is very much a part of a broader intellectual undertaking: with the decline of the modernist project, and the concomitant eclipsing of its avowedly ecumenical, but in actual fact highly class-, gender-, and race-specific claims to universality, attention has increasingly been focused on the unspoken and

---

embarrassingly uncritical rehash of every shopworn cliché imaginable—to Judy Mabro's very useful anthology, *Veiled Half-Truths: Western Travellers' Perceptions of Middle Eastern Women* (1991).

unwritten axioms underlying the great themes and narratives of post-Enlightenment Europe. Synthesizing earlier critiques and articulating powerful new ones, Edward W. Said's *Orientalism* (1978) constitutes a milestone in the deconstruction of European perspectives on "other" societies.[2] Although Said has been deservedly criticized for ascribing far too much coherence to his subject matter, and consequently neglecting or marginalizing some of its important constituents,[3] his work not only altered the course of cultural studies but also spawned a dynamic new field of critical writing, informed both by a burning need to challenge the arrogant solipsism of Eurocentric colonial and neo-colonial knowledge, and by deep epistemological concerns regarding the relation between knowledge and power, the modes of production of knowledge, and the role of representation in those modes of production.

Although Said only made passing reference to gender, later commentators such as Malek Alloula, Alison Blunt, Julia V. Douthwaite, Sarah Graham-Brown, Rana Kabbani, Billie Melman, Sara Mills, Jenny Sharpe, Margaret Strobel, Trinh T. Minh-ha, and others have either focused on the representation of women in orientalist (or, more generally, alteritist) discourse, or have investigated representations of the "other" *by* women. In so doing, they have begun the process of remedying a long-standing blind spot. Yet, and notwithstanding their unquestionable importance, these studies share to varying degrees a certain particularism, in that they each focus on a small subset of a much more general problem, and, like the proverbial blind men and the elephant, tend to generalize without the benefit of the overall picture.

To a certain extent, this reflects the limitations of some present-day scholarship on gender: for many researchers, studying gender means studying women, so that the domain of colonialism offers two more or less orthogonal areas of inquiry—native women and the feminization of colonies on the one hand, and European women and their role in race relations in the colonies on the other. Although a great deal of

[2] Publication dates appearing in the text, when they do not match those in the bibliography, denote the first edition in any language.
[3] For useful surveys of the critiques of Said's *Orientalism*, see Mani and Frankenberg, 1985; Sivan, 1985.

very interesting and valuable work has been conducted in each of these areas, it seems to me that the role played in the colonial project by *gender* as a category has not been adequately addressed. For example, are there commonalities between these two areas of inquiry? What are the flip-sides of native women (European men) and European women (native men) and how do they function in this representational universe? What about relations between native men and women, or, for that matter, between European and native men? Rather than trying to reverse centuries of masculinist neglect in social and cultural studies by privileging women, focusing on gender proper is more likely to shed some light upon the way in which the male-female axis was deployed throughout Europe's exploration and colonization of the rest of the world. It is necessary to go beyond a view of colonialism as purely masculine/masculinist, and to focus on the polymorphous ways in which gender and sexuality have historically structured colonial texts in both their production and reception. (Mills, 1993:198; Mills, 1994.)

Despite the large number of studies commenting on the various forms taken by gender and sexuality in colonial discourse, ranging from titillating accounts of harem life and the seduction of oriental women at one end of the spectrum, to captivity narratives and propaganda exploiting the so-called "sexual fear" at the other, the *unity* (which is not to say "invariance") of this discourse has not been adequately recognized. Take the example of Helen Carr's interesting study of the conflation of femininity and Indian-ness in New World narratives. Carr begins by stating that "colonialist, racist and sexist discourses have continually reinforced, naturalized and legitimized each other during the process of European colonization," and that "the model of the power relationships between men and women has been used to structure and articulate the relationship" of Europeans and colonized peoples so that "the difference man/woman provided a fund of images and topoi by which the difference European/non-European could be politically accommodated." Having made these very fitting observations, she then goes on to qualify captivity tales as "reversals," rather than seeing them as instances of a multifaceted totality. (Carr,

1985: 2: 46, 52.)[4] I would claim otherwise: it is not that the Orient/
Other was as a rule feminized (although this happened often enough),
but rather that gender and sexuality were deployed in various ways in
colonial discourse, to construct "the imaginative spaces that non-
Western peoples occupy and the tropes and stories that organize their
existence in Western minds." (Lutz and Collins, 1993: 2.) In this way, a
geography of contrasts was created that served both Europe's self-
definition and its imperial agenda.

Any mention of geography brings to the fore the question of
spatiality, a notion that is *implicit* in virtually all of post-colonial criticism, but is made *explicit* considerably less frequently. The idea that
place is not a neutral/inert location in which social relations unfold,
but that it rather both structures, and is in turn structured by, these
relations, has by now entered the counter-canon. To quote Edward
Soja's succinct summary:

> Spatiality is a substantiated and recognizable social product, part of a "second
> nature" which incorporates as it socializes and transforms both physical and
> psychological spaces.
> As a social product, spatiality is simultaneously the medium and outcome,
> presupposition and embodiment, of social action and relationship.
> The spatio-temporal structuring of social life defines how social action and
> relationship (including class relations) are materially constituted, made
> concrete. (Soja, 1989: 129.)[5]

It follows, therefore, that in contrast to physical space pure and simple,
places are not "objective" realities but exist only through particular
human spatial experiences. Social space must be viewed as more than
either a neutral medium for social practices or their passive resultant;

[4] On feminization and the discourse of discovery, see also Adorno, 1988; and Zamora,
1990–91. Noting that "when the Columbian texts of discovery are viewed as a unified
discourse and not in isolation from one another, these tropes of difference reveal a
hermeneutical strategy of feminization and eroticization that ultimately makes gender
difference the determining characteristic of the sign 'the Indies,'" Zamora argues that
this gender-coding permits not only a hierarchically informed characterization of natives
relative to Spaniards, but also the articulation of ambivalence wherein they are both
idealized and denigrated. (130, 143–4, 146.)

[5] For a different direction pursued in the reassertion of anthropocentricism, indeed
subjectivism, in geography, see Rodaway, 1994.

rather, it is "an active, constitutive, irreducible, necessary component in the social's composition." (Keith and Pile, 1993: 36.)

But given the complexity of the social, dissected as it is by myriad cleavages, how can one speak of spatiality in the singular? Surely there must exist a multiplicity of spaces—"cross-cutting, intersecting, aligning with one another, or existing in relations of paradox or antagonism." (Massey, 1994: 3.) In turn, there must be ways in which these multiple spaces can be differentiated, qualified, conceptualized, pitted against one another. This is the problem I address in this book.

The view of space as an active and constitutive component of the social has not yet been fully assimilated into social science practice. Spatial units are generally treated as given, and the socio-political forces underlying their selection or construction are not questioned. As Alexander B. Murphy writes, although "regional settings are social constructs that are themselves implicated in that which is being examined," too often "the regional framework is presented essentially as a backdrop for a discussion of regional change, with little consideration given to why the region came to be a socially significant spatial unit in the first place, how the region is understood and viewed by its inhabitants [or, for that matter, by people who live elsewhere], or how and why that understanding has changed over time." (Murphy, 1991: 24.) It is necessary, in other words, to problematize regionalization itself. That, however, is beyond the scope of the present volume: I do not go into the reasons for which the various regions discussed in this study— "Europe," "the Middle East," "Africa," "the New World"—are socially significant, nor into the historical (socio-economic, political) processes that led to their emergence; I hope, however, at least to shed some light on some of the ways in which they were, and continue to be, *conceptualized as distinct spatial units.*

As should be clear from this brief introduction, this book is written from an essentially social constructionist point of view.[6] It assumes, therefore, that a person's everyday relation to surrounding space is mediated by a complex edifice of shared significational structures that owe their existence to social practices; and it sets out to analyze some

---

[6] On the social constructionist perspective, see Berger and Luckmann, 1966.

of the tools with which this edifice is erected. Whether ancient or modern, societies know and signify themselves by telling themselves stories. The fundamental building blocks of these societal narratives, or their basic significational units, are myths. In particular, spatial myths have played a growing role in Europe during the modern period. The essence of spatial myths is difference—or, to be more specific, geographically structured difference. They embody beliefs that revolve around imagined contrasts between the "here" and the "there," and sexuality has been an important tool for encoding these contrasts.

In other words, gender and especially sexuality are fundamental (imputed) attributes of socially constructed space. Sexualized images of women *and* of men were used, in Europe's discourses of the other, as key markers of place, and hence as determinants of identity and alterity. To put it another way, and somewhat figuratively, the Linnean system of botanical taxonomy, which was based upon the reproductive organs of plants, was unsystematically extended, from the eighteenth century onward, to cover the sexual mores of peoples (nations, races) on the one hand, and places (regions, continents) on the other.[7] Thus, sexual tropes were among the building blocks with which a political discourse of spatiality was constructed.

Why "political"? As Keith and Pile write, "all spatialities are political because they are the (covert) medium and (disguised) expression of assymetrical relations of power." (Keith and Pile, 1993: 38, 220.) But, some might protest, sexuality is first and foremost the domain of psychology. In a study of European attitudes towards non-European peoples, Henri Baudet differentiated between "two relations, separate but indivisible"—the "concrete" world of political relations, and the psychological relations that only exist "in the minds of men." (Baudet, 1965: 6.) But the psychological and social/political realms need not (indeed, cannot) be distinguished from each other, as Gilles Deleuze and Félix Guattari (not to mention Wilhelm Reich) have shown.[8]

---

[7] See Linné, 1775, chapters 5 and 6. For a discussion of the relationship between Linnean taxonomy and travel writing, see Pratt, 1992, chapter 2.

[8] Indeed, Robert J.C. Young has recently proposed the Deleuze-Guattari model as a framework for the analysis of colonialism; see Young, 1995, chapter 7. On colonialism

Though spatiality and sexuality evidently figure prominently in people's psychological makeup, psychology is only relevant to the present study insofar as it overlaps with the political; it is not the individual that concerns me here, but the social. While I fully recognize that the two are not independent, I believe that the relationship between them, not unlike that between ontogeny and philogeny, is more problematical than it is sometimes claimed to be.

As space is humanized and infused with meaning, sites or groups of sites acquire symbolic significances and become metaphors for particular states of mind or value systems. In this manner:

> *real spaces are hypostatised into the symbolic realm of imaginary space relations.* The world is cognitively territorialized so that on the datum of physical geographic knowledge, the world is recoded as a set of spaces and places which are infinitely shaded with connotative characteristics and emotive associations. ... The resulting formation—half topology, half metaphor—is inscribed as an emotive ordering or *coded geography.* It is enacted in ritual, as gesture, and encoded in further guiding metaphors which define our relationship to the world. (Shields, 1991: 29, 264–5.)[9]

In other words, places have significances that transcend their physical/geographical characteristics, and these significances mediate our relations with our environment. But how does this come to be? How do places acquire these layers of meaning?

Foucault has introduced the term "technology" to denote the discursive tools with which knowledge of social realities and institutions is constructed, focusing on the technologies of power, sex, order, and so forth. In a paper delivered shortly before his death, he referred to "the different ways in our culture that humans develop knowledge about themselves" as "technologies," which, he argued, are of four types:

---

seen primarily from a psychological viewpoint, in addition to the well-known works of Frantz Fanon, Octave Mannoni, and Albert Memmi, see Nandy, 1983, chapter 1.

[9] An interesting application of such ideas can be found in recent debates on the concept of landscape in geography, and the argument that landscapes are not neutral physical objects but socially constructed representations. See, for instance, Cosgrove, 1985; Cosgrove and Daniels, 1988; Short, 1991. For a very interesting meditation on the interrelations between aesthetic and everyday constructions of space, see Harbison, 1977.

(1) technologies of production, which permit us to produce, transform, or manipulate things; (2) technologies of sign systems, which permit us to use signs, meanings, symbols, or signification; (3) technologies of power, which determine the conduct of individuals and submit them to certain ends or domination, an objectivizing of the subject; (4) technologies of the self, which permit individuals to effect by their own means or with the help of others a certain number of operations on their own bodies and souls, thoughts, conduct, and way of being, so as to transform themselves in order to attain a certain sense of happiness, purity, wisdom, perfection, or immortality. These four types of technologies hardly ever function separately, although each one of them is associated with a certain type of domination. (Foucault, 1988: 18.)

This terminology (and analytical approach) has been further developed in interesting directions: thus, for example, starting from the premises that "gender is (a) representation" and "the representation of gender *is* its construction," Teresa de Lauretis has put forward the notion of "technology of gender" to describe the discursive instruments and strategies by means of which gender is socially constructed and reconstructed. (De Lauretis, 1987: 3.) In this vein, I suggest using the term *technology of place* to describe the discursive instruments and strategies by means of which space is constituted as place, that is, place is socially constructed and reconstructed. Similar terminology has already been used in the literature, at least implicitly: for instance, Shields writes of "the specific technologies of manipulation and formation of everyday spatial notions and practices." (Shields, 1991: 8.) What I hope to do here is first to formalize this notion to some degree, and second to analyze just a few of the many technologies with which space has been, and is, socially constructed.

As Henri Lefebvre writes in his pioneering book *La Production de l'espace* [The production of space] (1974), "it is not the work of a moment for a society to generate (produce) an appropriated social space in which it can achieve a form by means of self-presentation and self-representation. . . . This act of creation is, in fact, a *process*." (Lefebvre, 1991: 34.) I refer, then, to the means of production of social space, that is, to the vehicles through which this process is effected, as "technologies of place," and argue that gendered and sexualized xenological[10] discourse is first and foremost a technology of place; this, I submit, both explains the highly variable forms that this discourse has taken in modern history, and sets forth the common thread that runs through these different forms.

It is difficult, if not impossible, to find precise and unique answers to such complex questions as "How is colonial discourse gendered?" or "How did women travellers' depictions of the Orient differ from men's?" After all, can one really compare *Robinson Crusoe* (1719) with Flaubert's nineteenth-century tales of Egyptian brothel-hopping?[11] Does it make sense to bunch together Lady Mary Wortley Montagu and Cristina Trivulzio, Princess of Belgiojoso, merely on the basis of their sex?[12] Instead of attempting such an undertaking, I focus on the multifaceted role of gender and sexuality in Europe's consciousness of the rest of the world, and attempt to formulate a framework into which these highly variable manifestations can be packed relatively comfortably. To this end, my analysis is limited not to women (native or European) in relation to men (European or native), but rather to natives (men and women) in relation to Europeans (men and women), as well as each other.

My focus is primarily on an ephemeral element of Western culture, namely erotic writings produced in Europe (and to a lesser extent in North America), but staged in or otherwise related to the Middle East and particularly Turkey. I must emphasize that the often posited distinction between erotica and pornography does not seem intellectually

[10] In using the term "xenology" I follow Harbsmeier, 1985, who takes it in turn from Wilhelm Halbfass. Along similar lines, I use *xenotopia* as shorthand for foreign or "other" lands.

[11] On the former, see for example Hulme, 1992; on the latter, see Flaubert, 1972.

[12] The proto-feminist writings of Lady Montagu are fairly well known; by contrast, the racist and misogynistic Principessa Barbiano di Belgiojoso (1808–71) is somewhat more obscure. For more information, see Desmet-Grégoire, 1983. For an interesting investigation of whether or not there is a specificity to women's travel writing, based in part on a reading of Lady Montagu, see Orr, 1994. For an essay that problematizes the political capital made by some Eurocentric feminists of Western women travellers' experiences, see Kaplan, 1995.

sustainable to me, and stems, in my judgment, from the dual wish to repress or control sexually explicit material while at the same time taking care not to offend liberal sensibilities. Since I share neither of these concerns, I use the two terms interchangeably. Although I originally set out to analyze erotica *per se*, it soon became clear that separating this literary genre from certain others—say, travelogues or ethnographies—that are rather less ingenuous about their sexual content is perhaps artificial; I have therefore allowed myself to be quite eclectic in my choice of material. However, I have chosen not to use visual sources, such as orientalist painting about which so much has been written lately,[13] nor to dwell at length on the well-known works of "great" writers, concentrating instead on the relatively unknown books often printed "for subscribers only" and distributed "privately." This choice is not meant to endorse the subdivision of culture into "high" and "low," and the canonization of the former—a practice which has, in any event, lost much of its legitimacy in recent years.[14] Rather, it reflects a *recognition* of this subdivision as constructed in the past, a recognition motivated by the fact that the popular (if not mass) culture of early erotica has suffered from considerable neglect.

For example, not one of the contributors to John M. MacKenzie's interesting volume *Imperialism and Popular Culture* (1986) dwells on erotica, despite the broad variety of subjects covered—ranging from Boy Scouts and juvenilia to journalism and propaganda, from the Empire Marketing Board and the British Broadcasting Company to cinema and popular representations of military campaigns. Worse, in an otherwise excellent book that probes the role of colonies and colonialism in the construction of European middle-class sensibilities, Ann Laura Stoler feels compelled to introduce her discussion of a work about Javanese women by Carl Heinrich Stratz (whose pseudo-encyclopedic book on women of all races I briefly discuss in chapter 3) with an apologia, declaring in a long footnote that while she is omitting "both the photos accompanying that piece and its most explicit descriptive obscenities,"

---

[13] On gender and sexuality in orientalist art, see for example Luebbers, 1993; Thornton, 1985.
[14] On the benefits of focusing on "minor" rather than canonical texts, see for example Rousseau and Porter, 1988: 9–11.

she "do[es] not hold that such pornographic texts should be buried or effaced from view." (Stoler, 1995: 184.)[15] This assertion seems so self-evident, that its articulation—and in a book on race and sexuality, no less!—provides food for thought as to the political pressures under which the academy labors nowadays.

Since they often enjoyed relatively limited circulation, the primary significance of works of xenological erotica lies not in the breadth of their influence, but rather in the fact that they present perhaps the purest, most distilled examples of the eroticization of the Orient and its inhabitants. As such, they both reflect and no doubt to some extent also contributed to a discourse that used gendered and sexualized language and imagery to construct a representation of world geopolitics and support the colonial enterprise.

In Part I, "Identity, Alterity, and Place," I propose an analytical framework for approaching the expansive and variegated literature in which foreign places and peoples are gendered and sexualized.

I begin by arguing, in chapter 1, "Constructing Self and World," that perceptions of the self are not simple truths unproblematically reflecting a material reality, but discursive constructions in which societal views, norms, and assumptions are (as it were) made flesh. I suggest that these perceptions are contained and stabilized through narrative, the medium by and through which social groups tell themselves and each other the stories and myths that give their existence coherence and meaning. I also note that identity is constructed as a dialectic in which the "other" plays a determining role as the antithesis, an embodiment of characteristics disavowed by the self that thereby paradoxically mirrors the self. Finally, I contend that notions of self and other are inextricably linked to notions of "here" and "there," and that the practice of constructing the self is therefore also a practice of reconstructing space in a manner that is socially meaningful and comprehensible. I

---

[15] Through a simultaneous reclaiming and critique of the place of colonialism in the work of Foucault, Stoler investigates the implicit racial grammar that underwrote the sexual regimes of bourgeois culture, showing that bourgeois sexuality and racialized sexuality were not distinct but "dependent constructs in a unified field." (Stoler, 1995: 97.) This book unfortunately appeared after most of the present text had been written, and I have only touched upon it briefly, in a handful of footnotes.

discuss the spatial narratives by means of which this has been accomplished in modern Europe, and stress the fundamental role played in their constitution by imperialism.

In chapter 2, "Spaces of Otherness," I focus on the discursive tools with the aid of which space is infused with meaning and made into place. I highlight the intimate relationship between the social construction of space and societal disparities of power, and suggest that place reflects and in turn reproduces power relations. I show that seemingly dissimilar stereotypes and binary oppositions can mutually reinforce each other, and in particular that sexuality has been a central instrument in the construction of spatial differentiation. I argue that the abstracting, archetype-making impulse present in much erotic writing is singularly well suited to that function. Finally, I underscore the conflation of spatial and temporal alterity in modern European discourse, and show that sexuality is made into a historical invariant that can be used to characterize East and West, North and South, self and other, here and there.

In Part II, "Inscriptions of Gender and Sexuality," I turn to concrete instances where geographical difference is gendered and sexualized.

In chapter 3, "Ethnopornography," I discuss the anthropological mode in sexually explicit literature and review the large body of writing that focuses on the sexual practices of "other" peoples. I show that this mode has its roots in medieval polemics against Islam and also in the travel literature, where an economy of meaning gradually took shape in which both traveller and destination were coded in unmistakably gendered and sexualized terms. I stress the variable, often mutually contradictory nature of these codes, and suggest that this incoherence is not a failing but a strength of alteritist discourse, whose driving force is epistemological rather than ontological.

I attempt to formulate a taxonomy of the sexual tropes in alteritist discourse in chapter 4, "Gendered Geography, Sexualized Empire." Providing examples ranging from the New World to India, the Middle East to black Africa, and the South Sea Islands to the Barbary Coast, I discuss instances where foreign women are alternatingly portrayed as sexually alluring or threatening, foreign men as effeminate weaklings or dangerous rapists, foreign lands as sexual idylls or hearts of darkness.

I underscore recurring themes such as masturbation, child sexuality, pathology, and miscegenation, in an effort to present both the enormous variability that characterizes this literature, and the underlying logic that permeates and unifies it.

Finally, in Part III, "Harem Women in Western Erotica," I focus as a case study on the representation of Muslim women in sexually explicit European writing.

I begin by discussing translations and pseudo-translations of "oriental" works in chapter 5, "Harvesting Clichés." I note that the popularity of works such as the *Thousand and One Nights* led to countless pastiches and imitations that made it very difficult, in their own day, to distinguish genuine translations from outright forgeries—a problem further compounded by the proliferation of fake foreign imprints from the eighteenth century on. Between this confusion, European writers' tendency to encourage their readers' fertile imaginations through innuendo, and the fact that even genuine translations were given literalist interpretations quite unwarranted in their original settings, I suggest that translations were an important source of stereotypes concerning harem women.

In chapter 6, "Thinly Veiled References," I describe some of the most common sexual tropes in this literature. These include the device of representing harem inmates as Europeans (and therefore in a certain sense safe); the tendency to portray them as unindividuated pluralities; the careful attention given to their grooming practices such as the application of henna and the depilation of pubic hair; the great popularity of images such as the Turkish bath and the slave market; the wildly exaggerated notions of harem women's sexual desires, including accounts of homosexuality, bestiality, and masturbation; and their characterization as scheming and devious. My purpose is once again to highlight the logic of variability that unifies sexualized alteritist discourse.

In his essay on Jeremy Bentham's *Panopticon* (1791),[16] from which I

---

[16] Bentham had proposed the "panopticon" as a circular prisonhouse in which authority and control would be exercised through the total, unobstructed visibility of the prisoners situated at the circumference, by the guardian situated at the center.

took the first epigraph of this introduction, Foucault spoke of "the formula of 'power through transparency,' subjection by 'illumination.'" (Foucault, 1980b: 154.) This applies all the more starkly to eroticized depictions of Muslim women, which are so often predicated upon the symbolic violation of the harem, the *making transparent* of its walls and of the veil. In this case, at least, the West's sexual panopticism is indeed the construction of power over the Orient; it is appropriation through voyeurism, subjection by denuding.

I conclude with the observation that the immense variability of narratives of space suggests the possibility of an emancipatory praxis that could potentially lead to the construction of non-hegemonic spatial discourses and practices.

Lefebvre has set forth a triad consisting of *spatial practices* comprising "production and reproduction, and the particular locations and spatial sets characteristic of each social formation"; *representations of space* related "to the relations of production and to the 'order' which those relations impose, and hence to knowledge, to signs, to codes, and to 'frontal' relations"; and *representational spaces* "embodying complex symbolisms, sometimes coded, sometimes not, linked to the clandestine or underground side of social life, as also to art." (Lefebvre, 1991: 33, 38–9.) My analysis cuts across this triad: I am concerned with regions of Europe's representational space (xenological discourse, gender) dedicated to the representation of space (xenotopia, the Orient), and intimately linked to certain spatial practices (colonialism, travel, sexual segregation). I concentrate on one particular element of this complex, the role of gender and sexuality in the construction of Europe's sense of self and otherness, spurred by the conviction that the cognitive separation of representation and reality, or of the metaphoric and the literal, are artificial and tend to obscure their mutual constitutivity. Meaning is not immanent, but is rather both marked and "in part *constituted* by the spaces of representation in which it is articulated. These spaces of representation subvert the representation of spaces so that the ground we stand on becomes a mongrel hybrid of spatialities; at once a metaphor and a speaking position, a place of certainty and a burden of humility, sometimes all of these simultaneously, sometimes all of them incommensurably." (Keith and Pile, 1993: 23.) Understanding the social construction of place, then, means understanding the ways in which we construct our selves.

My goal is not to re-place "subverted" representations of space with "correct" ones, but rather to explore some of the ways in which representations of space and spaces of representation partake in the construction of meaning and of geopolitical power. As bell hooks writes, "'the politics of location' necessarily calls those of us who would participate in the formation of counter-hegemonic cultural practice to identify the spaces where we begin the process of re-vision." (hooks, 1990: 145.) A clearer understanding of the ways in which sexuality inflects spatiality, in other words, is of more than intellectual interest: the decoding of hegemonic constructions of space is but a first step towards constructing emancipatory ones.

Part I

Identity, Alterity, and Place

La Femme
DANS LES
Colonies Françaises
PAR Petrus Durel.

1

Constructing Self and World

Identity is the socially constructed, socially sanctioned (or at least recognized) complex of self-significations deriving from an individual's membership in such collectivities as class, race, gender, sexuality, generation, region, ethnicity, religion, and nation. It plays a decisive role in human behavior: one acts from a certain positionality and in accordance with a certain worldview or set of values, interpreting data with the help of certain preconceptions or mental models, and reacting to them within certain parameters—all these deeply rooted in identity. At the same time, identity is never "complete"; rather, it is always under construction. To put it more explicitly, identity is not an object but a *process*. Furthermore, this process is not even: times of crisis or transition are often periods of particularly intensive identity construction. Thus, paraphrasing de Lauretis's formulation for gender, we can say that *identity is (a) representation, and the representation of identity, whether to oneself or to others, is in fact its very construction.*

In a critical overview of constructionist perspectives on the self, Ian Burkitt (1994) contrasts those who give primacy to language, that is to say the textual and discursive, such as Derrida and Foucault, with those who hold that lived experience and social relations shape the self, like Bourdieu and Norbert Elias. But why must these two alternatives be mutually exclusive? In what way are lived experience and social relations non-discursive? As I argue later in this chapter, the dualistic opposition of the discursive and the material is itself a historical artifact, which vanishes once it is recognized that no human experience can be viewed independently of the system of significations within which it is lived. Derrida's "text" need not be a *deus ex machina*: it is rewritten continuously by the very human practices that it shapes. There is no Kantian "transcendental subject" here; only a dialectic within which the self perpetually shapes and is reshaped.

Identity, therefore, comes to be through enactment, through performance, that is, through practices that construct it using a host of discursive instruments which might be called "technologies of identity." The image of a theatrical performance immediately brings to mind Erving Goffman's *The Presentation of Self in Everyday Life* (1956), in which he turned to dramaturgical principles to explain how individuals behave in the presence of others so as to conjure a certain image of themselves and thereby influence the outcome of the social intercourse in which they engage, and how the audience's response is also factored into the resulting performance. The self, according to Goffman, "is not an organic thing that has a specific location, whose fundamental fate is to be born, to mature, and to die; it is a dramatic effect arising diffusely from a scene that is presented," and bears the marks of the actor, the audience, and the stage. (Goffman, 1959: 252–3.)[1] Like Goffman, I argue that the performance of identity *is* its construction; I do not, however, postulate an independent will, an *ur*-self, which consciously chooses the play to be staged and recites its lines. In Goffman's formulation as I understand it, the performance appears to be an epiphenomenon of such an *ur*-self, and it is this latter that is presented, transparently or artifactually depending on the subject's intentions. True, the final outcome is determined by factors not entirely under the actor's control, but to call the *resultant* the "self" rather than the force that animates it seems to be a matter of definition. I am concerned not with the *persona* resulting from one's interaction with one's environment, that is, the way one "comes across" in society, but rather with how one defines oneself relative to surrounding collectivities.

Though identity is a permanent process of construction and reconstruction, this fluid or mutable nature does not mean that it never enjoys any stability. Clearly, a person's identity does not vary significantly from day to day, so that there must be a slowly varying envelope

---

[1] David Bell and Gill Valentine extend the idea to sexuality as a performative construction; see Bell and Valentine, 1995a.

containing (and constraining) the vicissitudes of self-enactment. This envelope is narrative: "while identity does not rest upon sameness or essence, it does acquire durability and permanence according to the stories we tell ourselves and others about our history." (Harvey, 1993: 59.) To be sure, this "durability and permanence" is only relative, a sustained period of construction (or sequence of reconstructions); nevertheless, narrative plays a central role in the constitution and preservation of identity. It is a carrier of meaning, the channel through which an individual tells him/herself and others the tale of his/her place in the world. It provides the self with inertia, endowing it with some measure of temporal continuity.

Human beings are social creatures, and from early childhood onward, narratives are an intrinsic part of their communal existence: "Individuals are born into a collective discourse comprising prohibitions, commands, roles, value judgements, exempla, fairy tales, and so on, which are absorbed through parents, school, the media, and other social institutions." It is through narrative that they receive "an unconscious pattern of cultural conditioning, a grammar of structuration, about which [they] reflect as little as about the grammar of [their] mother tongue." In other words, what may be called (inspired by Fredric Jameson) a "social unconscious," an informal body of knowledge that determines the limits of the possible and provides individuals with roadmaps to the societal landscape, is acquired, reproduced, and transmitted through narrative. Indeed, not only do such patterns or structures determine individuals' behavior in the world, they also define their identities: "In imposing a narrative pattern upon our experience and ideas, we create the meaning and significance of our lives and ourselves. In giving shape and form we determine sequence, allocate polarities, institute hierarchy, and thus reproduce the predetermined semantic blueprint of our culture. . . . [T]he world and the 'self' are mediated through the formal and semantic patterns this grammar of structuration imposes." (Boheemen, 1987: 13–14.)

Identity is its own construction, then, and narrative is the medium through which that construction is realized. But the construction of identity is inseparable from that of alterity—indeed, identity itself only makes sense in juxtaposition with alterity. If we tell ourselves and others the stories of who we are, we also tell those of who we are not. To put it more explicitly, of the infinite multiplicity of characteristics that describe a given group of individuals, it is those that are *unlike* another group that are socially significant—in the measure to which, needless to say, establishing difference between the respective groups serves a social function. Thus, "every version of an 'other,' wherever found, is also the construction of a 'self' . . . Cultural *poesis*—and politics—is the constant reconstitution of selves and others through specific exclusions, conventions, and discursive practices." (Clifford, 1986: 23–4.)[2] The construction of identity, therefore, is contingent upon the positing of a negative-identity, an "other," as the repository of opposites. Acknowledged qualities, whether real or imagined, are centered and taken as the norm; simultaneously, rejected qualities, whether real or imagined, are marginalized and exoticized. In short, the "other" is necessary as the "supportive scaffold for meaning and identity." (Boheemen, 1987: 30.)

The dialectic between "self" and "other," or "I" and "not-I," has a long history in European thought, going back at least to the eighteenth century.[3] Furthermore, the notion of *being* as a process (rather than a state), and the constitutive role of difference, have been much commented upon in recent years, particularly in their formulation by Heidegger and Derrida. I will therefore not dwell at length on this point, and only wish to emphasize that the "constitutive outside"—or, to use Bakhtinian terminology, the "transgredient" element of the self[4]—is central to my project. It is in fact precisely some of the ways in which this constitutive outside is *itself* constituted that I discuss in the pages that follow. I hasten to add, however, that this is not intended as an overarching statement about humanity at large. Not all societies conceptualize themselves or their individual members in like fashion,

[2] On passage from an enumeration of difference to a "rhetoric of otherness," see Hartog, 1988: chapter 6. See also Crapanzano, 1992: chapters 3, 4; Tucker, 1990.

[3] See for instance Buber, 1965: 209–24.

[4] The term is borrowed from Jonas Cohen and is used in counterposition to "ingredient" to denote constitutive elements whose origin is external to the self. (Todorov, 1984: 94–5.) On the constitutive role of difference and its connections with the representational episteme, see Stratton, 1990; also Laclau, 1990: chapter 1; Mouffe, 1994: 105–13.

and claims to the universality of the process of "othering" have been convincingly challenged, based upon anthropological and other evidence. Indeed, it would not be surprising at all to find that race, class, gender, or other differences produce different ways of conceptualizing society and its members, and that the significance of "othering" is therefore not a constant even within a given society. My argument is only meant to apply to dominant perspectives in Western Europe during the modern period.

Though "othering" and colonialism often go hand in hand, as we shall see, the discourse of the "other" in Western Europe during the modern period was not merely the intellectual arm of imperialism; equally—as emphasized by Fanon, Said, and others—it played a central role in the process of self-definition. Thus, while a view of alteritism as a rhetoric of control and domination is surely accurate to a certain extent, it is important not to lose sight of the fact that this rhetoric "often exists alongside (behind) a rhetoric of more obscure desires: of sexual desires or fears, of class, or religious, or national, or racial anxieties, of confusion or outright self-loathing." It is, therefore, "not just outer-directed" but "also inner-directed." The simultaneous inner- and outer-directedness of alteritist discourse informs much of the present study.[5]

We have seen that identity is central to human/social praxis; that it is not an artifact but a process, namely its own construction; that it only exists as the dual of alterity; and that both identity and alterity are contained and conveyed through narrative. Let us go one step further: the notions of identity and alterity, of "us" and "them," are closely linked to the sense of place, that is, to the notions of "here" and "there." The intimate relationship between identity and place has recently been the subject of considerable attention.[6] According to J. Nicholas Entrikin, for example, place is a "condition of human experience" since "as actors we are always situated in place and period and

---

[5] See Torgovnick, 1990: 192, where the subject is specifically primitivist discourse. On the role of stereotypes of the "out-group" in constructing the unity of the "in-group," see Allport, 1954: chapters 3 and 4.
[6] See, for example, Carter, Donald, and Squires, 1993; Bammer, 1994; Pile and Thrift, 1995.

... the contexts of our actions contribute to our sense of identity and thus to our sense of centeredness." It follows, Entrikin argues, that "our relations to place and culture become elements in the construction of our individual and collective identities." (Entrikin, 1991: 1, 4.) Similarly, Rob Shields has emphasized the "epistemic and ontological importance" of the spatial, since it is essential to the human experience and conceptualization of reality, truth, and causality. He has suggested that "a 'discourse of space' composed of perceptions of places and regions, of the world as a 'space' and of our relationships with these perceptions[, is] central to our everyday conception of ourselves and of reality." (Shields, 1991: 7.) Place, in other words, is a fundamental element of existence and hence of identity; the self unfolds in space, and therefore bears the indelible traces of the place it calls its "here."

But there is no single "here," nor even a simple "here/there" dichotomy, that defines identity; rather, it is an entire archipelago of places, with which one engages in discursive relationships of inclusion and exclusion, attraction and repulsion, acceptance and rejection. In their *The Politics and Poetics of Transgression* (1986), Peter Stallybrass and Allon White investigated "the question of displacements between *sites* of discourse—the fairground, the marketplace, the coffee-house, the theatre, the slum, the domestic interior of the bourgeois household." Arguing that "*the very drive to achieve a singularity of collective identity is simultaneously productive of unconscious heterogeneity,*" they showed that place plays a crucial role in that process: "The grouping together of sites of discourse, the acceptance and rejection of place, with its laws and protocols and language, is at once a coding of social identity." (Stallybrass and White, 1986: 194, italics mine.) The construction of identity, then, is at the same time the construction of a network of places—some tagged "here," others "there"—which are constituted by and simultaneously reproduce social cleavages such as gender (e.g. domestic and public), race (e.g. suburb and "inner city"), or class (e.g. club and pub).

Clearly, however, the "sites of discourse" with the aid of which European ruling classes defined themselves included not only the domestic social topography but also foreign lands. Indeed, these two were related: not only did race and ethnicity often function as metonyms for class, but class itself was often constructed in terms of racial difference. Noting that "in the European mind the affinity between race and class is . . . palpable," V.G. Kiernan wrote that in many ways, the English gentleman's "attitudes to his own 'lower orders' was identical with that of Europe to the 'lesser breeds.' Discontented native in the colonies, labor agitator in the mills, were the same serpent in alternate disguises. Much of the talk about the barbarism or darkness of the outer world, which it was Europe's mission to rout, was a transmuted fear of the masses at home." (Kiernan, 1969: 316.)[7] Thus, the representation of plebeian spaces such as the slum or the fairground had much in common with that of colonies. I shall return to the construction of such "spaces of otherness" in the next chapter.

The connections between identity, alterity, and place became more acute as the "known" world expanded, and Europe's consciousness became planetary. Increasingly, Europeans "indulged the exotic to redefine their own values and reassure themselves of their own locale as the world grew wider and more complex. Such dialectical reshaping was an inevitable result of increased accessibility." (Rousseau and Porter, 1990: ix.) The broadening of Europe's horizons and multiplying contacts with "different" societies provided not only disparate new objects of knowledge, but also new categories and paradigms. In turn, these categories and paradigms, as well as self-referential ones, assumed positions within an evolutionist hierarchy.[8] Indeed, Europe's exploration of the world during the colonial age was always productive of power assymetries; it followed "patterns [that] posit by definition an inside, a place geographical but also cultural and rhetorical from which all eccentricities were observed, articulated and, in effect, generated." (Pucci, 1990: 148.) The inevitable corollary of this inside was, of course,

[7] George W. Stocking, Jr. similarly writes that "both those who traveled overseas and those who read the literature they produced reacted to the experience of 'savages' abroad . . . in terms of prior experience with the changing class society of Britain." (Stocking, 1987: 234; see also 202, where parallels are drawn between Victorian analyses of the problems of modern urbanization and the "savages.") On the mutually constitutive nature of race and class, see also Lorimer, 1978: chapter 5; McClintock, 1995; Young, 1995; Stoler, 1995: chapter 4.

[8] See for example Street, 1975: chapter 3. On the emergence of taxonomy as a tool of scientific inquiry, and the evolutionism inherent in it, see Foucault, 1973: chapter 5.

an outside. As Europe explored the world, it represented the "other"; as it represented the "other," it defined itself. To paraphrase Gayatri Chakravorty Spivak, this was a process of "consolidating the self of Europe by worlding the world of the Other." (Spivak, 1985: 133.)[9]

But if identity goes hand in hand with place, and if identity further-more only makes sense in the context of alterity, what can one conclude about the relationship between the "here" and the "there"? First and foremost, that these two concepts define each other, by *delimiting* each other: the "there" begins where the "here" ends, and the "here" is where any travel must commence and terminate: "the economy of travel requires an *oikos* (the Greek for 'home' from which is derived 'economy') in relation to which any wandering can be *comprehended. . . .* In other words, a home(land) must be posited from which one leaves on the journey and to which one hopes to return." (Van Den Abbeele, 1992: xviii.) But there is more to it than that: taking a cue from Gaston Bachelard's *La Poétique de l'espace* [The poetics of space] (1957), we can say that the "here" is not only the "not-there," it is also the place where the "there" is imagined. It is therefore inextricably linked to the "there," as both its opposite and complement, and its construction site. To make this a bit more concrete, consider this example: the wood-panneled study in which the British gentleman, armed with his pipe and tweeds, his dog peacefully curled before the crackling fireplace, read his travel books and daydreamed of the fabulous Orient or the jungles of Africa, could not help being transformed by these thoughts, and infused with an entire array of meanings that would have never existed were it not for them. It is this oneiric dialectic that unites the "here" and "there": home is where one dreams of the world.

Narrative and Place

My reference to travel books is not casual. Like identity and alterity, the "here" and "there" are also constituted through narrative, and accounts of travel—both real and imaginary—played a central role in

---

[9] Spivak's use of the notion of "worlding the world" is of course inspired by Heidegger.

this process. Whether by themselves or as the frame stories of the "oriental trade," they created both the context and the substance of European perceptions of the rest of the world: "the growing interest in the objects of a culture far removed from the West and particularly of 'oriental' cultures was inextricably linked in both fiction and non-fiction to the narrative of voyage. Actual objects of beauty and curiosity plucked from foreign soil were brought by travellers to be sold, exchanged and inserted within the social and mercantile fabric of the West, whereas stories of these cultural objects in the form of adventures and travels were integrated into the narrative syntax of literature and document." (Pucci, 1990: 148.) In this manner, travel narratives provided Europeans with what phenomenologists would call a "pre-thematic" awareness of the world.

Let us make this more specific: Edmund Husserl held that we can only truly comprehend nature by factoring in our ordinary, intuited experience of it, in other words by grounding ourselves in our existence as creatures of nature in everyday contact with it, outside of—and indeed prior to—its being made the subject of scientific investigation.[10] This notion applies equally to history, since both the past and our consciousness of it are elements of our experienced world, we are historical beings first and historians second, and any philosophy of history must take into account the temporality of the historian. Narrative is the primary tool for organizing our experience of time, and therefore plays a key role in the construction of this temporality.[11] In the words of Paul Ricoeur, "time becomes human to the extent that it is articulated through a narrative mode, and narrative attains its full meaning when it becomes a condition of temporal existence." (Ricoeur, 1984: 1: 52.)

But the same must hold for our consciousness of *place*:[12] directly,

[10] See Husserl, 1970: Part III A, particularly paras 33–4 and 53–4.

[11] The extension of Husserl's phenomenology to time and history is due to Carr, 1991. Note that "temporality" is not synonymous with "historicity."

[12] In his 1946 presidential address to the Association of American Geographers, John Kirtland Wright gave an early—possibly the first—articulation of the idea that the lived experience of spatiality must be factored into the practice of geography as a "science." (Wright, 1966: 68–88.) On phenomenological approaches to geography and spatiality, see Pickles, 1985: parts 2 and 4.

because of the epistemic and ontological centrality of space; and indirectly, because time/narrative needs a location in which to unfold—as Bachelard puts it, "in its countless alveoli, space contains compressed time. That is what space is for." (Bachelard, 1964: 8.) Both place and our consciousness of it, then, are elements of our experienced world. Before becoming explorers of foreign lands—or geographers, cartographers, anthropologists, orientalists, tourists—we exist in space, in an immediate relationship with spatiality. Wide-scale spatial practices like colonialism can only be understood if that immediate relationship is given adequate consideration. But saying that the relationship is immediate does not mean that the ensuing consciousness is, say, purely instinctive. As with time, narrative is the primary tool with which we organize our experience of space; hence, it is again through narrative that human beings acquire their pre-thematic awareness of place. Space becomes human, that is, space is constituted as place, to the extent that it is articulated through narrative; and narrative attains its full meaning when it becomes a condition of spatial existence.

In his *L'Invention du quotidien: Arts de faire* (1980) [translated as *The Practice of Everyday Life*], Michel de Certeau has discussed what he calls "narratives of space" (*récits d'espace*), which organize places by describing displacements, and function to constantly transform space into place. These are the narratives that embody our awareness of spatiality, that humanize the space in which we live by infusing it with meaning. But the construction of social space is not merely an intellectual exercise, it also determines praxis: narratives, de Certeau writes, "'go in a procession' ahead of social practices in order to open a field for them." (Certeau, 1984: 116, 118, 125.)[13] Thus, the experiences of Europeans in foreign lands—ranging from the dilettante travelers,

---

[13] This subject is treated in some detail in chapter 9, where the term *récits d'espace* is translated as "spatial stories." De Certeau draws an analogy between the way in which narratives open a field for social practices and the Roman *fetiales*, specialized priests who carried out the rituals concerning *fas*, the deep sense of place that provides a foundation for human actions: before any action having to do with foreigners could be undertaken, a procession would be held designed to "*create the field* necessary for political or military activities." (Certeau, 1984: 124.) For a very interesting analysis of the narrative construction of the "other" and xenotopia, see also Certeau, 1986.

the writers and artists, to the occupying armies, surveyors, colonial administrators, and metropolitan officials—were overdetermined by the collective narratives that give normative significance to place, and thereby construct the "here" and "there." In short, just as the historical past exists and must be tackled prior to and independently of its thematization in historical inquiry, geographical location too is part of the Europeans' experienced world; narrative provides them with a pre-thematic, background awareness of their global positionality—or, to borrow a term from Bourdieu, a kind of geographical *habitus*[14]—which is key to understanding the politics of spatiality, then as now.

The practice of geography always entails a theory of reading:[15] because geography (in the sense of actual places) is intelligible to us only through our locally available ways of making sense of spatiality, geography (in the sense of knowledge of places) is accessible to us only through its production by means of readings that are inevitably grounded in and colored by our local ideological biases. In this sense, *reading is a material practice contributing to the construction of social reality*; any reading is first of all an ideological intervention in the ways of making sense of spatiality available to the subject in the subject's own locality. Geography as a discursive practice must be evaluated not in terms of its performance in recovering a particular place "as it really is," but rather in terms of uncovering the local socio-cultural relevance of that place in light of the interests served by the geographical narratives as material practices that act upon social reality.

To put it most starkly, "without a reading, there is no place." Place is a rhetorical construct, and geography is therefore an inherently literal

[14] Bourdieu defines *habitus* as "systems of durable, transposable *dispositions*, structured structures predisposed to function as structuring structures, that is, as principles of the generation and structuring of practices and representations which can be objectively 'regulated' and 'regular' without in any way being the product of obedience to rules, objectively adapted to their goals without presupposing a conscious aiming at ends or an express mastery of the operations necessary to attain them and, being all this, collectively orchestrated without being the product of the orchestrating action of a conductor." (Bourdieu, 1977: 72.) Another way of conceptualizing the implicit role of place to which I am refering, once again following Fredric Jameson, might be as a "*geo*political unconscious."

[15] This paragraph follows closely the argument about history and reading in Hennessy and Mohan, 1989: 326.

practice—"a grapheme or writing of the world: it provides the text or topics which specify places not as precise functions of minutes or seconds of latitude and longitude but as functions of humanly signifi- cant concerns. . . . [T]here simply are no places at all until they can become incorporated into a *vocabulary* of interests." (Daniel, 1989: 18, 21.) It might be objected that while time travel still eludes us, and our knowledge of the past is therefore necessarily contingent upon the reading of texts (in the broadest sense of the word), the same does not hold for space: one could, in principle, go to virtually any place on the globe and acquire knowledge of it first-hand. Thus, one might argue, spatial knowledge is accessible in a far more unmediated form than is temporal knowledge. At first, this would seem correct; but empirical observation does not yield knowledge unencumbered by the cognitive structures imposed by the subject's mind. Even the most unbiased traveler takes along a great deal of cultural baggage acquired prior to the journey which inevitably colors his/her perceptions; the acquisition of knowledge, in other words, is precisely an act of reading. Further- more, no one can visit every square-inch of the world, so that any *regional* knowledge is necessarily the result of an intellectual process of interpolation. And finally, the overwhelming majority of people acquire their geographical knowledge, such as it is, through the mediation of books, magazines, newspapers, movies, television, and so forth. In short, it is texts (in the broadest sense of the word) that provide us with the tools for making sense of place—both foreign lands and, dually, our home territory.

It is important to appreciate the fundamental nature of this geo- graphical awareness: "the cultural process by which people construct their understandings of the world is an inherently geographic concern. In the course of generating new meanings and decoding existing ones, people construct spaces, places, landscapes, regions and environments. In short, they construct geographies." Thus, like time and temporality, space and spatiality too guide human consciousness and praxis at a most basic level. Moreover, the construction/representation of place is a perpetual process: "human geographies are under continuous inven- tion and transformation by actions whose underlying fields of knowl- edge are themselves recreated through geographical arrangements.

People's cultures and their geographies intersect and reciprocally inform each other." (Anderson and Gale, 1992: 4–5.)

Because life itself depends on it, the element of space has of course been present in narrative since the earliest times; however, its meaning has not always been precisely the same. For example, space in Greek romances is generally abstract: it is deployed as the medium in which adventures take place—travel, pursuit, shipwreck, battle, captivity, et cetera—but individual places are largely interchangeable, for events have no essential ties to the countries or regions in which they are set. As Bakhtin writes, each occurrence is described "as if it were *isolated, single* and *unique*. Nowhere are we given a description of the country as a whole, with its distinctive characteristics, with the features that distinguish it from other countries, within a matrix of relationships. Only separate structures are described, without any connection to an encompassing whole. . . . The customs and everyday life of the folk are nowhere described; what we get instead is a description of some strange isolated quirk, connected to nothing." (Bakhtin, 1981: 101–2.) To put it another way, there is no *genius loci* in the Greek romance, and while the alien nature of the world is emphasized, little distinguishes home from foreign land, or one foreign land from another.

By contrast, emphasis on the specificity of place increased markedly during the eighteenth and early nineteenth centuries: in British rural fiction, for instance, works were set in a distinctive locality that took on an independent imaginative existence, rendering the story's setting at least as important as other narrative elements, and sometimes more so. Indeed, the fictional genres of the early nineteenth century generally put great emphasis on place, grounding their narratives in specific geographical regions that were seen (by both authors and readers) as embodying particular moral and cultural values. (Keith, 1988: 3; Perera, 1991: 35.)

In a series of lectures on the importance of place in fiction, the novelist Eudora Welty argued that "every story would be another story, and unrecognizable as art, if it took up its characters and plot and happened somewhere else. Imagine *Swann's Way* laid in London, or *The Magic Mountain* in Spain, or *Green Mansions* in the Black Forest." (Welty, 1957: 11–12.) Unthinkable? Perhaps, but why exactly? Is it

because each one of us has visited Proust's Combray, Mann's Davos, or
Hudson's Upper Amazon—not to mention London, Spain, and the
Black Forest—and can vouch from personal experience that the stories
would be irredeemably altered if transposed? I think not. As argued
above, knowledge of place largely derives from text, and it is important
not to lose sight of this circularity when assessing the relationship
between spatiality and literature. The reason Proust seems so quintes-
sentially French to us is precisely that our conception of what it means
to be French is in part derived (directly or indirectly) from his writings;
turn-of-the-century France, in other words, belongs to Proust just as
much as Proust belongs to it. Welty writes that location "is to be
discovered" by the writer (Welty, 1957: 25), but in fact it is to be
invented; not *ex nihilo*, of course—nothing ever is—but based upon a
combination of personal experience and ambient knowledge.

Travel narratives, colonial novels, and the like were therefore not
mere reflections of the Europeans' increased exposure to foreign
peoples and places, they were also "narratives of space" by means of
which spatial knowledge was encoded and the world was cognitively
constructed. Or, to put it another way, they were *writings* of the world,
through the *reading* of which space was made into place.

One of the principal ways in which spatial knowledge is encoded is
of course the map, which is precisely "the writing (the grapheme, the
character) implicit within the possibility of a reading. . . . Mapping
identifies a place within the context of a reading and, as such, reveals
how each reading expresses a trope, a figuration, a writing which
specifies the place only in distancing itself from the place in virtue of
its signification." Thus, "a place shifts attention away from its bare,
inchoate spatial coordinates to the mapping, signing, and writing
implicit within and misplaced by the reading by which it is a place."
(Daniel, 1989: 20–21.) Thus a map is not just a mimetic representation
of spatial reality; it is a vehicle through which meaning is infused into
people's perceptions of that reality—in other words an *emplotment* of
the human experience of space.[16] Beyond the graphical transcription
of empirical facts, the practice of cartography marshals a host of

---

[16] On the notion of emplotment, see Ricoeur, 1984.

mapping devices that act to convert chaos into coherence, experience into signification, uniformity into hierarchy. To consider but the simplest example, the cartographical symbols for desert or jungle are much more than purely ecological designations; they carry meanings that are culturally constructed and historically determined. Likewise, the particular projection technique used and the resulting relative sizes of the continents, their relative placement at the center or periphery of the frame, or the convention of placing a particular cardinal direction at the top or the bottom of the map, contain messages which are often subliminal but nonetheless highly significant. Moreover, as with any process of representation, mapping selectively includes and excludes, highlights and represses, centers and marginalizes, bringing to bear ambient power relations and thereby territorializing space. If maps are shaped by their conditions of existence, therefore, in turn they shape the minds of those who read them; they are, in short, "a way of conceiving, articulating, and structuring the human world which is biased towards, promoted by, and exerts influence upon particular sets of social relations." (Harley, 1988: 278.)[17]

But it is not only maps that are discursive constructs produced by and in turn reproducing social relations, so is the mapping process itself. Cartography as a practice has no independent existence outside of the discursive networks which produce it. (Marchitello, 1994: 35.) The act of mapping is therefore necessarily complicit in the discursive production of place. Whether commercial, military, scientific, or touristic, maps are produced with a purpose, by individuals invested in that purpose, and from a positionality consonant with that purpose: "there is an alterity which provokes the desire to map, to contain and to represent—which is to say, to make familiar. At the same time, the very mapping of this difference produces its differences in terms of the economy of the same. . . . *Mapping, as representation, is inextricably caught up in the material production of what it represents.*" (Diprose and Ferrell, 1991: ix, italics mine.) It is thus always necessary to problematize both the map and the map maker, to ask *qui bono?* and how cartographical

---

[17] See also Wood, 1992a; Monmonier, 1991.

techniques are articulated with social relations of domination and subordination to establish or perpetuate a particular world order.

Maps are enunciations in a language that derives its intelligibility from agreed-upon rules and sets of significations—that is, from social conventions. Consequently, they can only be "read" within the social/ cognitive context of their production. The concept of map, further-more, need not be restricted to its traditional and narrow sense of a graphic image, an abstracted two-dimensional depiction of a geographi-cal object. Any narrative representation of space—whether visual or verbal—can be viewed as a map, and that includes spatially structured descriptions of human difference: to assert that Asians are inscrutable or Africans lazy, orientals lascivious or Native Americans cruel, is to produce maps. In that sense, the present study is all about the act of mapping, and some of the cartographical devices that it employs.

But cartography, as Graham Huggan has suggested, exemplifies a structuralist procedure: "A simulacrum of the world (or part of it) is produced through the participation of the intellect in the abstract reorganization of its 'natural object': the external environment." As with travelogues, the work of the intellect is not in any sense "neutral"; in it inher the power relations that characterize the processes of acquisition and encoding of spatial knowledge. Thus, "what the 'imi-tated object' (the [Western] map) 'makes appear' in the 'natural object' it reconstructs (the world) is the anterior presence of the West." Both premise and product of dominant representational practices, this cartographic centering of Europe has had (and continues to have) profound political consequences. By contrast, "a deconstructive reading of the Western map is one which, focusing on the inevitable discrep-ancy between the 'natural' and the 'imitated' object, displaces the 'original' presence of the West in such a way as to undermine the ideology which justifies its relations of power." (Huggan, 1990: 129.)

Though I largely agree with Huggan, there is a crucial point on which our approaches perhaps differ. Focusing on discrepancies between the signifier and the signified, or, as he puts it, "between the 'natural' and the 'imitated' object," presupposes an Archimedean vantage point from which the signified can be observed "as it is," that is, without ideological occlusion. This is a tall order. Instead, I propose to focus on the discrepancies between different signifiers corresponding to the same signified; it is through these discrepancies, I submit, that we stand the best chance of achieving "a deconstructive reading of the Western map."

Writing the Empire

The overarching framework within which Europe dealt with the notions of place and geography, especially during the nineteenth and early twentieth centuries, was that of empire.

Much has been written lately about the role of narrative in the construction of European empires, based upon diverse sources like travelogues, novels, and maps. For example, Suvendrini Perera has reread the great cultural texts of English literature with an eye towards exposing their work to construct empire at the primary levels of vocabulary, image, character, place, and plot, arguing that they constituted the imperial experience at (and for) the center, and that empire was processed and naturalized by them. (Perera, 1991: x, 7.) Martin Green has contended that adventure novels were "the energizing myth of English imperialism," that their writers took them to be the counterpart in literature to empire in politics, by means of which they prepared the young men of England to rule over the colonies, and the public to support the imperial project. (Green, 1979: 1, 37–8.) Mary Louise Pratt has analyzed how travel writing produced "the rest of the world" for European readerships, as well as fostering Europe's differentiated conception of itself in relation to its others, how travel books created the domestic subject of European imperialism and how they engaged metropolitan reading publics to expansionist enterprises. (Pratt, 1992: 4–5.)

Of course literature is only one of the means by which empire was discursively constructed. Thomas Richards has focused on the "imperial archive," which he describes as a fantasy of knowledge compiled in the service of Empire which functioned both to imagine territory as representation and realize it as a social construction, thereby providing a means of "colonization through the mediated instrumentality of information." (Richards, 1993: 6, 16, 23.) Paul Carter has stressed the cartographic and toponymic construction of colonies, describing how a network of names defined a geographical region as a place to which travel was possible and in which settling was imminent; how, in other words, explorers and surveyors brought into being a country that readers could imagine and therefore inhabit, since space was transformed, by the act of naming, into place. (Carter, 1987: xxiv, 121–2.) David Spurr has likewise written that "the very process by which one culture subordinates another begins in the act of naming and leaving unnamed, of marking on an unknown territory the lines of division and uniformity, of boundary and continuity." (Spurr, 1993: 4.) And Eviatar Zerubavel has extended the scope of this argument, pointing out that the very "discovery" of America must be seen as encompassing not only Columbus's landfall on 12 October 1492 but also the three-century-long process, to which the history of cartography bears eloquent witness, through which Europe gradually came to recognize the true identity of what Columbus had called "the Indies" as a separate continent unconnected to Asia and hitherto unknown to Europeans. In other words, toponymy and cartography are key not only to imagining a piece of land as a potential object of colonization, but also to imagining a piece of land—period. (Zerubavel, 1992.)[18]

In each case mentioned above, the cultural artifacts of European high colonialism were not only reflections of imperial politics, but also direct instruments of that politics. From adventure novels to maps of Australia, they were writings of the world that enabled a particular reading of the world. By naturalizing empire and conjuring visions of colonies, they produced European domination.

It goes without saying that all this talk of the narrative construction of empire does not betray an idealist ontology wherein empire has no material referent nor existence outside the realm of discourse. Rather, it merely acknowledges the fact that "*every social community reproduced by the functioning of institutions is imaginary*, that is to say, it is based on the projection of individual existence into the weft of a collective

[18] See also O'Gorman, 1961.

narrative." (Balibar, 1991: 93.)[19] This argument may perhaps take the edge off of Richards's highly provocative, but nonetheless valid opening salvo, "an empire is partly a fiction" (Richards, 1993: 1): in the vast expanses that stretched between the network of widely scattered garrisons and command posts, in every spot where British or French or German soldiers *did not* stand guard and colonial officials *did not* oversee the workings of the imperial machinery, the empire nonetheless existed in the imaginations of both the colonizer and the colonized. It did so because the *fiction* of its existence was told and retold in narrative: "imperial relations may have been established initially by guns, guile and disease, but they were maintained in their interpellative phase largely by textuality, both institutionally . . . and informally. Colonialism (like its counterpart, racism), then, is an operation of discourse, and as an operation of discourse it drafts colonial subjects by incorporating them in a system of representation." (Tiffin and Lawson, 1994: 3.)

The Materiality of Discourse

I want to take a brief moment to elaborate on my understanding and use of the category of discourse in this study. Like moving bodies, intellectual debates too seem to obey the laws of Newtonian physics, and the flurry of publications in the poststructuralist mode has now brought about the inevitable reaction. It has become more or less *de rigueur* (at least on the Left) to criticize discussions that explicitly or implicitly appear to postulate the primacy of discourse, thereby running the risk of losing sight of the "material" underpinnings of history.

One of the more cogent statements of this line of criticism is articulated by Aijaz Ahmad in his critique of the chicken-and-egg problem that undeniably plagues Said's analysis of orientalism and imperialism:

[19] Balibar's succinct statement nicely generalizes Benedict Anderson's discussion of the birth of nationhood and nationalism—see Anderson, 1983. Also see Bhabha, 1990 for interesting applications and elaborations of this idea. On the role of culture in the conscription of both the colonizer and the colonized, see the works of Edward W. Said, particularly *Culture and Imperialism* (1993).

[T]here have historically been all sorts of processes—connected with class and gender, ethnicity and religion, xenophobia and bigotry—which have unfortunately been at work in all human societies, both European and non-European. What gave European forms of these prejudices their special force in history, with devastating consequences for the actual lives of countless millions and expressed ideologically in full-blown Eurocentric racism, was not some transhistorical process of ontological obsession and falsity—some gathering of unique force in domains of discourse—but, quite specifically, the power of colonial capitalism, which then gave rise to other sorts of powers. (Aijaz Ahmad, 1992: 184.)

Indeed, Eurocentricism more than met its match in the Sinocentricism of the "Middle Kingdom," and yet it was Britain and not China that established an empire over which the sun never set. The age of imperialism cannot be understood without reference to high capitalism.

So far, so good. But is political economy a "social materialit[y] of a non-discursive kind," as Aijaz Ahmad would have it? (Aijaz Ahmad, 1992: 182.) Does capitalism exist outside the realm of discourse? Surely not. After all, what is property, if not a discursive relation? What are commodities and value, if not discursive artifacts? Indeed, what is the first chapter of *Das Kapital* (1867) and its brilliant inquiry into commodity fetishism, if not discourse analysis?

The problem here arises, I believe, from the mistaken assumption that discursive and material are opposites—a misconception for which one may readily be forgiven, given some of the canons of poststructuralism, but a misconception nonetheless. Speaking about discourse is emphatically *not* tantamount to ruling out material causality; rather, it shows recognition of the simple truth that human beings' relations to materiality are not, and can never be, unmediated by language, and hence independent of the realm of discourse. After all, it was none other than Marx, whom Aijaz Ahmad follows, who on the one hand posited consciousness as the fundamental attribute of labor in its distinctively human form (Marx, 1970: 1: 178), and on the other argued that while humans possess consciousness, one cannot speak of "pure" consciousness, for it is from the very start burdened by language— adding: "Language is as old as consciousness, language is practical consciousness." (Marx and Engels, 1963: 19.) When he wrote that "the production of ideas, of conceptions, of consciousness, is at first directly *interwoven* with the material activity and the material intercourse of men, the language of real life" (Marx and Engels, 1963: 13–14, italics mine), Marx's intention may well have been to argue for the materiality of consciousness; but this assertion simultaneously reveals the discursiveness of the material. Without language, the material practices of human life are (quite literally) unthinkable; and since the constituents of language only acquire meaning within a discursive framework, they are unthinkable as well without discourse. Discourse does not float above materiality: it is the inextricable medium of human relations with the material world. That it is fundamental to both human perceptions of material reality and human praxis intended to act upon that reality leaves no doubt as to its own materiality.

To be sure, this is not to say that discourse is a *deus ex machina*: it is indubitably material relations that animate world-historical forces like colonialism. But after Gramsci and Raymond Williams, who will still set out to disentangle "base" from "superstructure," or separate relations of production from the systems of signification within which human beings enter them? Colonialism was not only spatial appropriation, military coercion, and economic exploitation; it was also narration, imagination, and interpellation. The experience of neither colonizer nor colonized can be abstracted from the discursive matrix framing the material reality of empire. This is precisely why post-colonial writing has been so concerned with discourse and textuality: empire is not just language, of course, but empire does owe its existence to language. Resistence to empire, then, must address the question of textuality, through, among other things, "motivated acts of reading. The contestation of post-colonialism is a contest of representation." (Tiffin and Lawson, 1994: 10.)

Though the age of colonialism was characterized by a vast array of socio-economic developments and material forces, it was thus also a time of tremendous meaning construction. As Europeans explored the world, as they came into contact with new lands and new peoples, they made sense out of what they encountered within the denotative parameters available to them. In other words, they discursively reconstructed it. By the seventeenth century, "a tradition of dividing the world into continents to which separate identities were attributed was deeply rooted in European thought about geography. Improbable as it might seem that a huge diversity of peoples over an immense area had significant features in common, this did not deter searches for what was regarded as the characteristics of 'eastern', 'oriental', or Asian peoples." (Marshall and Williams, 1982: 128.)

But to divide the world into regions invariably entailed marking some as "central" and others as "peripheral," some as "here" and others as "there." This process, and some of the tools of its practice, are the subject of the chapter that follows.

2

Spaces of Otherness

In a well-known essay, Homi Bhabha wrote that colonial discourse "is an apparatus that turns on the recognition and disavowal of racial/cultural/historical differences. Its predominant strategic function is *the creation of a space for a 'subject peoples'* through the production of knowledges in terms of which surveillance is exercised and a complex form of pleasure/unpleasure is incited. It seeks authorization for its strategies by the production of knowledges of colonizer and colonized which are stereotypical but antithetically evaluated." (Bhabha, 1994: 70, italics mine.) I take the notion of "the creation of a space for a 'subject peoples'" very literally, and argue that assymetries of power generate heterogeneities of space, which in turn validate and perpetuate the social imbalances that created them. Technologies of place, notably gendered and sexualized xenological discourse, are some of the tools by which this process is effected.

In Victorian England, for example, the discourse of gender was fundamentally spatialized: men and women were imagined as belonging to separate "spheres," which were pre-ordained, complementary, and mutually impermeable. (Houghton, 1957: chapter 13; Harrison, 1978: 56–61.) Such spatialization is not, of course, unique to Victorian England, and occurred in a wide variety of cultures. In the West, it has its roots in the dawn of modernity, as Foucault has shown in his discussion of what he calls the "great confinement"—the process whereby the pre-modern practice of eviction and some isolated instances of incarceration (as in the case of lepers) were replaced by the widespread and systematic confinement of the poor, the idle, the lame, the insane, and other social "undesirables" in hospitals, asylums, and prisons. In other words, in *spaces of otherness.* Starting with the 1532 decision by the Parliament of Paris to arrest beggars and press them into forced labor, and culminating with the royal edict of 1656 that led to the creation of the *Hôpital Général* where a vast assortment of "others" were incarcerated, this process ushered in a more consciously spatialized conception of society. "The walls of confinement," Foucault writes, "actually enclose the negative of that moral city of which the bourgeois conscience began to dream in the seventeenth century." (Foucault, 1965: 61.)

Likewise, although instances of the segregation of Jews in Europe had occurred for many centuries, the first time this was practiced as a permanent institution was in 1516, when the foundry (*ghetto*) quarter in Venice was enclosed by walls and gates, and Jews were compelled to live in it. This was emulated by Rome in 1555 and by many other cities of Europe, so that the expulsion of Jews (e.g. from England, Spain, and Portugal) and their occasional sequestration (as in the case of the *Judengasse* of Frankfurt) were replaced, in the sixteenth and seventeenth centuries, by their almost universal confinement within ghettos. (Wirth, 1969: chapters 2–4.) The significance of such spatial segregation cannot be overstated. In an analysis of the social construction of the outsider, and of the nature of the spaces to which outsiders are relegated, David Sibley has shown that marginalization "is associated not only with characterisations of the group but also with images of particular places, *the landscapes of exclusion which express the marginal status of the outsider group.*" (Sibley, 1992: 107, italics mine.)[1] In other words, segregation reproduces itself: spaces of otherness become not only repositories of "others" but indeed one of the primary indicators/producers of alterity.

The above examples are all instances of the construction of variegations

---

[1] In this article, Sibley's focus is on Gypsies (Rom) in contemporary Britain; he has further elaborated upon these ideas in his recent *Geographies of Exclusion: Society and Difference in the West* (1995). Similarly, Peter Jackson has discussed the spatial dimension of female prostitution, gay identity, and racism in contemporary Britain and the United States: see Jackson, 1989: chapters 5 and 6. On the spatial dimensions of racism, see also Hesse, 1993; and Goldberg, 1993: chapter 8. On spatiality and homosexuality, see also Bell and Valentine, 1995b.

within Western societies—what Foucault has called "heterotopias" (Foucault, 1986); it is clear, however, that differentiations of comparable significance were also constructed between Western European and Euro-American societies on the one hand, and the "rest of the world" on the other. The European outlook on the world during the Age of Colonialism—that is, the space of representations devoted to Europe's representations of space—was not only a reflection but a prime mover of the spatial practice that was colonialism. The transformation of the earth into a constellation of places—the filling in of the big blank spaces on the map,[2] so to speak—was intimately related to hegemony, and must be analyzed within that context.

Like eddies, the exercise of power spawns places of identity and alterity, both mimicking and reproducing the mechanisms of inclusion and exclusion prevalent in society. Asking rhetorically, "Is it conceivable that the exercise of hegemony might leave space untouched? Could space be nothing more than the passive locus of social relations, the milieu in which their combination takes on body, or the aggregate of the procedures employed in their removal?" Henri Lefebvre replies: "The answer must be no. . . . [S]pace serves, and . . . hegemony makes use of it, in the establishment, on the basis of an underlying logic and with the help of knowledge and technical expertise, of a 'system.' " (Lefebvre, 1991: 11.) Hegemony, then, moulds space, and hegemonic constructions of place in turn reproduce power relations.

Underscoring the intimate relationship between spatial practices and power, Foucault has similarly argued that "to trace the forms of implantation, delimitation and demarcation of objects, the modes of tabulation, the organisation of domains mean[s] the throwing into relief of processes—historical ones, needless to say—of power."

---

[2] Sir Arthur Conan Doyle wrote in *The Lost World* (1912): "The big blank spaces in the map are all being filled in, and there's no room for romance anywhere." (13.) Joseph Conrad's use of this image is perhaps better known: "At that time there were many blank spaces on the earth and when I saw one that looked particularly inviting on a map (but they all look that) I would put my finger on it and say: When I grow up I will go there." Later, he reflects, "it was not a blank space any more. It had got filled since my boyhood with rivers and lakes and names. It had ceased to be a blank space of delightful mystery— a white patch for a boy to dream gloriously over. It had become a place of darkness." (Conrad, 1988: 11–12.)

(Foucault, 1980a: 70.) Indeed, not only does power influence spatial practices, but the very existence of a discourse of spatiality is born out of the functioning of power. The territorialization of space is a discursive practice, as is our consciousness of those territories; they cannot be analyzed independently of the networks of power that generate them. Following the lead of Gayatri Chakravorty Spivak, therefore, I too take a crack at rewriting Foucault's "rule of immanence," as follows:

> One must not suppose that there exists a certain sphere of *spatial construction* that would be the legitimate concern of a free and disinterested scientific inquiry were it not the object of mechanisms of *exclusion and inclusion, or centering and peripheralization*, brought to bear by the economic or ideological requirements of power. If *place* was constituted as an area of investigation, this was only because relations of power had established it as a possible object; and conversely, if power was able to take it as a target, this was because techniques of knowledge and procedures of discourse were capable of investing it. Between techniques of knowledge and strategies of power there is no exteriority, even if they have specific roles and are linked together on the basis of their difference. (Foucault, 1978–85: 1: 98.)[3]

If gendered and sexualized xenological discourse is a technology of place, as I argue, then xenological erotica was instrumental in producing the spatial basis of geopolitics and Western hegemony. Indeed, Foucault's assertion that "heterotopias always presuppose a system of opening and closing that both isolates them and makes them penetrable" (Foucault, 1986: 26) acquires a new meaning in the case of tales of harems, oriental seductresses, and dark-skinned rapists.

Places that Mean

The significance of a particular representation of xenotopia derives in large part from the connotative power of the metaphors used to

---

[3] Foucault's subject is, of course, the "sphere of sexuality." I have indicated my modifications to Foucault's text by italics. See also Spivak, 1990: 224, which speaks of the "sphere of marginality." On the relation between the science of geography and imperial power, see Godlewska and Smith, 1994.

construct it. For example, "references to 'Jonestown' or to 'Chernobyl' have a 'semantic density' that extends far beyond the geographic locations to include the terrible events that took place there." It is impossible to hear names like Jonestown and Chernobyl, or Auschwitz and Hiroshima, or My Lai and Babi Yar, without instantly tapping into a large collective memory that endows such places with meanings transcending their physical/geographical realities. This is because places take on meanings according to events that occur there, becoming infused with human memories, hopes, values, fears. Indeed, the significances a location carries are established by social construction—whether through cultural consensus or hegemony—regardless of whether or not a given event really has occurred there: "the metonymic quality of our everyday concept of place has parallels in the characterization of place in myth." (Entrikin, 1991: 11.)[4] Thus, it is not merely events that have actually taken place at a given location that furnish it with layers of meaning; often, it is also "knowledge" of characteristics peculiar to that place which may have absolutely no basis in empirical fact. As Barthes has written in his *Mythologies* (1957), "*myth is a type of speech* . . . a system of communication . . . a message. . . . It is a mode of signification, a form. . . . Myth is not defined by the object of its message, but by the way in which it utters this message: there are formal limits to myth, there are no 'substantial' ones." (Barthes, 1994: 109.)

Yi-Fu Tuan has distinguished two principal kinds of mythical space. The first, corresponding to "a fuzzy area of defective knowledge surrounding the empirically known, . . . frames pragmatic space"; the

---

[4] Entrikin goes on to write that "the region or nation gains an identity through the increased density of the interconnectedness of group to place and place to other places." (Entrikin, 1991: 129.) Few must understand this better than the Serbian nationalists, who, at the time I was writing these lines, were completing their wholesale destruction of the entire cultural patrimony of Bosnia and Herzegovina, as they had done earlier in Dalmatia. No library, no archive, no site of historical or architectural significance escaped their barbarity. By driving out the non-Serbian inhabitants of each town they occupied and destroying each and every mosque, cemetery, bridge, or public building, the Serbian nationalists clearly aimed at severing the interconnectedness of nation and land, and thus destroying a people once and for all; and by their callous indifference, world powers became complicit in this genocide.

second "is the spatial component of a world view, a conception of localized values within which people carry on their practical activities." (Tuan, 1977: 86.) In other words, mythical space is either located at the margins of the known, or it consists of the socially reconstructed—that is, emplotted, mythologized—environment within which social practices unfold. Yet, these two kinds of mythical space are not necessarily mutually exclusive. A case in point is the practice of colonialism, which was aided and legitimated precisely by the attribution of mythical characteristics conceived in the center to the margins; the mythologized margins were, in other words, part and parcel of the metropolitan worldview.

A two-tiered cognitive process occurring during the Age of Exploration and its aftermath led to the successive construction first of an *absence of knowledge,* and then of knowledges in line with political imperatives. What does it mean to construct an absence of knowledge? Lack of knowledge, and consciousness of that lack, are of course two different things. Out of the infinity of facts about which we are ignorant, we give most no thought at all; it is only when we become aware of our ignorance of a particular thing that it acquires reality for us, and possibly (though not necessarily) becomes an object of desire, of a will to know. This I propose to call *unknowledge,* to distinguish it from ignorance, and to denote socially constructed lack of knowledge, that is, a conscious absence of socially pertinent knowledge.

The cartographic practice of representing the unknown as a blank in early maps is a good example, for it "does not simply or innocently reflect gaps in European knowledge but actively erases (and legitimizes the erasure of) existing social and geo-cultural formations in preparation for the projection and subsequent emplacement of a new order." Hence, for instance, "the antipodality of Australia joins with its construction as a *tabula rasa* to produce the continent as an inverted, empty space desperately requiring rectification and occupation." (Ryan, 1994: 153.)[5] This illustrates the power of representation in shaping

[5] For an interesting discussion of the emerging role of blank space in maps, see also Stratton, 1990: 68–9. On how the American continent gradually took shape in European maps, see Zerubavel, 1992. On cartography and the colonization of the New World, see Mignolo, 1995: chapter 6.

social and political practice. There is no obvious reason, after all, to construct maps that include entire areas denoted as *terra incognita*: indeed, one might even argue that there is something slightly perverse about producing representations only to simultaneously disavow them by admitting that they represent the unknown. One could claim that it would have made much more sense for cartographers to draw more narrowly focused maps limited to specific known territories (as was the case with portolans, for example), leaving the uncharted *beyond* the frame—out of sight, out of mind, as it were. Instead, they drew continental and global maps (*mappae mundi*) that necessarily incorporated large expanses of blank space, thereby constructing those lands *as unknown*, awaiting discovery and eventual appropriation. The reconstruction of parts of the globe as uncharted territory is, in this sense, the *production of unknowledge*, the transformation of those parts into potential objects of Western political and economic attention. It is the enabling of colonialism.

A related development was the population of certain areas of maps with monsters and other mythical creatures. In his analysis of Gerhard Mercator's *Atlas* (1585–95), José Rabasa has argued that this practice did not simply correspond to a lack of knowledge, but rather "points to sedimented symbolic associations of topographical regions with the fantastic and the demonic." (Rabasa, 1985: 2: 10.) In other words, mythical beings in maps represented not the absence of knowledge, but, on the contrary, a specific kind of knowledge: the inhabitants of those areas were not *unknown*, but rather *known to be monsters*. Empirical evidence was simply not germaine to the construction of that knowledge, and the failure of one explorer after another to find the amazons, astomi, cynocephali, blemmyae, or sciapods described by the ancients did not undermine belief in them. Instead, they were merely "relocated just beyond the receding geographical boundary of *terra incognita*, in the enduring European mental space reserved for aliens." (Montrose, 1992: 171.)[6] This space functioned, in a sense, as Europe's attic—a

---

[6] On the monsters with which, from Ctesias and Megasthenes to Pliny and Solinus and beyond, Europeans believed foreign lands to be populated, see: Wittkower, 1942; Friedman, 1981; Kappler, 1980; Hodgen, 1964; Campbell, 1988: 47–86.

place to which the frightening and the repulsive, the obscene and the grotesque could be relegated, the mess that made Europe's imagined order possible. Mary B. Campbell strikingly describes this phenomenon when she writes:

> Like the medieval manuscript and the medieval cathedral, the world itself has a margin, where the grotesque is free to frolic because it is perceived as somehow inherently beyond the power (or beneath the attention) of any integrative force ... Once firmly located in a margin, the grotesque poses little threat to the central order. It *need* not be integrated. (Campbell, 1988: 82.)

The monstrous races that populated foreign continents—much like gargoyles, forever excluded from sanctified space though roosted just outside it—marked the chaos that lay beyond the "here."

The *Libido Loci*

The mythical constructions of spaces of otherness extended to representations of the Orient. Like the copulating and defecating figures haunting the margins of medieval manuscripts, grotesque sexuality was a defining condition of Europe's margins.[7] It is not that empirical evidence was not available to challenge or revise the preposterous myths that had evolved around harems, public baths, et cetera, but rather that these latter were elements of (or perhaps conduits for) the "sedimented symbolic associations" between geographical regions and sexuality in European colonial discourse. Try as they might, Lady Montagu and her fellow eye-witnesses could not supplant the accumulated body of "knowledge" concerning oriental sexuality; at most, they were able to create alternative knowledges that co-existed alongside the former, but failed to gain the upper hand.

A case in point is the following caption in an early twentieth-century book, below a photograph depicting a fairly typical, Western-looking, bourgeois interior: "This photograph was taken expressly for a London

---

[7] For a fascinating study of margins in medieval art and architecture as licensed spaces of transgression, see Camille, 1992.

paper. It was returned with this comment: 'The British public would not accept this as a picture of a Turkish Harem.' As a matter of fact, in the smartest Turkish houses European furniture is much in evidence." (Zeyneb, 1913: facing 192.) The picture to which this caption refers was probably taken by Grace Ellison and sent to the *Daily Telegraph*, for which she wrote a series of essays on harem life in Turkey during the early part of the century. (Ellison, 1915.) Evidently, an indoor pool with myriad nude women reclining on pillows and smoking water-pipes would have been more in line with the expectations of "the British public" than some stuffy European furnishings. At first sight, what is striking here is the frankness with which a newspaper publisher would acknowledge that he was more anxious to pander to readers' preconceptions than to inform them. But this incident can also be seen in a different light: the publisher's frame of reference was fundamentally different from Ellison's. He was, so to speak, speaking from a different significational layer, and his commitment was to a different "truth."

Harems are a clear-cut case of a more general pattern: the process by which spaces of otherness were constructed was often deliberately sexualized—as for instance in the case of world fairs and expositions, which not only went out of their way to create "authentic" bubbles of extra-territoriality in the heart of the European metropolis, but moreover invariably featured such exotic/erotic spectacles as belly dancing as their main attraction: "Catering to fantasies about harem life, belly dancers attracted great crowds and achieved major commercial success; in 1889 in Paris, the '*danse du ventre* made all of Paris run [in its orbit],' and an average of two thousand spectators flocked to watch the belly dancers every day." (Çelik, 1992: 24.)[8]

In eighteenth-century London, where libertinism ran rampant and many forms of sexual entertainment were available, brothels catering to certain specialized tastes such as flagellation were known as *bagnios* and *serails*; there were also "shows which featured naked dancing and

[8] A very nice elaboration of this subject is in Çelik and Kinney, 1990. See also Buonaventura, 1989: chapter 5. On the deep influence that the World Fair of 1889 had on Paul Gauguin and his quest for "the primitive," see Brooks, 1993: 163. On the construction of spaces of otherness in world fairs and expositions, see Mitchell, 1988: chapter 1; and Armstrong, 1992–93.

copulation, as for example that run by Mrs Hayes where—she advertised—'at 7 o'clock precisely 12 beautiful nymphs, spotless virgins, will
carry out the famous Feast of Venus, as it is celebrated in Tahiti, under
the instruction and leadership of Queen Oberea (which rôle will be
taken by Mrs Hayes herself).'" (Porter, 1982: 9.)

Although Steven Marcus devoted no fewer than twenty pages of his
classic *The Other Victorians: a Study of Sexuality and Pornography in Mid-
Nineteenth Century England* (1966) to the anonymous pre-Victorian
epistolary novel *The Lustful Turk* (1828),[9] he said virtually nothing
about the novel's setting—the harems of the Dey of Algiers and the
Bey of Tunis, on the Barbary Coast. To be sure, this omission is
consistent with his concept of "pornotopia," the nowhere-place in
which sexual acts described by pornographic works occur:

> The isolated castle on an inaccessible mountain top, the secluded country
> estate set in the middle of a large park and surrounded by insurmountable
> walls, the mysterious town house in London or Paris, the carefully furnished
> and elaborately equipped set of apartments to be found in any city at all, the
> deserted cove at the seaside, or the solitary cottage atop the cliffs, the inside
> of a brothel rented for a day, a week, or a month, or the inside of a hotel
> room rented for a night—these are all the same place and are identically
> located. (Marcus, 1966: 271.)

At first reading, this seems correct—at least for the mass-produced
pornographic videos filmed in a few hours at seedy motels; after all, of
what importance can the backdrop be, when the sole purpose of
pornography is to display the sexual act? More careful consideration,
however, calls Marcus's assertion into question, for it seems to ignore
the fetish value of certain places—the outdoors, a public space, a
moving train, a musty attic, the kitchen floor. Place, in other words,
emphatically does carry a certain "value-added" in pornography. And if

[9] On *The Lustful Turk* and its early editions, see Ashbee, 1885: 134–6. Ashbee also
mentions a work entitled *Scenes in the Seraglio* (London: W. Dugdale, [ca. 1855–60]),
apparently by the same author, but I have not seen it. According to his summary, the plot
is similar to that of *The Lustful Turk*: a young Sicilian woman by the name of Adelaide is
abducted by pirates, who sell her to "Achmet, Sultan of Turkey." An imbedded story
concerns the "Amours of Euphrosyne," another inmate of the harem. (Ashbee,
1885: 136–7.)

attics and kitchens can contribute "semantic density" to sexual narratives, how could sexualized spaces of otherness like the harem fail to do so? "The aura of the harem 'swells' the phallic order by suggesting a *locus sexualis* that has no equivalent in Western expression," writes Emily Apter. "The scopic intrusion into interior space, when 'haremized,' produces an 'other' eroticism that folds the power dynamics of female sequestration in with the thrilling transgression of cultural voyeurism." (Apter, 1992: 210, 212.) Setting an erotic story in a harem thus deploys pre-established connections between sexuality and the Orient, conjuring an exclusively female space filled with compliant and desirous naked women, a taboo place into which the vicarious entry of the reader or viewer evokes all the excitement of the forbidden.

For his analysis of the human value attached to places, Bachelard coined the word "topophilia" (Bachelard, 1964: xxxi); apparently independently, Tuan proposed using the same term to describe a human being's affective ties to the material environment, which couple sentiment and place. (Tuan, 1974: 93, 113.) In like fashion, I would suggest that the fetishistic effects elicited in Western consciousness by harems, Turkish baths, slave markets, and the like, could perhaps be described as *topolagnia*—libidinous attraction to a place. There are countless examples of topolagnia in literature, a handful of which I now describe.

The Marquis de Sade situated the sexual excesses he described in his *Les 120 journées de Sodome, ou l'école du libertinage* [The 120 days of Sodom, or the school of libertinism] (written in 1785, first published in 1904) in "a splendid antechamber adjoined by four superb apartments, each having a boudoir and wash cabinets; splendid Turkish-style beds canopied in three-colored damask with matching furniture adorned these suites whose boudoirs offered everything and more of the most sensual that lubricity might fancy." (Sade, 1966: 238.)[10] Why "Turkish" beds? The contribution of this oriental connection to the novel's sexually charged ambiance becomes all the more evident when one considers that beds in Turkey have no special features, least of all

---

[10] I have slightly altered the translation. On the narrative structure of *Les 120 journées de Sodome* and the interesting fact that Sade owned a copy of the *Thousand and One Nights*, see the editor's notes in Sade, 1990: 1: 1124.

are they canopied! In similar vein, the sadomasochistic novel *The Pleasures of Cruelty* (ca. 1880) is set in Turkey, even though none of the characters are Turkish and there is nothing in the text, except for a couple of fleeting references to Constantinople and a spurious imbedded "harem tale," to distinguish it from countless other pornographic works of its kind. It was only the mystique of an Orient where "the language is strange and barbarous" (Anon./*Pleasures*, n.d.: 6)[11] and walls and veils delimit an impregnable sexual *topos* that was signified by the geographical setting.

Gustave Flaubert wrote in his *L'Éducation sentimentale* [The sentimental education] (1869) of a brothel owner known as "*La Turque*" [the Turkish woman], a nickname that, he contended, "added to the poetic character of her establishment." (Flaubert, 1904: 2: 237.) And only a few years after the publication of *L'Éducation sentimentale*, in 1875, a play written by Guy de Maupassant and possibly inspired by Flaubert— his mentor and patron—was privately performed in Paris; it was entitled *À la Feuille de Rose, Maison turque* [At the Rose Petal, Turkish house], and was set in a brothel that featured a "harem" theme, with all the prostitutes dressed in Turkish fashion. In the first scene, upon learning of this new theme, the errand-boy compliments the pimp for his clever idea, exclaiming: "A Turkish brothel—one doesn't find that every day. And what's more, the bourgeois is partial to Turkish women." (Maupassant, 1984: 36, translation mine.)[12] In fact, the theme of prostitutes costumed and brothels decorated in Turkish style recurs in pornography, for instance in the anonymous *La Rose d'Amour; or the Adventures of a Gentleman in Search of Pleasure* (1849).[13]

[11] According to Pascal Pia, this book consists of the English translation of "fragments of the *Nouvelle Justine* and the *Story of Juliette*." (Pia, 1978: col. 1057, translation mine.) The earliest edition I have been able to find dates from 1898; however, a section of text was published in *The Pearl: a Journal of Facetiae and Voluptuous Reading* in 1880, so I assume that earlier editions must have existed.

[12] While the word "maison" literally means "house," it also carries the connotation of brothel (*maison close*). The name of the brothel, "*feuille de rose*" (rose petal), is slang for anilingus, or what is nowadays called "rimming." See Guiraud, 1978: 333; Richard, 1993: 98–9.

[13] This work was serialized in *The Pearl: a Journal of Facetiae and Voluptuous Reading*. Although it is subtitled "Translated from the French," Rolf S. Reade [Alfred Rose] lists a similarly subtitled edition published in 1864 and states that it is a reprint of an "original

It is not surprising, therefore, that in French and British parlance, the foreign, and in particular the "oriental," came to signify sexuality: "the popularity of terms like 'seraglio figure', 'Turkish beauties' (meaning female buttocks), and 'Asiatic ideas' (meaning sexual desire) in the discourse of male British writers on sex and male responses to femininity [brought] the oriental theme back to Europe, giving a significant new dimension to discourses of sexuality there." (De Groot, 1989: 106.)[14] Reference to a particular location could thus be shorthand for a vast array of significations, and, as Lisa Lowe has argued, by invoking a pre-existing association between the oriental and the erotic, a colonial text could signify orientalism in order to signify erotic desire. (Lowe, 1991: 94.) By the same token, such a text could signify *erotic desire* precisely in order to conjure a certain vision of the *Orient*—a vision in line with the current (but ever-changing) Western geopolitical agenda. Like Jonestown and Chernobyl, such places as Baghdad, Constantinople/İstanbul, or Cairo also embodied multiple layers of signification. They existed dually, in reality and in myth, their "semantic density" augmented by the tropes of gendered and sexualized xenological discourse.

Erotica as a Technology of Place

Spaces of otherness—spaces, that is, where "others" live, and at the same time spaces that endow "others" with alterity—were thus constructed in part through the instrumentality of the discourse of sexuality. On the one hand, xenotopia was sexualized; and on the other, sex was exoticized. Sexuality became one of the axes along which identity and alterity could be constructed—a practice that survives to this day in contemporary American political culture, in the form of the dis-

---

American work" published in 1849. (Reade, 1936: no. 4026.) Indeed, the tone of the narrative is far too English for the French attribution to be credible.

[14] Of course such imagery was also used considerably earlier; see, for instance, the entry for "Turk" in Rubinstein, 1984: 284–5; also Chew, 1937: 144.

course surrounding sexual promiscuity, teenage pregnancy, and single motherhood in the "inner city."

In his study of eighteenth-century pornography, Jean Marie Goulemot qualified the notion of tableau as "one of the indispensible elements for the production of [the] effect of desire by the reading of the pornographic novel," writing that "there is tableau, it seems, essentially because there is mise-en-scène, that is, inscription of bodies into a space which they saturate. The tableau exists only by virtue of this occupation of the space of narration." Language, he asserted, gives depth and dynamics to space and "ends up *creating a descriptive space without a description of the act itself.*" (Goulemot, 1991: 142–3, translation and italics mine.) Place is not merely a neutral setting, it is a participant actor that makes its own contribution to this process. Furthermore, the effect works both ways: for instance, can anyone ever look at a French château the same way again, after having read Pauline Réage's *Histoire d'O* [Story of O] (1954)? There is a dialectic, a production–reproduction cycle at work here: the *topos* in which an erotic tale is set is transformed by the tale; the erotic *reconstructs* the place in its own image. The château becomes a place where women are imprisoned in dungeons, whipped, and trained to be sex slaves; likewise, the Orient (or xenotopia in general) is reconstructed in a particular image by the actions of erotica functioning as a technology of place. In Suzanne Rodin Pucci's catchy phrase, the "mystery" of the exotic Orient is embodied in the representation of the harem, "*a realm of seemingly radical political, and especially erotic, alterity.*" (Pucci, 1989: 115, italics mine.)

The question is, "why erotica?" Why have recourse to sexuality for the narrative construction of spaces of otherness? Foucault provides at least a partial answer when he writes that sexuality is endowed with tremendous instrumentality, and can serve to construct various realities and to bolster diverse strategies. (Foucault, 1978–85: 1: 103.) For example, George L. Mosse has argued that nationalism played a crucial role in the emergence of manners, morals, sexual attitudes—in short, "respectability": as sexual "abnormality" was increasingly viewed as alien, nationalists came to feel that the survival of the nation hinged upon the careful delineation of normal and abnormal. This attitude became more acute in the second half of the nineteenth century, as Darwinism added fuel to the nationalist campaign against the abnormal: "Natural selection, which Darwin had seen at work among animals, would reward a healthy national organism free of hereditary disease and moral weakness." In other words, the sexually "abnormal" was seen as threatening the continued well-being of the nation, and had to be excised. For the nationalists, "lack of control over sexual passions [was] part and parcel of that lack of self-control thought characteristic of the enemies of ordered society. The enemies of society and the inferior race were identical in racist thought, while the superior race possessed the attitudes, manners, and morals of existing society." Thus, Mosse concludes, "the relationship between racism and sexuality must be set in this wider context. Sexuality was not just one more attribute of the racist stereotype, but by its attack upon respectability threatened the very foundation of bourgeois society." (Mosse, 1985: 33, 151.)[15]

I find this argument in large measure convincing, except for one detail: it takes sexuality as *given*. In fact, sexuality was—or better still, *sexualities* were—*produced* precisely in order to be able to draw boundaries between "us" and "them." After all, nationalism is an ideology based upon *exclusion* at least as much as community; sexual "abnormality" provided a set of criteria with which to draw lines of demarcation.[16] It mattered little that homosexuals and other so-called "deviants" did not pose a genuine threat to the nation; neither, for that matter, did Jews in Weimar Germany. (It is no coincidence, of course, that Jews were deeply sexualized in much anti-Semitic discourse—where, as Mosse and Sander Gilman have shown, incest, circumcision, and the corruption of Christian women were common polemical springboards.) What was important was to erect walls, to *produce* the nation by a process of sifting, of retaining some and rejecting others. Sexual propriety was a tool with which to imagine difference between the nation and the "other."

It is not, therefore, that sexual "normalcy" was a necessary condition

---

[15] On eugenics and the feminization of decadence, see also Low, 1993a.

[16] For two interesting collections of essays dealing with sexuality and the construction of nationhood, see Parker, Russo, Sommer, and Yaeger, 1992; and Moon and Davidson, 1995. See also some of the contributions to Grewal and Kaplan, 1994.

or a natural consequence of the emergence of nationalism, but rather that nationalists produced and used it as a litmus test for inclusion and exclusion—a technology of identity and alterity. For example, the development of English national identity was related to "an emerging language of racial difference in which skin color and physiognomy became overdetermined markers of a whole range of religious and sexual and cultural differences by which the English were distinguished from various non-European 'others.'" (Howard, 1994: 102.) Simultaneously, "the representation of British women's sexuality [was] seen as an essential component in the construction of Britishness, and, particularly, male Britishness within the colonial context." (Mills, 1993: 58–9.) These processes were coterminous with a change in the perception of female sexuality, as the image of woman was transformed during the eighteenth century from one of willful carnality to one of idealized domesticity. (Poovey, 1988: 9–10.) As gender was thus redefined (for any change to the definition of woman necessarily entails a change to that of man), societal differences—such as those imagined along the lines of race, class, and gender—were recast as sexual: for instance, though sexual desire was acknowledged to exist in some women, these came to be viewed as lacking in propriety and morality by virtue of either class provenance or ethnic or racial origin. (Mabro, 1991: 11.) The sexuality of "other" women, including both working-class Europeans and non-European natives, was thus an important constituent of the European bourgeoisie's self-construction. It allowed Western Europeans to disown characteristics they considered undesirable in themselves by reflecting them onto the "other." In this manner, "textual stereotypes that construct the oriental as 'Other' serve[d] a unifying function for the culture that produce[d] them, a culture which, in the service of a coherent and idealized self-definition, denie[d] those qualities that threaten or undermine its own self-image and project[ed] them on to extracultural groups (or on to marginal groups, like women, within the culture)." (Hurley, 1993: 196.) The sexual difference of the European *bourgeoise* was constructed not only in opposition to men, but as importantly in opposition to women whose class or racial affiliation, or social behavior, were flagged as unfeminine. (Kaplan, 1985: 166–7; Levy, 1991: 69.)

In this context, sexually explicit writing was used to set up Goulemot's "descriptive spaces," and thereby to construct self and other as
well as place. In Hector France's *L'Amour au pays bleu* (1880) [translated
first as *The Chastisement of Mansour*, and subsequently as *The Amatory
Adventures of Sheik Mansour*], the narrator warns the European readers
that the amorous passions of the novel's characters will be quite beyond
their grasp: "You of the North, you cannot understand these whirlwinds
[of] fiery passion. In your cold land, love is a puny dwarf; it makes
humble slaves of you, with bent head and downcast eyes. . . . But it is
very different with the sons of Arabia, whom the hot sun scorches with
the breath of flame, and fires the blood." (France, 1932: 48, 50.) France
took up this theme again in the Preface to his collection of short stories
Sous le burnous (1886) [translated as *Musk, Hashish and Blood*], where he
wrote that "the great world, mankind at large, cannot be judged by the
standard of the familiar folk of everyday whose whole life is passed
within view of the steeple of their Parish Church." (France, 1900: xiii.)
In short, any Westerners who dare venture into the exotic East should
brace themselves as they will encounter incomprehensible, fiery
passions, wild emotions, and strange sexual practices. Xenotopia is
what Europe *is not*, the antithesis of bourgeois austerity, respectability,
and temperance. This is the profoundly didactic message underlying so
many seemingly frivolous romances and erotic novels set outside of
Europe.

The instrumentalization of sexuality is closely related to the infusion
of the human body with socially significant meanings, that is, to its
"textualization." In the modern era, the human body has become the
locus and carrier of a whole range of significations, a process that has
led to "a semioticization of the body . . . matched by a somaticization
of story." (Brooks, 1993: xii.) Elizabeth Grosz argues that "as a *material*
series of processes, power actively marks or brands bodies as social,
inscribing them with the attributes of subjectivity," and that "the
'messages' or 'texts' produced by such procedures construct bodies as
networks of social signification, meaningful and functional 'subjects'
within assemblages composed with other subjects." This corporeal
intertext produces, in other words, body-subjects that are social texts
which may be read and interpreted, and which are articulated within

the narrative fabric and mythology that are the foundations of social intercourse and self-representation. (Grosz, 1990: 62–3, 65–6.)[17] The domain of sexuality being a manifestation of the body *par excellence*, it should come as no surprise that sex and gender have evolved into fundamental carriers of signification: for instance, the female body, sexuality, and pathology became organizing tropes in eighteenth- and nineteenth-century French politics,[18] and like anti-aristocratic ideology, anti-clericalism too was often manifested in erotic form.[19]

Many stereotypes in Western culture, during this period and thereafter, were constructed in the form of gendered polarities—for example, dichotomies like culture/nature, mind/body, intellect/feeling, logos/chaos, form/matter, or truth/lie, where, of course, the first element was coded masculine/central, and the second feminine/marginal.[20] Such mutual reinforcement—or *articulation*—of two systems of stereotypes is fairly common; as Cora Kaplan has noted:

Masculinity and femininity do not appear in cultural discourse, any more than they do in mental life, as pure binary forms at play. They are always, already, ordered and broken up through other social and cultural terms, other categories of difference. Our fantasies of sexual transgression as much as our obedience to sexual regulation are expressed through these structuring hierarchies. Class and race ideologies are, conversely, steeped in and spoken through the language of sexual differentiation. Class and race meanings are not metaphors for the sexual, or vice versa. It is better, though not exact, to see them as reciprocally constituting each other through a kind

[17] Grosz also writes that "consciousness is an *effect* or result, rather than the cause of the inscription of flesh and its conversion into a (social) body," and here I think she is going a bit too far: it would seem that there is a dialectic, rather than a one-way effect, in the relationship between consciousness and the "textualization" of the body; otherwise, who (or what) does the textualizing?

[18] See Hunt, 1991; Baecque, 1991; and Wagner, 1988: 87–112, which covers both French and English erotica.

[19] An extensive survey of anti-clericalist erotic literature is in Ashbee, 1879. See also Wagner, 1988: 47–86. It is worth noting that anti-Mormon polemics in nineteenth-century America were also strongly sexualized, with a proliferation of books and pamphlets about "Brigham Young and his harem," "the blighting curse of polygamy," and so forth.

[20] See Boheemen, 1987: 29; Cixous, 1986: 63–4. On a more general note, for a feminist critique of binarism, see Jay, 1981.

of narrative invocation, a set of associative terms in a chain of meaning. (Kaplan, 1985: 148.)

Indeed, it can be argued that to carry out successfully its significational functions, a stereotype actually requires constant reference to other systems of stereotypes from which it draws epistemic support. (Bhabha, 1994: 77.) Robert Young puts it as follows: "class, gender and race are circulated promiscuously and crossed with each other, transformed into mutually defining metaphors that mutate within intricate webs of surreptitious cultural values." (Young, 1995: xii.)

But mutually reinforcing systems of stereotypes draw upon and reproduce *both* systems: thus, through a circular logic, gendered polarities serve to naturalize and reproduce not only gender but other forms of domination as well. A case in point: in a well-argued critique of mainstream feminist attacks on pornography, Mariana Valverde has stressed that focusing only on sexual domination is a narrow course of action that white middle-class women tend to follow because they are not subject to other forms of domination. By contrast, "a feminism which is more broadly based and which takes into account the experience of women of color and women in the Third World will have to take a serious look at the glamorization of racism and capitalism, not just the glamorization of sexual subordination. *Pornography often eroticizes several forms of domination at once.* Consider, for example, the cliché scenes about white male explorers coming upon a 'primitive' society whose women are portrayed as 'natural' sex objects free of the inhibitions of white Protestant ladies." (Valverde, 1987: 131–2, italics mine.) In this example and in many others like it, stereotypes based on race and gender are articulated together, mutually inflecting and reinforcing each other. Thus, in power relations between nations and power relations between the sexes inheres a kind of dialectic that ought to imply a feminist agenda: the critique of the eroticization of colonialism is also part and parcel of the struggle against gender oppression in the societies where these ideologies originate.

Beyond the instrumentality of sexuality, beyond the doubling of gender and racial or ethnic stereotypes, there is yet another reason why erotica was especially well suited for use by xenological discourse: as

Angela Carter aptly observes (in an otherwise very tiresome book), "pornography involves an abstraction of human intercourse in which the self is reduced to its formal elements." Pornography is, in other words, a screen on to which are projected Platonic ideals; "since all pornography derives directly from myth, it follows that its heroes and heroines, from the most gross to the most sophisticated, are mythic abstractions, heroes and heroines of dimension and capacity. Any glimpse of a real man or a real woman is absent from these represen-tations of the archetypal male and female." This process of archetyping, Carter continues, functions "to diminish the unique 'I' in favor of a collective, sexed being which cannot, by reason of its very nature, exist as such." (Carter, 1988: 4, 6.)

That pornography derives from myth must be placed in the context of Barthes's assertion that myth "abolishes the complexity of human acts, it gives them the simplicity of essences, it does away with all dialectics, with any going back beyond what is immediately visible, it organizes a world which is without contradictions because it is without depth, a world wide open and wallowing in the evident, it establishes a blissful clarity: things appear to mean something by themselves." (Barthes, 1994: 143.) All depth and individuality are thus subordinated to the fundamental typology of fucker/fuckee, giving rise, in Nabokov's words, to "the copulation of clichés." (Nabokov, 1970: 315.) The personae at best distinguish themselves by their physical character-istics—the 12-inch penis, the 39D bust, the shaven pubis, and so forth.

Given the basic essentialism that thus permeates pornography, it stands to reason that culturally recognizable stereotypes such as the oversexed African or the lascivious harem girl should be extremely compelling: in pornography, a man is just a penis, but a black man can be a veritable sex machine; a woman is just a vagina, but an oriental concubine promises pleasures beyond imagination. In this fashion, writers of what we might call *ethnopornography*[21] availed themselves of a whole new palette of archetypes with which to construct their scenes of

---

[21] Although I was quite pleased with myself for having coined this term, I have discovered of late that Walter Edmund Roth used it many decades ago as title to his study of sex in the South Sea Islands; see Burton, 1935.

abstracted, ritualized sex. In this sense, xenological erotica is not unlike the cartoon strip, which, "with its caricaturing simplifications, is a vehicle for stereotypes or prejudices, for archetypes, a carrier of ideology, sometimes propaganda through drawing." (Servantie, 1989: 49, translation mine.)

The perception of national "types" as embodiments of national character, sexual or otherwise, has deep roots in European culture: "just as flowers and birds in the Middle Ages were studied not for their own sakes but as symbols of moral and metaphysical principles, so the differing breeds of men assumed an emblematic quality." (Hodgen, 1964: 179–80.) To get an idea of how strongly-held ethnic stereotypes were, it is instructive to note that the eminent critic Hippolyte Jules Pilet de la Mesnardière actually listed, in his *La Poëtique* [Poetics] (1640), the national attributes that should be associated with characters in a literary work in order to ensure its plausibility and propriety: "An Asian is timid, an African unfaithful, a European wise, and an American stupid." He went on to caution writers not to violate these rules by "making a warrior of an Asian, a faithful African, an impious Persian, a truthful Greek, a generous Thracian, a subtle German, a modest Spaniard, or an uncivil Frenchman." (la Mesnardière, 1640: 38, 125, translation mine.)[22] Discussing la Mesnardière's typology, Julia V. Douthwaite points out that "just as the dramatists of the classical age represented human society on stage as an assortment of French 'types' drawn from aristocratic experience (e.g., the master, the servant, the courtier, the lover), so seventeenth-century writers represented members of other cultures as exotic 'types' drawn from a stock collection." (Douthwaite, 1992: 27.) Such typologies found fertile ground in pornography, which is by its very nature reductionist.

As an aside, I might note that this pattern was by no means limited to the seventeenth or eighteenth centuries, and continues even today: the write-ups that accompany pictorial features in *Penthouse* magazine, for instance, often use racial/ethnic stereotyping to conjure the (sexual)

---

[22] See also la Mesnardière, 1640: 122–3, where the author painstakingly lists the "correct" qualities of the French, Spanish, English, Italian, German, Persian, Greek, Egyptian, Moorish, Thracian, and Scythian nations.

personalities of the women portrayed. For example, "Teneil attributes her active social life to her unusual Ukrainian-British heritage. 'My Ukrainian side makes me outgoing and lusty,' she confides, 'But fortunately my British side makes me very particular about who I'm outgoing and lusty *with*.'" (July 1991); or "Partly descended from Apache warriors, 'I'm as wild as the wind and ready to take the warpath for anything I believe in,' says the dark-eyed beauty." (April 1990.) And then there are wonderful non-sequiturs like "Part Cherokee Indian, French, and New Zealand Maori, 21-year-old Jisél has no patience for school." (May 1990.) Needless to say, these part Apache, part Cherokee, part Maori women are blonde and fair enough to make the Aryan Brotherhood proud! But this is for another book.

It is of course the principal function of ideology to mystify the political by naturalizing it, and what is more natural than sex? To quote Barthes again, "myth does not deny things, on the contrary, its function is to talk about them; simply, it purifies them, it makes them innocent, it gives them a natural and eternal justification, it gives them a clarity which is not that of an explanation but that of a statement of fact." (Barthes, 1994: 143.) Naturalization of what is political and man-made thus both absolves actors from responsibility and makes their construction seem inevitable and pre-ordained. In geopolitics, it is colonial discourse that carries out this function, acting "to dehistoricize and desocialize the conquered world, to present it as a metaphysical 'fact of life,' before which those who have fashioned the colonial world are themselves reduced to the role of passive spectators in a mystery not of their own making." (JanMohamed, 1986: 87.) The sexualized body, literally the embodiment of "nature," is an effective channel for such mystification, laying the foundation for what Pratt has called the "anti-conquest"—that is, "the strategies of representation whereby European bourgeois subjects seek to secure their innocence in the same moment as they assert European hegemony." Sex and slavery, two central themes of colonial literature, blend into one another as love becomes a naturalizing and absolving metaphor for colonial domination. (Pratt, 1992: 7, 86, 97.) Consequently, while sexual ethnic stereotypes provided useful material for pornography in the form of recognizable archetypes, they simultaneously acted to mystify and naturalize global inequalities and Western hegemony.

In the great works of "domestic" fiction of the nineteenth century, order was brought to social relationships by subordinating all social differences to those based on gender. (Armstrong, 1987: 4.) By the same token, ethnopornography reduces all global differences to those based on sexuality, and thus functions to bring order to the geopolitical balance dictated by the hegemonic powers. It does this by constructing sexualized spaces of otherness, spaces whose sexuality is interpreted, with the right ideological "spin," as justifying colonial rule: "the definition of otherness, the degree to which others can be persuasively shown to be discordant with the putative norm, provides a rationale for conquest." (Deane, 1990: 12.) Describing difference—or, more accurately, constructing socially significant difference—serves to construct the norm itself, an important function of xenological erotica.

How are these sexualized spaces of otherness constructed? Michel de Certeau has emphasized the role of *boundaries*, arguing that:

> it is the partition of space that structures it. Everything refers in fact to this differentiation which makes possible the isolation and interplay of distinct spaces. From the distinction that separates a subject from its exteriority to the distinctions that localize objects, from the home (constituted on the basis of the wall) to the journey (constituted on the basis of a geographical "elsewhere" or a cosmological "beyond"), from the functioning of the urban network to that of the rural landscape, there is no spatiality that is not organized by the determination of frontiers. (Certeau, 1984: 123.)

But it seems to me that it is not, strictly speaking, the *boundary* that defines a place, rather the imagined *contrast* between the "inside" and the "outside." Encircling an arbitrary acre of Antarctica with a picket fence would not appear particularly meaningful to most observers, since there would be little or no difference between what lies within and without the fence. Likewise, what makes the home is not the four walls that delimit it, but rather the fact that it is that unique place where we can be together with our loved ones, sleep at night, enjoy our belongings, or keep warm in the winter and dry during rain. Doreen Massey makes this argument more precise: she proposes an alternative interpretation of place based upon the premise that "what gives a place its specificity is not some long internalized history but the fact that it is constructed out of a particular constellation of social relations, meeting and weaving together at a particular locus." Thus, she writes, instead of "thinking of places as areas with boundaries around, they can be imagined as articulated moments in networks of social relations and understandings." (Massey, 1994: 154.)

It is *difference*, then, that makes place; to imagine a place, it is not even necessary to know explicitly the precise location of its boundary. Take for example the "Orient": in the nineteenth century, it was sometimes held to begin at the river Leitha, a small tributary of the Danube just downstream of Vienna. (Armstrong, 1929: xii.) But how literally must such an assertion be taken? Surely it was not a real or imagined line passing through the southeastern suburbs of the Austrian capital that divided East from West, but rather the differences between the respective characteristics attributed to each region. In other words, in contrast to physical locations, whose boundaries can be expressed in degrees and minutes, the distinctions between *socially constructed* spaces are primarily *qualitative*. And once again, those qualitative differences define the "here" as well as the "there": "the lines on the map produce borders beyond which things are seen to be different. Yet, the difference of the 'outside' also defines what is 'inside' the border." (Diprose and Ferrell, 1991: ix.)

When de Certeau goes on to say that "a narrative activity, even if it is multiform and no longer unitary, thus continues to develop where frontiers and relations with space abroad are concerned. Fragmented and disseminated, it is continually concerned with marking out boundaries" (Certeau, 1984: 125), I would claim, instead, that narratives of space are continually concerned with *mapping out difference* between the "here" and the "there"—this indeed is what lies at the root of "the metropolis['s] obsessive need to present and re-present its peripheries and its others continually to itself." (Pratt, 1992: 6.)

Sexuality, that element of power relations endowed with the greatest instrumentality according to Foucault, played a key role in mapping out difference: "here" and "there" were distinguished, if not principally, at least significantly, by the imagined differences between the sexual practices of "us" and "them." Harems, eunuchs, public baths, dancing girls, concubines, slave markets, all relentlessly provided evidence of the Orient's alterity. This construction of difference served both domestic and global political imperatives, defining the self as well as representing the other as a territory to be conquered: "the 'Otherness' which was central to Westerners' concept of the Orient—it was what they were not—[was] expressed in terms which are both racial/cultural and profoundly sexual, both elements combining to define a terrain— the Orient—for control, power, and domination." (De Groot, 1989: 104.)

The Foreign Country Is a Past

Another axis along which spaces of otherness were constructed was that of time. In the now famous opening line of L.P. Hartley's novel *The Go-Between* (1953), the narrator says: "The past is a foreign country: they do things differently there." (Hartley, 1954: 3.) In a classic study whose title was inspired by this very line, David Lowenthal pointed out that past and present were not differentiated throughout most of history, and that ancient events, when referred to, were portrayed as contemporaneous: "Only in the late eighteenth century did Europeans begin to conceive the past as a different realm, not just another country but a congeries of foreign lands endowed with unique histories and personalities." (Lowenthal, 1985: xvi.)

Paradoxically, one of the consequences of this new historical consciousness in Europe was an *ahistorical* perspective on non-European societies. As distance was increasingly experienced in what one might call a time–space continuum, it came to be measured interchangeably in miles and centuries. Thus, in October 1904, on his way back from two years in the South Sea Islands, Victor Segalen—one of the most prominent figures in the turn-of-the-century exoticist movement— jotted down a note to himself, in which he proposed to write a book on exoticism: "Argument: parallelism between regression into the past (historicism) and the spatially remote (exoticism)." This was apparently the earliest reference to his unfinished *Essai sur l'exotisme* [Essay on exoticism] (written in 1904–18, published in 1978), in which he set out to "gradually extend the notion of exoticism . . . to history. Past or future." Asserting that "exoticism is not only given in space, but equally as a function of time," Segalen recalled an analogy drawn by André Gide between epoch and homeland, and saw temporal exoticism as a "flight from the wretched and despicable present" into "the elsewheres and the once-upon-a-times." (Segalen, 1978: 13, 19–20, 23, 28, 57, translation mine.)

To be sure, this equivalence between temporal and spatial distance was not, in itself, a particularly recent phenomenon: in the preface to the 1676 edition of his play *Bajazet*—a tragedy about the Ottoman prince Bayezid, who was executed in 1635 on the orders of his brother Sultan Murad IV—Racine justified his choice of such "recent" subject matter by pointing out that physical distance compensated in this case for the temporal proximity of the events portrayed:

> for if I may say so, people scarcely distinguish between what is a thousand years and what is a thousand leagues away from them. Thus it is that Turkish people, for example, however modern they may be, have a dignity upon our stage. One sees them as ancient before their time. Theirs are completely different mores and customs. We have so little commerce with the princes and the other people who inhabit the Seraglio that we consider them, so to speak, people living in another century than our own. (Racine, 1991: xiv.)[23]

But the association of time with progress, that is the erection of a value hierarchy associated with temporality, *is* a later phenomenon. Foreign countries were no longer just geographically remote, they now also corresponded to particular points on linear time; and since Europe represented the furthest stage of human evolution, other countries were necessarily identified with its past. Asians and Africans were not merely different, in other words, they were the way Europeans used to be in some semi-mythical, long-gone era. This was actually a solution to the puzzling plurality of humanity with which the Age of Exploration had confronted Europe: as scholars "struggled to form some kind of

[23] I have modified the translation somewhat. See the French edition of 1885–88: 2: 491–2. On the interesting case of a Peruvian society that does not clearly distinguish between distance in time and space, see Skar, 1981: 35–49.

synthesis of the peoples of the New World from the avalanche of descriptive materials which descended on their desks," they advanced the argument that these were "men in an early stage of development, primitive Europeans in a sense." In Peter Heylyn's *Microcosmos* of 1636, this claim was given great precision: "He that travelleth in any part of America not inhabited by Europeans shall find a world very like to that we lived in, in or near the time of Abraham the Patriarch about three hundred years after the flood." (Cited in Marshall and Williams, 1982: 191.)

The very historicism that endowed Europeans with the capacity to perceive their own change and the conceptual apparatus to interpret it as development or progress, thus made them deny non-European societies those same processes, and view them as timeless, mired in the past. Through this conflation of chronology and chorography, this tendency to view anachorism as anachronism, the West condemned the rest of the world to eternal stasis. An instructive example is Bernhard Stern's *Medizin, Aberglaube und Geschlechtsleben in der Türkei* [Medicine, superstition, and sex life in Turkey] (1903), a massive work with encyclopedic pretensions whose second volume (the one on sex, naturally!) was translated into English and "printed for subscribers" in 1934.[24] Beginning with a 25-page annotated bibliography and ending with a 41-page index, the German original at first sight gives every indication of being the fruit of serious scholarship. Upon reading it, however, the fact that perhaps stands out the most is the way in which anachronistic sources such as Ovid, Pliny, or the Bible are blended with contemporary folklore and personal observation to explain the social and sexual mores of Ottoman subjects around the turn of the century. For example, chapter 14 of volume 2 (to pick one at random) covers the following sources and topics, in precisely this order: the Bible, ancient Persia, the Qur'ān, Druses, modern Persia, Albania, Bosnia,

[24] In this edition, the text was supplemented by numerous nude photographs, mostly taken from Carl Heinrich Stratz's *Die Rassenschönheit des Weibes* [*The Racial Beauty of Women*] (1901), of what can only be described as "non-Western-European" women—ranging from Greeks and Algerians to Indians and Japanese, but excluding the main topic of the book, namely Turks; by contrast, both the bibliography and the index were left out, suggesting that despite the scholarly-sounding publisher and the title of "M.D." appended to the author's name, this translation's sole purpose was to titillate.

Bulgaria, Turkey, Serbia, Africa, Estonia, ancient Greece, ancient Rome, India, and Australia. Chapter 16 covers similar topics, this time drawing upon Herodotus (on Babylonia and Assyria), the Bible, the Qur'ān, Ovid, Martial, Hesiod, Propertius, and Lucian.

Today, this collection of subject matter seems totally incongruous; in past centuries, however, this was the norm rather than the exception: "The Bible, or the writings of Herodotus, Pliny, Strabo and Ptolemy remained authorities on Asia which, for many, needed little if any revising or supplanting until the nineteenth century." This was due to a firm belief in the unchanging nature of the non-European world: "the customs of the people of the Near East were of some interest because they were the same people who had lived in the area in Biblical times and it was assumed that Asian peoples did not change their mode of life. . . . Nearly all European commentators agreed that the distinguishing feature that they had in common above all others was imperviousness to change. Asians were intensely conservative. They never adopted new ideas or new practices. Thus descriptions of Asian peoples in the Bible or by the Greeks were virtually identical with those given by contemporary travelers." (Marshall and Williams, 1982: 7, 10, 128.) As a result, Walter B. Harris could write "a wonderful life these Bedouins live, wandering from place to place, . . . [p]assing their days as their ancestors passed it when Rebecca was found at the well" (Harris, 1889: 56), while Edward S.D. Tompkins thought that the fountain he and his party encountered was "perhaps the very fountain from which Mary drew water" (Tompkins, 1889: 248), a view echoed by Sir Frederick Treves, who stated that "the primitive villages differ probably but little from the village of the days of Christ." (Treves, 1912: 24.) Indeed, the Rev. Edward John Hardy was moved to make such parallels explicit in a book whose very title said it all: *The Unvarying East: Modern Scenes and Ancient Scriptures* (1912). He wrote that "the best commentary on the Bible is the Bible itself, and the next best is residence in the East. . . . The acquisition of knowledge of Eastern ways gives us, if not a Fifth Gospel, certainly a setting of the four we have, in newer and more clearly cut type." (Hardy, 1912: 15.)[25] But if houses,

---

[25] It is astonishing that Hardy, who had served as chaplain to the British forces overseas,

wells, and fountains had not changed since Biblical times, how could sexual practices have? Little wonder, then, that Stern used the Bible to explain the sex lives of present-day Middle-Easterners.

The same mentality is at work in a much more recent book, Gabriele Mandel's *Oriental Erotica* (1983), where the author incongruously identifies sexual positions depicted in nineteenth- and twentieth-century Persian, Kurdish, and Turkish popular art by their Sanskrit names. (Mandel, 1983: 16–17, 52–5, 62–3, 79–80.)[26] To be sure, a number of Indian classics were known (in translation) to the Middle East, and some medieval Arabic erotic works may well have been inspired by them; still, it is difficult to imagine that Sanskrit names of sexual positions would have been particularly meaningful to a late-nineteenth-century folk artist in Iran or Turkey! This is a meaningless display of pedantry which can only be explained, it would seem, in terms of a homogenizing vision that melds societies separated by thousands of miles and almost fifteen centuries into a single undifferentiated "Orient." Indeed, Pinhas ben Nahum, the pseudonymous author of *The Turkish Art of Love* (1933), went as far as to claim that sexuality is a historical invariant that characterizes the East:

> The love-life of any people ... teaches one much more about the people than its political, social, or economic life. For these factors change with almost every generation, certainly with every passing century, whereas the love-life of a people is as fixed and immutable as its soil and climate. Therefore, to know the Turkish Art of Love is to know Turkey itself. And to know Turkey is, in large measure, to know the Orient, the other half of this strange world. (Pinhas, 1933: 258.)

The historicist perspective that viewed each society as representative of a particular stage of human development defined an agenda for

---

sought (and found) analogies between the Scriptures and contemporary life not only in Palestine, but also in China! Someone else might have attempted to explain such similarities by invoking the invariants of the "human condition" or some such, but not Hardy; to him, the Bible and China were similar because they were both oriental. (I should note in passing that Hardy's book is far from unique: a number of other works similarly attempted to shed light upon social life and material culture as depicted in the Bible by drawing parallels with the contemporary Middle East.)

[26] A comparable work is Robert Surieu's *Sarv é Naz* (1967), which, though it does venture into India and Turkey, better manages to stay focused on its declared subject matter.

early anthropologists: for instance Joseph-François Lafitau wrote, in a book significantly entitled *Mœurs des sauvages ameriquains, comparées aux mœurs des premiers temps* [Mores of the American savages, compared to the mores of the earliest times] (1724): "I was not content to get to know the character of the savages, and to inform myself as to their customs and practices, I sought in these practices and in these customs, vestiges of the most remote antiquity." (Lafitau, 1724: 1: 3, translation mine.) In other words, Père Lafitau hoped that native Americans would provide him with information about Europe's own past. That European travelers' accounts tended to place foreign societies in a temporal order other than their own had profound political implications: "descriptions of foreign peoples as an iconic 'they' imply that 'their' actions are motivated not by historically specific local events but are typical examples of common custom or rites." Thus stripping "others" from all depth and complexity, "the European observer negates inter-nal conflicts within a foreign society by describing the native population as a collective 'they' whose activities take place not in a particular historical moment, but in a timeless present tense, implying that all 'their' actions are merely repetitions of pre-given, unchanging cus-toms." (Douthwaite, 1992: 16, 76.) As the idea of "progress" gained centrality in Western thought, it is easy to imagine the consequences of such a belief on Europeans' attitudes towards non-European peoples.

It has recently been argued that modern thought has privileged time (in the form of an inordinate preoccupation with historicity) at the expense of space. (Soja, 1989.) Indeed, Fredric Jameson has written that the transition to postmodernism has been accompanied by "the waning of the great high modernist thematics of time and temporality, the elegiac mysteries of *durée* and memory," that "we now inhabit the synchronic rather than the diachronic," and that "it is at least empiri-cally arguable that our daily life, our psychic experience, our cultural languages, are today dominated by categories of space rather than by categories of time, as in the preceding period of high modernism." (Jameson, 1991: 16.) But the primacy of the temporal in high modern-ist thought was not achieved by the elision of the spatial, rather by its subsumption under the temporal. After all, the modern era ushered in vastly increased global accessibility and an explosion in the physical scope of spatial practices. Europeans became conscious of other places to an unprecedented degree, and if the social sciences managed during this period to ignore the spatial and focus on the temporal, it is in large part because they viewed spatial and temporal distances as interchangeable. Since, say, Asia or Africa were perceived merely as versions of Europe at different stages of evolution, it was sufficient to formulate a single (necessarily Eurocentric) explication of the human experience to cover a wide diversity of social formations. (This is, incidentally, one reason why Marx was never able to adopt a coherently anti-imperialist position, and also why post-colonial theory today is so preoccupied with the category of space.)[27]

In his very interesting book *Time and the Other: How Anthropology Makes Its Object* (1983), Johannes Fabian coined the term "allochronism" to denote this "denial of coevalness," that is, "a persistent and systematic tendency to place the referent(s) of anthropology in a Time other than the present of the producer of anthropological discourse." Through this tendency, "relationships between parts of the world (in the widest sense of both natural and socio-cultural entities) can be understood as temporal relations. Dispersal in space reflects directly ... [a] sequence of Time." This practice was a dimension of the secularization of time, and "the construction of anthropology's object through temporal concepts and devices is a political act; there is a 'Politics of Time.'"

Fabian explains the roots of this politics of time in terms of a colonial imperative:

> It is not difficult to transpose from physics to politics one of the most ancient rules which states that it is impossible for two bodies to occupy the same space at the same time. When in the course of colonial expansion a Western

[27] For example, in an article entitled "The British Rule in India" published in the *New York Daily Tribune* of 25 June 1853, Marx wrote: "England, it is true, in causing a social revolution in Hindostan, was actuated only by the vilest interests, and was stupid in her manner of enforcing them. But that is not the question. The question is, can mankind fulfil its destiny without a fundamental revolution in the social state of Asia? If not, whatever may have been the crimes of England she was the unconscious tool of history in bringing about the revolution." (Marx, 1968: 89.) On post-colonialism, space, and displacement, see for example Ashcroft, Griffiths, and Tiffin, 1989: 8–11.

body politic came to occupy, literally, the space of an autochthonous body, several alternatives were conceived to deal with that violation of the rule. . . . Most often the preferred strategy has been simply to manipulate the other variable—Time. With the help of various devices of sequencing and distancing one assigns to the conquered populations a *different* Time.

Thus, anthropology justified colonialism by endowing politics and economics with an evolutionary concept of time, and by promoting "a scheme in terms of which not only past cultures, but all living societies were irrevocably placed on a temporal slope, a stream of Time—some upstream, others downstream." (Fabian, 1983: x, 11–12, 17, 29–30, 31, 32.)[28] I think this goes a long way towards explaining the obsessive, aggressive ahistoricism that permeates all of xenological discourse, and xenological erotica in particular.

Having outlined a framework for the study of xenological erotica based upon the construction of sexualized spaces of otherness, I now turn to the literary genre itself.

[28] On the elision of the temporal dimension in anthropology, see also Thomas, 1989.

Part II

Inscriptions of Gender and Sexuality

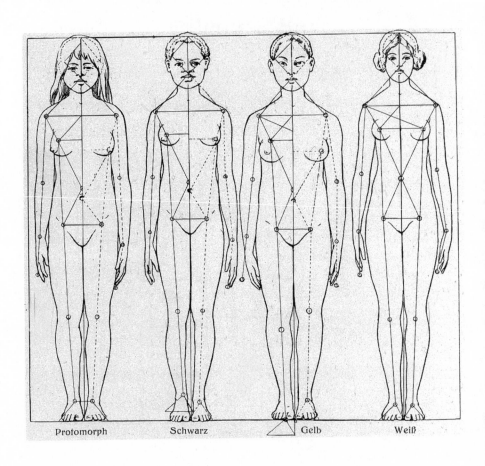

Protomorph   Schwarz   Gelb   Weiß

3

Ethnopornography

"Toward the beginning of the eighteenth century," writes Michel Foucault, "there emerged a political, economic, and technical incitement to talk about sex." The resulting regime of sexual discourses differed from earlier manifestations primarily by the preponderance of its modalities: "the Middle Ages had organized around the theme of the flesh and the practice of penance a discourse that was markedly unitary. In the course of recent centuries, this relative uniformity was broken apart, scattered, and multiplied in an explosion of distinct discursivities which took form in demography, biology, medicine, psychiatry, psychology, ethics, pedagogy, and political criticism." (Foucault, 1978–85: 1: 23, 33.) A notable omission in Foucault's catalogue of the areas in which these discursivities took form is anthropology.[1] Indeed, if "discourses on sex did not multiply apart from or against power, but in the very space and as the means of its exercise," as Foucault writes (Foucault, 1978–85: 1: 32), then clearly the anthropological/ethnographic discourse on sexuality was an instrument of the exercise of geopolitical power.

It has been argued that ethnography and pornography share common elements as representational practices and discourses of power.

---

[1] I use the terms "anthropology" and "ethnography" loosely, to indicate discursive practices concerned with representing peoples not of European descent. This is not to say that the impressionistic narratives of early travelers and the more rigorous, "scientific" methodologies utilized today constitute an undifferentiated homogeneous whole; however, it is certain elements of continuity that I wish to stress. See also Douthwaite, 1992: 8–9.

(Hansen, Needham, and Nichols, 1989.)[2] There are also much more direct and much less subtle ways in which ethnography and pornography overlap, ranging from ethnographic works that venture deep into the domain of the erotic, to erotic works endowed with "a surface narrative of anthropological documentation" that permits the articulation of Western male fantasies in remote and therefore socially acceptable settings. (Dijkstra, 1986: 114.) As Peter Gay writes:

> The nineteenth-century bourgeoisie ... found reassurance in displacing its erotic needs as far from home—literally—as possible. ... [T]he doctrine of distance was a mechanism for licensing what was impermissible under ordinary circumstances. The bourgeois century, like other centuries, abounded in assertions that 'Jewesses' or gypsies or other 'exotics' were 'hot-blooded' or that redheads were passionate—principally because they were rare creatures. Figures remote in space or time or appearance could release sexual desires and overcome, or at least reduce, inhibitions against erotic fantasies. ... A provocative, barely clothed girl lounging in an Algerian doorway was exotic; the same girl in the same attitude in a Parisian doorway would have been obscene. (Gay, 1984–93: 1: 392.)

What could be called the "anthropological mode" in sexually explicit art and literature, then, at once provided an alibi for commercially successful erotic works and, at the same time, was one thread in the plethoric regime of sexual discursivities that proliferated in modern Europe.

Sexual Anthropology

One might justifiably ask if it is fair to group sexual ethnography with xenological erotica, to lump together, say, an eminent anthropologist like Bronislaw Malinowski and a pornographic novel like *The Lustful*

---

[2] Although I found some of the reasoning in this article somewhat contrived, it makes interesting points regarding the structures and codes (both formal and significational) that govern ethnographic and pornographic films. See also Stewart, 1991: 241–8, who suggests that ethnology is a suitable "scientific paradigm for a metadiscourse of pornography," and proposes to investigate its three constituents: "the articulation of the space; the positioning of actors within the space; [and] the invention of the social."

Turk. At a certain level, I think the answer is yes. Consider this: in the introduction to his famous *The Sexual Life of the Savages* (1929), Malinowski solemnly declared that "in Anthropology the essential facts of life must be stated simply and fully, though in scientific language, and such a plain statement cannot really offend the most delicately minded nor the most prejudiced reader; *nor can it be of any use to the seeker after pornography.*" (Malinowski, 1929: xxiii, italics mine.) Having uttered these pieties, however, he went on to dedicate the book "To my friend E. Powys Mathers," a man who made a career of publishing xenological erotica. Now, I am not suggesting that Malinowski is thereby guilty by association of being a pornographer, but clearly the connection must have occurred to him when he chose so to dedicate the book. Besides, as his diaries have shown, "scientific language" was not the only form in which sex entered his mind during his long and apparently celibate stay in the Trobriand Islands.[3]

Ethnographic publications were, in fact, a good source of erotica and especially of images of female nudity. Bare-breasted women first made their appearance in the pages of the *National Geographic* in 1896, according to Catherine A. Lutz and Jane L. Collins, who write that "nothing defines the *National Geographic* for most older American readers more than its 'naked' women. . . . [T]he magazine's nudity forms a central part of the image of the non-West that it purveys." Indeed, "until the phenomenal growth of mass circulation pornography in the 1960s, the magazine was known as the only mass culture venue where Americans could see women's breasts." (Lutz and Collins, 1993: 115, 172.)[4]

Predictably, compilations of such pictures soon followed. For example, Hermann Heinrich Ploss's monumental *Das Weib, in der Natur- und Völkerkunde: Anthropologische Studien* (1885) [translated as *Woman: An Historical, Gynaecological and Anthropological Compendium*] was reissued

---

[3] See, for example, Torgovnick, 1990: chapters 1 and 12. Torgovnick, incidentally, describes her aim as "opening the seam between 'ethnographic authority' . . . and a vaguer, emotional or 'intuitive' response to the primitive often at odds with scientific or scholarly knowledge." (23.) Surely a good part of that "emotional or 'intuitive' response" was (and remains) of a sexual nature.

[4] See also Rothenberg, 1994.

several times with ever increasing numbers of pictures, the overwhelming majority of which featured nudity. A wide-ranging study of woman—from a distinctively masculine perspective—*Das Weib* contained chapters on such topics as the female genitalia, breasts, puberty, menstruation, pregnancy, and childbirth. It was a commercial success, and although Ploss died a mere two months after its initial publication, expanded editions by Max and Paul Bartels as well as a substantially altered translation by Eric John Dingwall were subsequently published, all augmented by large numbers of often explicit illustrations.[5] Perhaps the outstanding example of the genre is Carl Heinrich Stratz's highly systematic *Die Rassenschönheit des Weibes* [*The Racial Beauty of Women*], which first appeared in 1901 and went through some twenty printings in three decades.[6] It is a veritable gallery of multiracial nudity featuring over four hundred photographs of mostly nude women and girls from all over the world, as well as line drawings purporting to show the physical "proportions" of women of different races. The pseudo-scientific language of the text mingles freely with the frankly pornographic nature of the photographs, offering the reader/viewer/voyeur a virtual harem designed to cater to every taste imaginable. Ferdinand Freiherr von Reitzenstein's *Das Weib bei den Naturvölkern: Eine Kulturgeschichte der primitiven Frau* [Woman among primitive peoples: a cultural history of primitive woman] (ca. 1923) is another illustrated volume where the erotic and the anthropological maintain a highly precarious balance.

A relative latecomer into this genre is John Everard's *Oriental Model* (1955), an incongruous pastiche of modern Asian and African nudes photographed by Everard himself, and turn-of-the-century orientalist images by the likes of Lehnert and Landrock. Perhaps to make up for the heavy airbrushing, the commentary by the photographer's wife, Jane Everard, assures the reader that "in spite of rumours to the

[5] Some of the sexually explicit passages and illustrations were collected in *Femina Libido Sexualis: Compendium of the Psychology, Anthropology and Anatomy of the Sexual Characteristics of the Woman* (1965). Another interesting and quite opinionated selection is Paula Weideger's *History's Mistress: a New Interpretation of a Nineteenth-Century Ethnographic Classic* (1985).

[6] Part of this book dealing with the women of Java was published separately; for an interesting discussion of that volume, see Stoler, 1995: 184–90.

contrary that ignore the simplest rules of anatomy, there is no fundamental difference in the bodily structure of the Oriental and the
Occidental woman." (Everard, 1955: 14.) Be that as it may, the recent
catalog of a pornographic video distributor from Southern California
specializing in imports and "international" themes lists an item entitled
United Nations Nude with a cast of over forty women; according to the
blurb, the film is "a celebration of the beauty of the races of humanity.
Naked Asians, Africans, Arabs, Indians, Islanders, Mediterraneans, and
more. . . . Every kind of open pussy and ass. A cornucopia of breasts.
. . . Every style of clit imaginable." This item is listed next to another
one, entitled *Lips: The Movie*, promising "100 different pussies, all close
up" from "30 different nationalities." It is sobering to see that in nearly
a century, only the degree of explicitness has changed.

Other works of this kind include *Women of All Nations: A Record of
their Characteristics, Habits, Manners, Customs, and Influence* (1908) by T.
Athol Joyce and N.W. Thomas, both Fellows of the Royal Anthropological Institute, and *Das Weib im Leben der Völker* [Woman in the life of
nations] (ca. 1910) by Albert Friedenthal. While the former is somewhat more tame, offering both a larger volume of text and a greater
proportion of dressed women, the latter features an endless succession
of bare-breasted women from exotic places, in addition to elegantly
dressed Europeans. Jules Gourdault's *La Femme dans tous les pays*
[Woman in all countries] (1882) begins with the promise that "the
romantic is absent from this book; it pushes aside the fantasies of story-
tellers and poets, in order to draw exclusively from the real," but soon
turns to "the oriental harem, whose mysteries were made popular early
on among us by the famous tales of *The Thousand and One Nights*" and
to "the beautiful golden cages in which the Muslim detains the birds of
his fancy [that] remain as hermetically closed as in the past." (Gourdault, 1882: vi, 34–5, translation mine.) *Die Frauen des Orients, in der
Geschichte, in der Dichtung und im Leben* [The women of the Orient, in
history, poetry, and life] (1904) by Amand Freiherr von Schweiger-
Lerchenfeld has a more modest scope, as its title indicates, but is no
less voluminous or richly illustrated. Covering the "Orient" from North
Africa through Turkey and Persia to India, it mixes art history with
harem fantasies, though the amount of nudity it offers is, as in

Gourdault's work, infinitely more restrained. Photographs of "oriental" women were, incidentally, not limited to books: postcards, for instance, constituted a prolific and lucrative industry.[7]

Another photograph album, this one entitled *A Private Anthropological Cabinet of 500 Authentic Racial-Esoteric Photographs and Illustrations*, "collected, annotated, arranged by the Anthropologist Robert Meadows" and "privately issued for mature subscribers only" in 1934, is a truly bizarre and quite disturbing hodge-podge of female nudity, genitalia, childbirth and nursing, illnesses and deformities, rituals, chastity belts, body modification, et cetera—indeed it is difficult to fathom the criteria employed by the compiler in deciding what sort of material to include in this strange assemblage. What *is* common to all these collections, though, is an encyclopedic approach to female sexuality, wherein individual women of different nationalities or races are presented as paradigmatic of their respective national or racial groups, and their multiplicity itself carries the unspoken implication of offering the (generally male) reading public the full range of sexual experience possible.[8]

Besides the better-known works of Malinowski and other anthropologists, many books on the sexuality of the "other" were published in the late nineteenth and early twentieth centuries. *Les Fastes de l'amour et de la volupté dans les cinq parties du monde* [The festivities of love and voluptuousness in the five parts of the world] (1839), published pseudonymously by Alfred de Theille,[9] is an early collection of supposed sexual customs from places as diverse as Africa, Turkey, the Carribean, Japan, Tahiti, and India. *La Femme dans les colonies françaises: Étude sur les mœurs au point de vue myologique et social* [Women in the French colonies: a study of mores from a myological and social viewpoint] (1898), by Pétrus Durel, similarly covers Africa, Asia, America, and

---

[7] For a creative (if problematical) reading of French colonial postcards of Algeria, see Alloula, 1986; but see also my review, Schick, 1990.

[8] It is worth noting that though women figured very prominently in anthropological photography, they were by no means its only subjects; see, for example, Edwards, 1992; Corbey, 1989.

[9] This attribution is due to Joseph-Marie Quérard, who calls it a "dirty production reproduced under the perfidious title of 'Souvenirs de voyages.'" Note that Quérard erroneously cites the pseudonym as "Saint-Elme." (Quérard, 1964: 3: cols. 525–6, translation mine.)

Oceania, and is adorned with charmingly naive erotic etchings. As its title suggests, the "musculature" (read: physique!) of women of different races receives special attention from the author.

Mœurs orientales: Les Huis-clos de l'éthnographie [Oriental mores: the closed doors of ethnography] (1878), published under the pseudonym "E. Ilex" and attributed to a Colonel Emile Duhousset (Pia, 1978: cols. 607–8), discusses sexual practices such as genital mutilation in Egypt and the Levant. *L'Amour aux colonies: singularités physiologiques et passionnelles* (1893) [translated as *Untrodden Fields of Anthropology: Observations on the Esoteric Manners and Customs of Semi-Civilized Peoples*] is one of several books published under the pseudonym "Jacobus X"—supposedly a French army surgeon who wrote of his experiences in Indochina and other French colonial territories. It covers such topics as prostitution, homosexuality, and the supposed characteristics of the genital organs of Asian and African peoples, and runs the gamut of stereotypes concerning size, odor, and lustfulness, all couched in the illusory authority of the eyewitness. *Curious Byways of Anthropology: Sexual, Savage and Esoteric Customs of Primitive Peoples* (1932) by Elie Reclus, well known in anarchist circles, offers some case studies from India as well as the Far North.

Paolo Mantegazza's *Gli amori degli uomini: Saggio di una etnologia dell' amore* (1900) [translated as *Anthropological Studies of Sexual Relations of Mankind*] sets out to present "all the curiosa in the sexual life and customs of mankind," dwelling particularly on "savage and uncivilized tribes, for it is in these scala that are most easily traced the roots and the infinite divergencies of the sexual life of humankind." (Mantegazza, 1932: 5.) The subjects it treats range from the rituals of puberty, deflowering, and forms of coitus, through courtship, marriage, and polygamy, to sexual "perversions," genital mutilation, and prostitution, and hardly any race or nationality is spared the author's panoptical attention. A comparable work is Iwan Bloch's *Beitrage zur Aetiologie der Psychopathia Sexualis* (1902–3) [Contribution to the etiology of the psychopathia sexualis; first volume translated as *Anthropological Studies in the Strange Sexual Practises in All Races of the World* (1933), and second volume as *Anthropological and Ethnological Studies in the Strangest Sex Acts in Modes of Love of All Races* (1935)]. The author of many books on sexuality and touted as "the founder of sexual science," Bloch aimed here to counter Krafft-Ebing's theory that sexual "aberrations" resulted from neuroses stemming from modern civilization. He covered roughly the same geographical area as Mantegazza, but with significantly greater emphasis on "vice" and "perversity," in an effort to show that societies at "lower" stages of evolution were also prone to sexual variation. Presumably to increase sales, the English translation of the second volume was supplemented with "A private anthropological cabinet of 181 erotic curiosities . . . including a rare section of 50 fetichistic [*sic*] photographs and scenes"—an incongruous collection featuring images of tribal warriors with weapons as examples of sadistic blood lust, "primitives" with elaborate hairstyles as examples of hair fetishism, and so forth.

Neger-Eros: ethnologische Studien über das Sexualleben bei Negern (1928) [translated first as *Voodoo-Eros: Ethnological Studies in the Sex-Life of the African Aborigines* and subsequently as *Dark Rapture: The Sex-Life of the African Negro*] was written by Felix Bryk, who, in addition to a book on the subject of male and female circumcision, also wrote about the naturalist Carl von Linné, plant species, lepidoptera, et cetera. The book was not without influence, and Marie Bonaparte records that Freud gave it to her when it first appeared, drawing her attention to Bryk's discussion of clitoridectomy. He pointed out that Bryk must have been familiar with his own theory of the transfer of erotogenic sensitivity from clitoris to vagina at puberty, "and thought Bryk's hypothesis worth examining, and checking, in the light of the facts. In any case, he said, this operation should not suppress the erotistic or orgastic potentiality in the woman; otherwise the Nandi men would never have allowed a custom which deprived them of mutual participation in voluptuous pleasure, which all men prize in all climes." (Bonaparte, 1953: 191–2.) Setting aside the fact that Freud appears to have gotten it exactly wrong, since the most likely motivation for clitoridectomy is precisely the control of women's sexuality, it is interesting to see how the study of the sexuality of "other" women here came back to haunt that of Europeans. Another professional "sexologist," Magnus Hirschfeld, published a part-travelogue, part-sexual ethnography entitled *Die Weltreise eines Sexualforschers* (1933) [translated as *Men and Women: The*

World Journey of a Sexologist], where he noted his observations on sexual customs in various parts of the world, as well as his interpretations of them.

In a sense, it is possible to consider Bob Slavy's strangely prescient novel *Le Harem océanien* [The harem in Oceania] (1935) the mutated offspring of this genre. Set in the aftermath of a eugenicist holocaust, it describes life in the dystopian "harem" of a sociopathic "mad scientist," drawing upon the mass of ethnographic fact and fiction assembled in books like those discussed above. No cliché is spared, nor ethnic or racial stereotype neglected, as Chinese eunuchs and Russian "Skoptzis," amazons and concubines, Polynesian dancers and Turkish harem superintendents all come together in a phantasmagoric tale of sadomasochism, pedophilia, homosexuality, and transsexualism. Science fiction blends with ethnography, as grafts of sexual organs alternate with footbinding and depilation, to create a story that definitively blurs the line between sexual anthropology and pornography.

If it is difficult today to determine where the scholarly ends and the prurient begins, we may find some solace in the fact that the distinction was equally unclear at the turn of the century: acknowledged publishers of erotica, like Falstaff Press, Panurge Press, and Charles Carrington, and publishers of a more ambiguous nature, such as the Anthropological Press, the Eugenics Publication Company, and the American Ethnological Press, routinely reprinted each other's works; and the defensive prefaces sometimes added to the books did less to establish their scientific legitimacy than to betray their questionable standing.

These kinds of books, incidentally, continued to be published well past the twilight of colonialism. Boris de Rachewiltz's *Eros Nero* [Black Eros] (1963), for instance, is a lavishly illustrated survey of sexuality in Africa, covering art and religion, body modification and genital mutilation, and sexual practices of various kinds, all the while showcasing hundreds of black and white and color photographs, most of which of course depict nude women. Armand Denis's *Taboo: Sex and Morality Around the World* (1967) is, like Hirschfeld's book, a travelogue of sorts. It relates the author's observations on several continents, including the inevitable stories about sexually uninhibited South Sea Islanders and Middle Eastern harems that hark back to the earlier history of the genre. As late as 1994, Richard Zacks published *History Laid Bare*, a compilation of sexually explicit tidbits from antiquity to the present, including the predictable accounts of harems, public baths, and so forth. Depressingly, Zacks writes: "The Turkish harem was not the figment of some overheated Victorian pornographer's imagination. It really existed for almost five hundred years, from 1453 forward. The basic setup: One Ottoman sultan with three hundred or more beautiful half-naked virgins at his beck and call." (Zacks, 1994: 177.) Myths die hard. Let us now turn to some of the earlier history of ethnopornography.

Jewels that Speak in Foreign Tongues

If ethnopornography reached its apogee around the turn of the century, its origins go back much earlier, to the vaguely titillating descriptions of the Ottoman seraglio given by so many travelers to the East. Indeed, to borrow a phrase from Foucault, from the seventeenth century onward, the image of the harem has "not ceased to provoke a kind of generalized discursive erethism." (Foucault, 1978–85: 1: 32.) Works such as Michel Baudier's *Histoire générale du serrail, et de la Cour du Grand Seigneur Empereur des Turcs* (1624) [translated as *The History of the Imperial estate of the Grand Seigneurs*], Ottaviano Bon's *A Description of the Grand Signor's Seraglio, or Turkish Emperours Court* (written in 1608, first published in 1650), and Jean-Baptiste Tavernier's *Nouvelle relation de l'intérieur du Serrail du Grand Seigneur, contenant plusieurs singularitez qui jusqu'icy n'ont point esté mises en lumière* (1675) [translated as *The six voyages of John Baptista Tavernier (. . .) to which is added A new description of the Seraglio*] laid the basis for fantastic and eroticized descriptions of imperial harems, so that by the eighteenth century, an array of stock motifs was available from which writers could pick and choose.[10]

---

[10] Thus, Mitchell Greenberg argues that by the seventeenth century, sexuality and politics were conflated in the European view of the Turks; see Greenberg, 1992. For a detailed study of the interweaving of exoticism and eroticism in early orientalist German literature, see Kleinlogel, 1989. On British literature, see Chew, 1937; on French literature, see Rouillard, n.d.

And so they did, in large numbers; indeed, the very work that supplied Foucault with the metaphor he used to describe the modern Western obsession with talking about sex was, perhaps not coincidentally, a novella set precisely in an "oriental" harem (more exactly, in the Congo)—Denis Diderot's *Les Bijoux indiscrets* [The indiscreet jewels] (1748), a tale based on the rather amazing premise that a magic ring caused women's "jewels" (that is, their genitalia) to speak out and confess their sexual escapades.[11] In turn, one of the works that apparently inspired Diderot, Crébillon's *Le Sopha, conte moral* [The sofa, moral tale] (ca. 1745), is likewise set in the Orient (this time in India), and tells the equally improbable story of a man whose past avatars included an incarnation as a series of sofas; the tenor of the book can be surmised from the narrator's comment that "just as it is true that few men are heroes to those who can see them up close, so I may safely affirm that there are, to their sofas, a precious few virtuous women." (Crébillon, 1745: 1: 31, translation mine.)[12]

Norman Daniel has shown how the Islamic institutions of polygamy and divorce, as well as certain religious motifs such as Paradise, were insistently interpreted by medieval Christian polemicists as incontrovertible proof that Islam is a sensuous religion which grants its adherents boundless sexual license, that its prophet was hopelessly debauched and corrupt, and that it is therefore a false faith.[13] The accounts of Baudier, Bon, Tavernier, and many others thus merely rode the coat-tails of earlier anti-Islam polemics, and even apparently serious and scholarly works unabashedly flirted with the erotic. For example, Aaron Hill's *A Full and Just Account of the Present State of the*

[11] See Foucault, 1978–85: 1: 77, 79. Diderot's novella was first published anonymously in 1748 probably in Paris, but with the fictitious imprint "Au Monomotapa." Reade reports that an English translation was published in 1749 under the title *The Indiscreet Toys* (Reade, 1936: no. 515), but I have not seen it. Other English translations include *The Talking Pussy* (1968) and, most recently, *The Indiscreet Jewels* (1993). On erotic accounts of the "Orient" dating from the eighteenth century, see Martino, 1906: 66–73, 265–72; and Dufrenoy, 1946–7: part 2. This latter discusses *Les Bijoux indiscrets* in chapter 7.

[12] I have preferred a literal translation to that in *The Sofa: a Moral Tale* (1927). On Crébillon and his many imitators, see Dufrenoy, 1946–47: chapters 5, 7, and 8.

[13] See Daniel, 1960: chapter 5, particularly 135–46 and 148–52; also Setton, 1992: chapter 1.

Ottoman Empire in All its Branches (1709)—dedicated to royalty and subscribed to by countless dignitaries—includes lengthy passages describing with relish the various adventures with Constantinopolitan women of the Master of an English Merchant Ship, an English Sailor, and a French Embassador's Secretary. (Hill, 1709: 105–7, 112–15.) Similarly, Elias Habesci's *The Present State of the Ottoman Empire* (1784) contains an "Entertaining Anecdote of a young Frenchman and the Wife of a Turk." (Habesci, 1784: 389–93.)

The manner in which exhaustive (and exhausting) descriptions of the palace bureaucracy, the structure of the military, and the religious hierarchy are followed by such silly stories of trysts with Turkish women is at first sight incongruous. It may be that even eighteenth-century travelers knew that "sex sells," but I would think that there is more at work here than pure commercialism. Bridget Orr has noted that while such accounts "follow a fairly rigid generic pattern, moving from accounts of the Turkish polity through religion and only latterly turning to 'manners and customs'[, *t*]*heir claims for authority stem from the completeness of their survey and the accumulation of empirical observation.*" (Orr, 1994: 157, italics mine.) This suggestion is borne out by Sir Paul Rycaut who wrote, in yet another book entitled *The Present State of the Ottoman Empire* (1666):

> Since I have brought my Reader into the quarters of these Eunuchs, which are the Black guard of the sequestred Ladies of the *Seraglio*, he may chance to take it unkindly, should I leave him at the door, and not introduce him into those apartments, where the Grand Signiors Mistresses are lodged: And though I ingenuously confess my acquaintance there (as all other my conversation with women in *Turky*) is but strange and unfamiliar; yet not to be guilty of this discourtesie, I shall to the best of my information write a short account of these Captivated Ladies. (Rycaut, 1668: 38.)

The titillating stories about harem women, and particularly those concerning the doings of Western men with native women, could therefore lay claim to being the authors' concession to scholarly thoroughness, constituting in a sense the meeting grounds of the erotic and the encyclopedic. From anti-Islam polemics to "thorough" scholarship, descriptions of the sexuality of "orientals" has, then, a rather long history in European thought. But why is it that it became such a central leitmotif in Western Europe during the eighteenth and nineteenth centuries?

The early modern period in Europe witnessed several phenomena that together laid the groundwork for the gendering and sexualization of world geography. In France, according to Georges Van Den Abbeele, there occurred "a remarkable conjunction between the vogue of exoticism and imaginary voyages, on the one hand, and the philosophical trends of skepticism, relativism, and *libertinage*, on the other." Furthermore, "the same age that saw the birth of nation-states and that sent men scouring the four ends of the earth also shut women up within the home, a historical coincidence perhaps but one that legitimated the gendered topography of the male imaginary in the very organization of daily life." (Van Den Abbeele, 1992: xxiii, xxviii.)[14] Neither was this development limited to France; in Britain, the changing class structure that underlay the colonial project also led to the emergence of gender as an important fount of metaphors for economic and political development. As Laura Brown writes, the late seventeenth and early eighteenth centuries were "the first major age of English imperialism, the age of the powerful consolidation of a consensus on the universal benefits of economic expansion, and of an energetic, wide-ranging, but incomplete ideological hegemony. The female figure, through its simultaneous connections with commodification and trade on the one hand, and violence and difference on the other, play[ed] a central role in the constitution of this mercantile capitalist ideology." (Brown, 1993: 3.) Needless to say, the female figure was deeply sexualized in this discourse, as it often is in androcentric thinking. Thus, a synchronicity encompassing the Age of Exploration, the confinement of women, the rise of the bourgeoisie, and the decline of the moral and ideological hegemony of the church created a context wherein the sexual practices of the "other" became a topic commanding great interest. One manifestation of this interest was a proliferation of books on matrimonial practices around the world. These ranged from Louis de Gaya's early and somewhat bawdy *Marriage Ceremonies, as Now Used*

[14] See also Jacob, 1993.

in All Parts of the World, originally written in Italian and first published in French in 1680, to Theophil Löbel's remarkably comprehensive *Hochzeitsbräuche in der Türkei* [Marriage customs in Turkey] (1897), which covers not only Turks but virtually every ethnic and religious group in the Empire, from Serbs in the West to Kurds in the East. (Incidentally, Löbel was for a time Sultan Abdülhamid II's chief censor.)

As travel gained currency and visibility as a strictly male domain, the discourse of travel became increasingly imbued with patriarchal values and conceptions, functioning as a technology of gender. In other words, travel came to comprise discursive practices that construct and reconstruct gender. (Van Den Abbeele, 1992: xxvi.)[15] Moreover, as a consequence of its own gendered nature, travel came to be imbricated with what Eric J. Leed has called a "sexual economy": "the *erotics of arrival* are predicated on certain realities in the history of travel: the sessility of women; the mobility of men. . . . Historically, men have traveled and women have not, or have traveled only under the aegis of men, an arrangement that has defined the sexual relations in arrivals as the absorption of the stranger—often young, often male—within a nativizing female ground." (Leed, 1991: 113–14, italics mine.) This is not to say that women never traveled, of course; a considerable number of women both traveled and wrote about their experiences during the Victorian era, for instance, as stressed by several recent studies. Still, many of them were viewed as eccentrics and until very recently travel remained by and large a male business.[16] The discourse of travel was thus profoundly sexualized, Leed's "erotics of arrival" applying both to the traveler's home and to the lands to which his travels took him.

Ronald Hyam has also suggested that empire may have had a corrupting influence and unfrozen restraint, since "it can hardly be an accident that all the classics of British erotic literature were written by men who were widely traveled inside and especially outside Europe." He cites the examples of John Cleland, author of *Memoirs of a Woman*

---

[15] On the gendering of travel and its discourse, see Wolff, 1993, and the references cited therein.

[16] For a historical perspective on the sexual economy of travel, see McNelly, 1975; for an attempt to subvert this traditional economy, see Pollock, 1994. For a titillating account of sex and travel, see Schidrowitz, 1927.

of Pleasure (1749, better known as *Fanny Hill*), perhaps the most famous work of pornography in the English language, who was for some time consul in the Ottoman port city of Smyrna (İzmir) and spent many years in India; Henry Spencer Ashbee (pseud. Pisanus Fraxi), the author of important bibliographical works on erotica, who traveled in Asia, Africa, and America; the anonymous author of the monumental *My Secret Life* (ca. 1890), who journeyed around Europe, America, and Egypt;[17] and many others. (Hyam, 1990: 90–91.) Though these facts hardly establish *causality*—for it seems equally likely that travel and the colonies tended to attract independent-minded, adventurous, and imaginative individuals, some of whom may have tried their hand at writing erotica—nevertheless, whether their interest in matters sexual preceded or derived from their experiences abroad, it is certainly true that there were a sizeable number of people who had traveled or lived overseas, and had the inclination, if not always the talent, to write sexually explicit material.

Intrepid explorers and armchair travelers alike applied themselves to the task, leading to a proliferation of romances and erotica which titillated their Western readers with juicy fantasies about oriental women and accounts of clandestine exploits in well-guarded harems.[18] Of course there was no unanimity as to the merit or accuracy of these works. For instance, an article in the *British Review* in 1817 criticized Thomas Moore, author of the popular "oriental" romance *Lalla Rookh* (1817), for writing a work based upon "fictions of Oriental extravagance [which] proceeds without moral, or purpose, or plan . . . in a tissue of flowery language, amorous description, and rambling vehemence." It pointed out that such works tend to whitewash the oppression and misery of the Orient, since "where so much is made of corporeal delights, and the various gratifications of sense; where we

---

[17] The 11-volume "autobiography" *My Secret Life* was first published anonymously in Amsterdam in a private edition of only six copies, and is sometimes attributed to Henry Spencer Ashbee. It has been reprinted numerous times both in its entirety and in abridged versions.

[18] In addition to the books discussed in later chapters, many more titles of such works can be found in the bibliographies of erotic works compiled by Ashbee, Hayn, Gay, and others; see Deakin, 1964.

hear of nothing but of groves and of baths and fountains, and fruits and flowers, and sexual blandishments, we are too apt to figure to ourselves a paradise of sweets." (Cited in Sharafuddin, 1994: 136–7.) Still, and despite such occasional criticism, the attraction of these works for the Western public seemed irrepressible, and the number published was correspondingly very high. Next to more mainstream creations like *Lalla Rookh*, popular editions also proliferated, such as Maturin Murray Ballou's *The Turkish Slave or the Dumb Dwarf of Constantinople* (ca. 1863), which appeared in a series of "Ten Cent Novelettes," and George W.M. Reynolds's *The Loves of the Harem: A Tale of Constantinople* (1855), a slightly racy historical romance "published in weekly penny numbers and monthly sixpenny parts." Hence, the genre transcended class boundaries, reaching an audience of sizeable proportions.

The process greatly intensified during the nineteenth century, when the sexual realm became "a central structuring feature of systems that relate difference to pathology." (Gilman, 1985: 37–8.) To be sure, sexuality was not invented in the nineteenth century; but its deployment was generalized to an unprecedented degree, and it became more explicit than ever before in dominant European systems of representation—particularly in the context of constructing difference. Not surprisingly, therefore, numerous pseudo-scholarly books on sex in the Orient were published during the late nineteenth and especially early twentieth centuries. Bernhard Stern's *Medizin, Aberglaube und Geschlechtsleben in der Türkei* is, as mentioned earlier, an ambitious work; after discussing medicine—formal and popular—in the first volume, Stern turns his attention in the second volume to sexuality. In no fewer than thirty-three chapters, he covers a vast range of subjects including polygamy, divorce, adultery, eunuchs, the imperial harem, sexual customs and terminology (presenting with great relish the relevant vocabulary in numerous languages from Bulgarian and Serbo-Croatian, through Turkish, Arabic, and Persian, to Hindi), homosexuality, masturbation, prostitution, venereal diseases, impotence, infertility, abortion, pregnancy and confinement, and the list goes on. The style of writing is quite chaotic, unsystematically drawing upon classical sources, collections of folklore, histories, and the writings of such "orientals" as Fâzıl Bey and Omer Haleby (to whom I shall return in chapter 5), not to mention hearsay and personal experience. While Stern is careful to distinguish, say, the Balkans from Asia Minor, an enormous territory is united in his book by its knowability, by its capacity to be reduced to a collection of facts. In that sense, this is an interesting book not only for its contents, but perhaps more so for its form.

A roughly comparable though more limited work is *The Turkish Art of Love*, ostensibly written by a certain Pinhas ben Nahum, but actually almost entirely plagiarized from Stern's book, with the addition of a few ribald tales from a French anthology, and a good deal of racist claptrap. In *Sittengeschichte des Orients* [Moral history of the Orient] (1932), Paul Englisch, author of several books including a voluminous history of erotic literature, sets out to cover a subject both temporally and spatially diverse: starting with the early Near East (including Egypt, Assyria, and Babylonia), he proceeds to Turkey, Arabia, and Persia, and thence on to India, China, and Japan. Once again, it is only the uniformity and unchanging nature of the Orient that holds together this dissonant collection of times and places. The topics are by and large the same as all the other books of this kind, including harems, sexual acts, and "perversions," as well as white slavery and sexual violence.

Though published a couple of decades later, Carl van Bolen's *Erotik des Orients* [Erotic of the Orient] (1955) is squarely in the same category as Englisch's book—covering "primitive" eroticism as well as that of Arabia, Persia, India, China, and Japan. Indeed, a number of new titles made their appearance during the late 1950s and the 1960s. For example, *Ladies of the Harem* (1955) by James Cleugh offers anecdotal accounts (mostly based on travelogues) of sexuality in Turkey, Egypt, Arabia, Persia, India, and Africa, counterposing these societies' "natural" polygamy to the "European Heresy" of monogamy. George Allgrove's *Love in the East* (1962), dedicated "to the memory of Sir Richard Burton," shows the Victorian explorer's unmistakable influence. Allgrove's views concerning race and gender are somewhat more enlightened than those of his mentor, but his general approach is quite similar: though he starts with the dialogues of Lucian, with the Hebrews and early Christians, and with pre-Islamic poetry, and ends with the post-colonial Middle East, his main source is still *The Thousand and One*

Nights, which he qualifies as "a guide to the present, as well as the past; . . . a shaft let down into the collective unconscious of the Arabs." (Allgrove, 1962: 52, 149.)

Based upon the writings of Burton and other even less reliable nineteenth-century travelers, Allen Edwardes's *The Jewel in the Lotus: A Historical Survey of the Sexual Culture of the East* (1959) sets out to survey sexuality in the vast region ranging from North Africa to India. Taking its informers' claims at face value, it offers an impressive collection of myth and hearsay, stereotype and fabrication, covering such topics as "woman," eunuchs, genitalia, circumcision, masturbation, prostitution, "perversions," and hygienic practices. This book would have been a useful survey of nineteenth-century British writing on "oriental" sexuality if only the author had been more conscientious about indicating his sources; still, though it is little more than a pastiche of quotations as it stands, it does convey the mentality that underlies the whole discourse. *The Cradle of Erotica: A Study of Afro-Asian Sexual Expression and an Analysis of Erotic Freedom in Social Relationships* (1963) by Allen Edwardes and Robert E.L. Masters is presented as a survey of more recent sexual customs in Africa and Asia, but the subject matter, as well as the sources, are quite similar to Edwardes's earlier volume. In "A Historical Survey of Sex Savages and Sexual Savagery in the East" (1963), published as an appendix to a volume entitled *Sex Crimes in History,* Edwardes argues that systematic sexual violence is endemic in the "Orient," due to the region's religious and cultural characteristics.

The Eunuch and the Virgin: A Study of Curious Customs (1962) by Peter Tompkins is a chatty, journalistic account of precisely the two topics mentioned in its title, once again largely based on the travel literature. Lo Duca's *Die Erotik im fernen Osten* [The erotic in the Far East] (1969), despite its title, covers Persia and India in addition to Japan. As for Joseph R. Rosenberger's *Sex in the Near East* (1970), its paperback cover is shaped like a camera lens focused on the crotch of a mostly nude "harem woman," setting the stage for a book with hardly any redeeming value. Very much in the tradition of eighteenth-century libertinism, though a couple of centuries too late, the author claims to have written this book in order to demonstrate to puritanical Americans the value of moral and cultural relativism. The concluding passage, "Sex should be like the wind. It should be free. It *is* in the Near East . . ." (Rosen-berger, 1970: 156) will no doubt come as something of a surprise to those familiar with that part of the world!

Though written with various degrees of care and reflecting different levels of learning, the books just described do have a great deal in common. They all seem to cover roughly the same geographical areas, use the same sources, and express more or less the same opinions about the same aspects of sexuality. Yet, it is important to bear in mind the fact that they comprise only a small subset of the literature, and a very homogeneous one at that. When taken in its entirety, sexualized xenological writing is considerably less uniform, as I will show in the chapter that follows. Before doing so, however, I wish to clarify the sense in which these works can be said to constitute a discourse.

Tropology and Variability

Reading through the enormous corpus of orientalist travelogues, romances and erotic novels, and pseudo-scientific treatises, one is struck by two qualities that are at first sight contradictory, and yet somehow seem to coexist. On the one hand, one finds a recurrence *ad nauseam* of the same motifs, anecdotes, and stereotypes over and over again, each culled from a previous work that was merely quoting yet another—in short, a process of reality-construction through the instrumentality of citation and repetition. On the other hand, one is confronted by a dizzying wealth of mutually contradictory assertions that, by a curious mechanism of intellectual denial, mysteriously fail to undermine the credibility of the literature *in toto*. Thus, for instance, "the oriental woman" is described as both sylph and harpy—both alluring and repulsive, crude and refined, disgustingly filthy and obsessed with bathing, unspeakably ugly and fabulously beautiful, elegant and ragged, shapeless and perfectly proportioned, graceful as a gazelle and clumsy as a duck, languorous and a beast of burden, a helpless prisoner and a scheming evil-doer.

Of course this tension is not limited to orientalist literature, and women are often ascribed conflicting attributes in patriarchal discourse. Toril Moi convincingly argues that this is related to the marginalization of women, which causes them to:

> share in the disconcerting properties of *all* frontiers: they will be neither inside nor outside, neither known nor unknown. It is this position that has enabled male culture sometimes to vilify women as signifying darkness and chaos, to view them as Lilith or the whore of Babylon, and sometimes to elevate them as the representatives of a higher and purer nature, to venerate them as Virgins and Mothers of God. In the first instance the borderline is seen as part of the chaotic wilderness outside, and in the second it is seen as an inherent part of the inside. (Moi, 1985: 167.)

Still, despite this tremendous variability, one also invariably encounters sweeping statements that deny it outright, like the 1866 claim by Suzanne Voilquin that "one peculiarity of Arab women is the physical and moral uniformity which produces but one single type." (Voilquin, 1978: 241, translation mine.)[19] Now, if Arab women can be all of the above and still belong to "one single type" in the mind of a European traveler, then the functioning of orientalism must be much more complex than is often assumed.

An increasing number of critics have argued in recent years that colonial discourse was not nearly as homogeneous or coherent as first suggested by Said in *Orientalism.* They have challenged the notion of a "consistent, univocal discourse that dominates, manages, and produces cultural differences," asserting that "figurations of an oriental Other are not unified or necessarily related in meaning; they denote a plurality of referents, do not necessarily have a common style in the production of statements about their Orients, and are engendered differently by social and literary circumstances at particular moments." (Lowe, 1991: ix-x.) This is true, furthermore, not only of different stages of the colonial project, but of particular times as well. Take, for example, the European discovery of the New World: two contradictory discourses co-existed in the initial European response to the native

---

[19] This idea, incidentally, dates back at least to the fifth century B.C., when Hippocrates affirmed that "the physique of Europeans varies more than that of Asiatics" because seasons are more uniform in Asia. (Hippocrates, 1923–28: 1: 131.) To Hippocrates, "Asia" meant Asia Minor.

Caribbean, a discourse of Oriental civilization and a discourse of savagery, both of which can be traced back to the classical period. (Hulme, 1992: 21.)[20] Failure to give proper consideration to such variability, both across and within specific colonial situations, entails the risk of missing some of the important mechanisms with which colonial discourse addressed a reality that was, after all, hardly static. Indeed, as Ali Behdad has emphasized, the homogeneity and coherence attributed by Said and some of his followers to orientalist discourse "cannot account for the complexities of its *micro*practices; that is, the specific but crucial points of its dispersed network of representations that include strategic irregularities, historical discontinuities, and discursive heterogeneity." (Behdad, 1994: 12.)

Before probing the significance of the variability that characterizes colonial discourse, let me address the more fundamental question of its very *discursivity*. After all, given the different and at times mutually contradictory assertions that run throughout the colonial literature, one could justifiably wonder if there is even grounds to speak of a single discourse. In *L'Archéologie du savoir* [The archeology of knowledge] (1969), Foucault argued that a large group of statements that constitutes a "discursive formation" is characterized not by a unity of object, type of statement, conceptualization, or thematic, but rather by the presence of a regular system for the dispersion of these statements. (Foucault, 1972: 31–9.) It is, in other words, not necessary for a body of representations to be homogeneous in order to constitute a discourse in the Foucauldian sense; what *is* necessary is that it be *deployed in a systematic way*.

In this respect, focusing, for instance, on the writings of women travelers tends to miss the point. Although Billie Melman has argued against the tendency to view Europe's attitude towards the Orient as unified and monolithic, progressing linearly, deriving from "a binary vision sharply dividing the world into assymetrical oppositions: male–female, West–East, white–nonwhite and Christian–Muslim, [or] from that universal propensity to 'think in pairs,'" she has indulged in some binarism of her own in writing that "in the eighteenth century there

---

[20] On the discourse surrounding the discovery of the New World, see also Todorov, 1984.

emerged an alternative view of the Orient which developed, during the nineteenth century, alongside the dominant one," and whose expression can be found in the hitherto largely untapped "mammoth body of writings by women travelers to and residents in the Middle East." (Melman, 1992: 7.) But this "mammoth body" was itself hardly homogeneous. Rather than positing *an* alternative view running alongside *the* mainstream one (one plus one still equals two), I would argue that many conflicting threads run through a single discursive fabric in the deployment of gender and sexuality in colonial discourse. This presents a good illustration of what Foucault has called the "rule of the tactical polyvalence of discourses," which he enunciates as follows: "Discourses are tactical elements or blocks operating in the field of force relations; there can exist different and even contradictory discourses within the same strategy; they can, on the contrary, circulate without changing their form from one strategy to another, opposing strategy." (Foucault, 1978–85: 1: 101–2.)

In the sense outlined above, gendered and sexualized representations of xenotopia and the "other" clearly constituted a discursive formation. Indeed, the polyvalence of this discourse—far from putting its existence into question—is integral to it, and the contradictions and splits within Orientalism therefore do not constitute a challenge to its unity and hegemony. As Meyda Yeğenoğlu notes, one must not "look for the re-statement of the Orientalist topos in the act of simple repetition of earlier ideas and images, but also in displacements, divergences, and even in the dissemination of dissenting ideas." (Yeğenoğlu, 1992: 46–7.)[21] Along the same lines, Behdad has argued that orientalism "depends for its economy on a 'principle of discontinuity' that makes possible the production of a whole series of discursive practices in various epistemological domains." Difference, ambivalence,

---

[21] Although I think this is a very profound point, I find Yeğenoğlu's metaphysical insistence that "orientalism establishes its *unity* despite the polymorphous nature of the texts that constitute it" (Yeğenoğlu, 1992: 58) rather less than convincing. In particular, her efforts to deny Lady Montagu's writings any sort of specificity (as argued, for instance, by Lowe, 1991: chapter 2, or by Lew, 1991) are at best questionable: as a British ambassador's wife living in the early eighteenth century, it is hardly surprising that Montagu's *Letters* are not devoid of sexist or imperialist attitudes; but proving that two things are not mutually exclusive is not the same as proving that they are identical.

and heterogeneity are, according to him, fundamental attributes of orientalist representations, in that they allow the possibility of the multiplication and dispersion of statements. Thus, "the discourse of power depends on discontinuity and specification to produce new sites of authority. In this sense, *heterogeneity is an enabling force* in the production and transformation of colonial power, one that ensures its currency in new historical conjunctures." (Behdad, 1994: 13, 140, italics mine.) To put it even more forcefully, "orientalist hegemony could not possibly sustain itself without its unique articulation and rearticulation in various forms and in different historical periods." (Yeğenoğlu, 1992: 47.) Thus, the plurality of gendered and sexualized images used by colonial discourse is testimony to its adaptability, and offers important clues regarding the problems confronting the colonial project at various times and in various places. Each colonial relation engenders its own narratives particular to its setting and history, drawing on an entire range of discursive practices, and reflecting the characteristics, duration, and stage of the particular situation. (Mills, 1993: 87–8.)

The power of orientalism (or, more generally, of alteritism) derives not from its manifest content (specific images, individual stereotypes) but rather from its epistemology. Abdul R. JanMohamed has suggested that this epistemology is based on the "Manichean allegory," which he considers the central feature of colonialist representational systems. Colonial discourse is characterized by its dualistic structure, and not by any individual claim it may posit: "the imperialist is not fixated on specific images or stereotypes of the Other but rather *on the affective benefits proffered by the Manichean allegory,* which generates the various stereotypes [and], . . . with its highly efficient exchange mechanism, permits various kinds of rapid transformations." (JanMohamed, 1986: 82, 87, italics mine.)[22] As we shall see, the dichotomy form is a potent instrument independent of any particular content, a form systematically deployed in Europe's self-exploration and self-construction in the colonial period.

To be sure, it has become something of a new orthodoxy to criticise

---

[22] JanMohamed follows Frantz Fanon's use of the term "Manichean" in *The Wretched of the Earth.* (Fanon, 1968: 41.)

analyses that implicitly or explicitly postulate some form of dualism, based upon the undeniable fact that the reality of colonialism was much more nuanced than allowed by simple dichotomies like white/ black or colonizer/colonized. Thus, it has been argued that "to interpret the configurations of colonialism in the idiom of such ineluctable divisions is to deny the impact of narrative on a productive disordering of binary dichotomies." (Suleri, 1992: 4.)[23] Yet, extant cultural artifacts suggest that these binary dichotomies were very much on the minds of those who lived the reality of colonialism; recognizing them as valid cognitive or analytical tools, that is, as devices with which those involved in that reality attempted to make sense of their own existence, is not tantamount to denying the multiplicities of that existence. While the poles often changed place, *polarity* remained a central feature of this discourse; to describe *moments* of colonial discourse as dualistic is thus *not* equivalent to positing ineluctabilities. It is not reality that was dichotomous, but people's perceptions of its various facets.

Like JanMohamed, Bhabha has argued that "the chain of stereotypical signification is curiously mixed and split, polymorphous and perverse, an articulation of multiple belief." For instance, "the black is both savage (cannibal) and yet the most obedient and dignified of servants (the bearer of food); he is the embodiment of rampant sexuality and yet innocent as a child; he is mystical, primitive, simpleminded and yet the most worldly and accomplished liar, and manipulator of social forces. In each case what is being dramatized is a separation—*between* races, cultures, histories, *within* histories—a separation between *before* and *after* that repeats obsessively the mythical moment of disjunction." In other words, it is the very existence of difference that is operative, not particular differences. Mutually contradictory stereotypes can co-exist without undermining one another's effectiveness; indeed, they reinforce each other even while they reciprocally contradict or negate one another. It is "the *process of subjectification* made possible (and plausible) through stereotypical discourse" that gives xenological discourse its effectiveness. (Bhabha, 1994: 67, 82.) In short, it is the ability to make—with absolute impunity—a claim such

[23] See also Lowe, 1991: chapter 1.

as Voilquin's that lies at the root of the representational violence inherent in xenological discourse. Recall Barthes: "Myth is not defined by the object of its message, but by the way in which it utters this message: there are formal limits to myth, there are no 'substantial' ones." Correspondence to the "truth," or even internal consistency, are simply not germane to its functioning; on the contrary, their absence bears witness to its triumph—an almost Cartesian "I represent, therefore I am."

Polyvalence therefore does not correspond to the failure of xenological discourse, but is largely integral to it. The great achievement of this discourse was not the creation of a coherent tissue of representations—whether a "realistic" simulacrum of a given society, or its deliberate or unintentional "mis"representation—but rather its ability to pass arbitrary and sometimes mutually contradictory statements as fact. In other words, the most fundamental product of xenological discourse was its own credibility, and thanks to that credibility, it provided a seemingly inexhaustible supply of stereotypes that could be made to serve the structures of power.

That the credibility of the discourse was not undermined by the internal contradictions that permeated the literature is a historical verity; saying so, however, begs the question of how this came to be. How, for example, was it that a person could read in one place that the oriental woman is revoltingly dirty, and in another that she is obsessed with her toilette, and not question the truth-value of both texts at once? I think the answer is that xenological discourse was really nothing more than a collection of tropes which, while not necessarily mutually consistent, each fulfilled a certain function in the process of Europe's self-definition through othering and/or in the colonial project. For instance, the trope of the dirty oriental woman was central both to the self-consciousness of the rising European bourgeoisie as clean and proper (as distinct from the filthy working classes, "the great unwashed") and to the imperial effort that justified itself in part through its claim to bring hygiene and health care to the "primitive" colonies; on the other hand, the fixation of orientalist discourse upon Turkish baths served the function of portraying the oriental woman as inordinately preoccupied with her body, hence excessively sensual, licentious, *ergo* once again unlike the hard-working, self-sacrificing, essentially asexual European *bourgeoise*; moreover, such inveterate sexuality militated against the "other's" ability to self-govern, and hence argued in favor of colonization. Each product of orientalist discourse, each travel book or novel or ethnography, was at the most fundamental level a medley of such tropes, whose effectiveness derived from membership in a larger entity. That is to say, each text benefited from the aggregate authority of alteritist discourse as a whole, and while individual works frequently took issue with one another or criticized earlier writings, the truth-value of the discourse itself and its episteme were not called into question. Commenting on the inconsistencies that characterize anthropology, Anita Levy thus notes: "To enter into this debate is to assume that anthropology's contradictions indeed represent all sides of the argument; instead, I believe that they reveal a strategy whereby intellectuals agree to disagree on issues within a framework, so that the framework itself remains the more firmly in place and far-reaching in scope." (Levy, 1991: 56.) This is true of all xenological discourse.

In a certain sense, this corresponds to a radial rather than longitudinal version of Derrida's *différance*—the constitution of meaning through difference/deferral. (Derrida, 1973: 129–60.) Rather than a potentially infinite linear referential chain, in other words, Europe signifies itself as a many-spoked wheel, a hub linked to a rim not by a simple binary relationship, but by a plethora of dichotomies not necessarily logically consistent with each other. The self is suspended, as it were, in mid-air, held in place by countless dialogical forces that link it to other, equally unfixed referents. In a manner not unlike Engels's infinite series of parallelograms of forces whose resultant propels history,[24] it is the resultant of many, often mutually incoherent, significative inputs that infuses the self with meaning; Europe floats within its constitutive

[24] In a well-known letter to Joseph Block dated 21 September 1890, Engels wrote: "history is made in such a way that the final result always arises from conflicts between many individual wills, of which each in turn has been made what it is by a host of particular conditions of life. Thus there are innumerable intersecting forces, an infinite series of parallelograms of forces which give rise to one resultant—the historical event." (Marx, Engels, and Lenin, 1972: 295.)

outside, buoyed by myriad contrasts that distinguish it from its "others." And thus we are back to the Panopticon:

> Panopticism constitutes a succint geometry of a society that defines its primary mental and social relationships in terms of radial lines. The dialectic between the core and periphery establishes a single-valued logic: madness is known as an absence of sanity, crime as a lack of virtue, ignorance as thought in want of knowledge. The line connecting these paired opposites is aggressive and progressive. There is no middle term or golden mean but only a temporary horizon that serves partly to advance, partly to defend. (Kunze, 1987: 10.)

This resolves the apparent contradiction between the citationary aspect of orientalism, emphasized by Said, and the internal inconsistencies that characterize it: there were many times more motifs to cite than any single work could accommodate; an individual author would pick and choose from this vast repertory—by a process that was, of course, not arbitrary but determined by the conditions under which he or she labored—and would often end up with a set of motifs that contradicted another writer's choices. This did not matter, for, as Said puts it, "every one of them kept intact the separateness of the Orient, its eccentricity." (Said, 1979: 206.)[25] In other words, each one of them was a technology of place.

---

[25] Said adds "its backwardness, its silent indifference, its feminine penetrability, its supine malleability," but I will show in the pages that follow that the discourse was more complex than that.

Ducourtioux sc.

Chrétiennes captives des Turcs

H.Daragon.Ed.

4

Gendered Geography,
Sexualized Empire

To affirm that space, geography, and empire are socially constructed implies, *inter alia*, that they necessarily bear the imprint of society's systems of signification; it is hardly surprising, then, that they are profoundly gendered and sexualized. Going back at least to the gynecomorphic map of Europe first published by Joannes Bucius (Johann Putsch) in 1537,[1] the gendering of place has a long history in Western culture; the sexualization of foreigners—whether real or fictitious—likewise goes back many centuries, to Cleopatra, Salomé, the Queen of Sheba, Helen of Troy, Dido, Monostatos, Othello, and Caliban. As Paul Brown puts it, the discourse of sexuality offered "the crucial nexus for the various domains of colonialist discourse." (Brown, 1985: 51.)[2]

---

[1] There is some question as to whether the original map was intended to represent a woman or to be a fanciful portrait of Charles V of Spain. Nevertheless, in the hands of Sebastian Münster, Heinrich Bünting, and other subsequent mapmakers, it acquired unmistakably feminine features. See Hill, 1978: 39. Although I have something of an aversion to unquestioning applications of psychology to social and cultural phenomena, some interesting discussions of gendered and sexualized geography and geopolitics may be found in Stein and Niederland, 1989. For an analysis of the highly sexualized (but fictitious) map in Henry Rider Haggard's *King Solomon's Mines* (1885), see McClintock, 1988; and Stott, 1989: 77–9, 84–5. On sexualized representations of place in literature, see Lutwack, 1984: chapter 3. For interesting discussions of gender, sexuality, and space, see Rose, 1993; Massey, 1994; Betsky, 1995; Blunt and Rose, 1994; and Colomina, 1992. For a useful review of the literature, see McDowell, 1993.

[2] A good survey of the sexualization of historical personages, both fictional and real, is Kabbani, 1986. See also Hulme, 1992: 89–134. On medieval romances involving Christians and Muslims, see Metlitzki, 1977: 136–60.

For instance, a strong intertextuality existed between the British discourses of exploration and anatomical science during the late sixteenth and early seventeenth centuries, linking "the anatomist's opening and exposing to the eye the secrets or 'privities' of women and the 'discovery' or bringing to light of what were—from a Eurocentric perspective—previously hidden worlds." In particular, Francis Bacon, the principal theorist of the new epistemology, often used Columbus, Magellan, and the motif of travel "through which 'many things in nature have been *laid open and discovered*' as emblems of the potential development of science itself as a 'masculine birth of time,' opening and laying bare 'the remoter and more hidden parts' of a feminized 'nature.'" (Parker, 1994: 86–7.)[3] This point is made starkly, if lyrically, in John Donne's elegy "To His Mistress Going to Bed," thought to have been composed in the mid 1590s and first published in 1669: instructing his lover to disrobe and naming each article of clothing along the way, Donne writes:

> License my roaving hands, and let them go,
> Before, behind, between, above, below.
> O my America! my new-found-land,
> My kingdome, safeliest when with one man man'd,
> My Myne of precious stones: my Emperie,
> How blest am I in this discovering thee!(Donne, 1985: 184.)

With this punning use of the verb "discovering," and the preceding reference to America, the parallelism could not have been drawn more clearly.

Travel books frequently described the Orient as "The Eternal Feminine." Indeed, Douglas Sladen declared in his 1906 travelogue *Carthage and Tunis: The Old and New Gates of the Orient*—and apparently with a perfectly straight face—that in North Africa, "the women are far more Oriental than the men." (Sladen, 1906: 2: 324.) In this and other such statements, the quality of "being Oriental" was defined by the perceived differences relative to Western European (that is, primarily white male bourgeois) norms, and since women in the "Orient" appeared to be

---

[3] See also Dufrenoy, 1946–47, I: chapter 6.

more different from those norms than men, they were necessarily qualified as "more oriental."

But the Orient was not always depicted as female. Sometimes Christendom was pictured as a vulnerable woman, desecrated or in danger of desecration at the hands of a distinctly male oriental "other." In February 1454, for instance, a much-publicized "Feast of the Pheasant" was held at Lille to garner support from European sovereigns against the Turks who had recently conquered Constantinople. This was a lavish affair, rich in nourishment and symbolism; serving dishes alternated with floats and constructions, and:

> directly opposite the duke's table the figure of a woman stood on a high pillar. She wore one hat of gold, studded with precious stones, and another on top of the first garnished with flowers. Her blond hair fell loosely to her feet, and around her body was draped a veil with Greek letters painted on it. Throughout the banquet spiced wine flowed from her right breast. Next to her on a lower pillar was chained a live lion, described by [Mathieu] d'Escouchy as a most beautiful beast. Against the column, upon which the lion stood guarding the woman, was a placard with the following words in gold letters: *Ne touchiés à ma dame* [Touch not my lady]. The figure of the woman represented Constantinople, and the live beast, the Turk, who had captured and ravaged the capital of Byzantium. (Schwoebel, 1967: 86–7.)[4]

Somehow I doubt that the noble lion, that "king of the animals," was intended here to symbolize the enemy; it seems more likely that it stood for the power of the Western sovereigns that the Duke of Burgundy hoped to mobilize in support of Byzantium. Be that as it may, here Constantinople was portrayed as a woman, and descriptions of its fall were accompanied by gruesome stories of sexual violation. For instance, it was related by one chronicler that upon entering Hagia Sophia, the Turks found many Byzantine ladies and young girls of whom "they had carnal knowledge, by force and against their will"; another decried "the shamefull ravishment of women and Virgins ... perpetrate and done by the unmerciful Pagans and cruell Turkes." (Schwoebel, 1967: 12, translation mine, and 13.)

---

[4] On some of the sexual tropes in Renaissance Europe's response to the Ottoman threat, see also Hampton, 1993.

Now, such stories are of course common by-products of war, and I am not suggesting that these passages are in any way unique to this particular conflict. They do show, however, that the "Orient" was not always feminized. Though the practice of gendering and sexualizing geography may be ancient, its manifestations through the course of time have exhibited a great deal of mutability; indeed, to use a fashionable metaphor, it has been a veritable *palimpsest* on which the vicissitudinous history of Europe's contacts with non-European societies has been inscribed and re-inscribed.

In the pages that follow, I discuss the common thread of sexualization—paradoxically, perhaps—by highlighting the many *different* forms it has taken in xenological discourse. It has been suggested that the way the medieval *Wonders of the East* "jumps around the map from Africa to Asia and back indicates that its focus is not on the East as a travelable geographic area, notable for its strangeness, but on that strangeness itself." (Campbell, 1988: 63–4.) This, of course, is a trademark of xenological writing, where the similarity of the fundamentally dissimilar is taken for granted, so long as each is different from "us." It seems to me that the analysis of such material requires similar eclecticism: in this chapter, I am interested not in the depiction of a particular geographical area or period, but in the representational processes underlying these images. In other words, without suggesting that xenological literature constitutes an undifferentiated whole—indeed, while emphasizing the great variability that characterizes it—I aim to present a certain mindset common to European discourses on non-European peoples and places, one that persists under widely differing conjunctures, and whose very persistence is as noteworthy as any other attribute.

That narratives of travel at different times and to different parts of the world were viewed *in their own day* as constituting a unified *corpus* is evidenced by the numerous major collections which were published, from Richard Hakluyt's *The Principal Navigations, Voiages, Traffiques and Discoveries of the English Nation* (1589) to Robert Kerr's monumental *A General History and Collection of Voyages and Travels, Arranged in Systematic Order* (1811–24). Moreover, the interest commanded well into the twentieth century by grand theories concerning foreign regions and peoples—such as those expounded by Count Joseph Arthur de Gobineau or Sir Richard Burton—shows that this attitude has persisted until fairly recent times. For this reason, I too approach this material as a totality: the examples I give span a broad range of historical periods and geographical regions,[5] as my goal in this chapter is to underscore the manifold uses of sexual themes and imagery that appear *throughout* Europe's relations with the rest of the world, starting with the early modern period. The fact that examples from the sixteenth and the twentieth centuries, say, or from India and the Americas, follow each other in quick succession must not be interpreted as insensitivity to historical or geographical specificity.[6]

Making no effort to be exhaustive, and in no particular order, I will now list some different manifestations of the trope of sexuality in xenological discourse. I am not concerned with the causes of each manifestation, and therefore do not attempt to correlate them with underlying "material" conditions. I hope to demonstrate that what unites all the different forms taken by the trope of sexuality over the course of some four centuries is its utilization as a technology of place.

Xenotopia as a Woman to be Conquered

In a popular version of this trope, xenotopia was represented as a pure virgin awaiting deflowering; not surprisingly, this motif was primarily used in the context of New World exploration and colonization, as illustrated, for instance, by Sir Walter Ralegh's well-known metaphor, "*Guiana* is a Countrey that hath yet her Maydenhead, never sackt, turned, nor wrought," (Ralegh, 1596: 96) and Thomas Morton's complaint in 1632 that New England had been neglected by colonists and left

---

[5] I have left out East and Southeast Asia, although the analysis could (and probably should) be extended to that area as well.

[6] I have in mind, for example, John MacKenzie's (quite unfair) criticism of Lisa Lowe, in which he suggests that the very act of juxtaposing historically distinct manifestations of orientalism, even with the intention of underscoring their differences, somehow makes her analysis ahistorical. (MacKenzie, 1995: 24.)

Like a faire virgin, longing to be sped,
And meete her lover in a Nuptiall bed. (Morton, 1637: 10.)

In *The Lay of the Land: Metaphor as Experience and History in American Life and Letters* (1975), Annette Kolodny provides an excellent survey of these and many other feminine metaphors for the land of North America.[7] Such imagery occulted the colonial relation by sexualizing it: the masculinized colonizer and the feminized colony were depicted in a sexual, that is, natural/biological encounter, establishing a sense of necessity, of harmony, that justified Western domination. (Knibiehler and Goutalier, 1985: 40.)

Ironically, the New World was not the only virgin in sixteenth-century British political discourse: Elizabeth I, "the virgin queen," was after all the monarch in the name of whom the entire colonization enterprise had been undertaken. Indeed, she was made the emblem of the territorial integrity of England in Thomas Heywood's *The Fair Maid of the West* (ca. 1600–4), where she is referred to as "the mighty empress of the maiden isle." (Howard, 1994: 108.) This makes the simple male-Europe/female-xenotopia binarism difficult to sustain; the female body was in fact an extremely important trope in Elizabethan culture, and its areas of application were not limited to the colonies and their inhabitants. Images like the virginal land and the naked women of America came together with "the pure and dangerous, politic and natural bodies of the queen of England" in a semiotic matrix that rendered Englishmen not as the territorial aggressors they were, but rather as "passive beneficiaries of the animated land's own desire to be possessed." (Montrose, 1992: 163, 182.) Reconciling such tropes with the towering figure of the queen required some fairly creative rhetorical acrobatics on the part of British ideologues such as George Chapman, a challenge to which they ably rose. (Hulme, 1992: 159.)

Since America was of course known to be inhabited, albeit by so-called "savages," speaking of its virginity required another leap of logic; in large measure, that leap was realized by viewing the natives as part

---

[7] In particular, chapter 2 is about the virgin land trope and covers the years 1500–1740. For a nice discussion of this discourse, see also Montrose, 1992: 155–7; on the Spanish analogue, see Zamora, 1990–91.

of nature itself, and therefore as integral to the continent's putative virginity—unlike the "civilized" Europeans who had come to deflower it. In this context, the native population of the new world, both men and women, were seen as pure, uncorrupted, simple, child-like; this perception was quickly discarded when political expediency required recasting the natives as cruel and violent ravishers and rapists of the land and of white women. I will return to this point.

That the world was already inhabited was of little consequence to Thomas Carlyle, who wrote in his essay "Chartism" (1839):

> Over-population? And yet, if this small Western rim of Europe is overpeopled, does not everywhere else a whole vacant Earth, as it were, call to us, Come and till me, come and reap me! ... [T]o the overcrowded little Western nook of Europe, our Terrestrial Planet, nine-tenths of it yet vacant or tenanted by nomades, is still crying, Come and till me, come and reap me! [. . .] Is it not as if this swelling, simmering, never-resting Europe of ours stood, once more, on the verge of an expansion without parallel: struggling, struggling like a mighty tree again about to burst in the embrace of summer, and shoot forth broad frondent boughs which would fill the whole earth? (Carlyle, 1848: 382, 385–6.)

The phallic and ejaculatory metaphors in Carlyle's prose are almost overwhelming; but rather than Freudian keys to his subconscious, these images must be seen as *political* signifiers. As Perera has noted, "if Carlyle's vision of effortless and natural occupation conceals some of the violent realities of colonial settlement, closer attention suggests that this effect is accomplished largely by the sexualization of his language. The heaving fecundity of a supine earth, the struggle of Europe 'like a mighty tree' to 'shoot forth broad frondent boughs which would fill the whole earth' deliberately invoke the opposition of European/ Other, virility/passivity and masculine/feminine." (Perera, 1991: 55.) It is such oppositions that Carlyle and writers like him marshaled to make the colonial project comprehensible, compelling, and, ultimately, a reality.

But though such dichotomies do characterize *moments* of discourse, they are highly unstable. One must not lose sight of the fact that the figure of "woman" was widely used throughout this period, to signify extremely diverse concepts: yes, nature was symbolized by a woman, but so were knowledge, and law, and victory; America, Asia, and Africa were symbolized by women, but so was Europe. Even Britannia is, after all, a woman. Indeed, during most of this period, spaces and landscapes were generally coded as feminine in the Western political imaginary.[8] The female figure was not, in other words, confined to the colonies.

This is not to say that there was no difference between female figures representing Europe and those representing other parts of the world. The hierarchical arrangement and dress (or undress) of these figures pointed unmistakably to European supremacy: "dressed and learned in the sciences," Rabasa writes, "Europe rules and supercedes Asia, the origin of science, art and religion. In contrast, Africa and America in their nudity testify to the dominance of the feminine and tipify barbarous states which are, nonetheless, full of treasures for Europe." (Rabasa, 1985: 11–12.) Thus it was not gender but rather sexuality that distinguished the representations of Europe from those of other continents, and nudity (*ergo* sexuality) functioned here, as it often does, as a technology of place. In many nineteenth- and twentieth-century descriptions of Africa, for instance, the continent itself is anthropomorphically "endowed with a teeming female sexuality which affects everything within her. . . . African vegetation is abundant and luxuriant, African women are tempting, reproductive sex objects, who both allure and repel." (Busia, 1986: 364.) Europe and Africa are both women, then, but not the same woman: if Europe was characterized by the demure temperance of the model *bourgeoise*, Africa embodied the indomitable sexuality that white middle-class consciousness tried very hard to relegate to the working class, the natives, the "other."

Another version of this trope represented xenotopia not as a compliant virgin but as a wild woman to be tamed: as Alison Blunt has noted, "nineteenth-century travel writers often used sexual imagery to create and sustain the heroic stature of many male explorers and travelers

[8] See Gregory, 1994: 131. A notable (albeit later) exception is Albert Camus's *La Femme adultère* [The adulterous woman] (1954), where the French-Algerian woman's Danaë-like "adultery" is not with a native man but with the countryside. On the symbolic uses of the figure of woman, see Warner, 1985; on the representation of the continents as women, see Le Corbeiller, 1961. On the feminization of space, see also Rose, 1993: 56–61.

who wrote of conquering and penetrating dangerous, unknown continents, often characterized by the fertility of the indigenous vegetation
and women." (Blunt, 1994: 28.) Here, then, is an example of the
coexistence of mutually contradictory motifs within colonial discourse:
the land is both virgin and shrew, the colonizer both ardently desired
lover and tamer of resisting wilderness. The old cliché of the woman-
child, the virgin and the whore, is deployed to naturalize the colonial
relation: "Whereas virginity underlines the status of availability, thus
'logically' calling for a fecundating penetration, the libidinousness
subliminally requires the use of force. Colonial discourse oscillates
between these two master tropes, alternately positing the colonized
'other' as blissfully ignorant, pure and welcoming as well as an uncontrollable savage, wild native whose chaotic, hysteric presence requires
the imposition of the law, i.e., the suppression of resistance." (Shohat,
1991a: 51, 55; Shohat, 1991b.)

Whether compliant or wild, virginal or shrewish, xenotopia was thus
represented as a woman to be "taken," to be domesticated, by the
European *qua* man. In this way, "the construction of a sexual domain
was complementary to the construction of a domain to be colonized."
(Blunt, 1994: 29.) This duality between sexual and colonial conquests
played several roles simultaneously: on the one hand, it framed the
colonial project within a recognizable context, that of man's sexual
domination over woman; on the other, it reduced a complex political
act necessitating legitimation to an interpersonal relation that was its
own justification. Tzvetan Todorov puts it nicely when, citing Pierre
Loti's characterization of a man who supplied French officers with
native girls as an "agent for the intercourse of races," he comments
that "the country is reduced to its women, which makes it all the easier
to reduce the encounter with a country to a strictly individual relationship." (Todorov, 1993: 314–15.)

But the identity worked both ways. As sexual desire was deployed in
support of Europe's discovery and colonization of foreign lands, the
colonies in turn partook in the formation of sexual desire: "These
images began to construct the body that would constitute a mysterious
goal for men whose desires were armed for an imminent voyage, a
body that was to be more enticing than all the rest of the world put

together. It was the fountain men drank from after crossing the arid terrain of their adventures, the mirror in which they sought to recognize themselves." (Theweleit, 1987: 1: 296.) The foreign lands, in other words, moved back into the deep recesses of the self, colonizing European men's desires. The often-quoted 1926 statement by Freud that "after all, the sexual life of adult women is a 'dark continent' for psychology"[9] is indicative of the connections between femininity, sexuality, and Europe's colonial relations with xenotopia. This image naturalized colonialism by situating it within an established tropology and system of signification, that of gender.

Xenotopia as Sexual Idyll

Asking himself what Europe has retained from its long history of travels—from the Argonauts to the discoverers of the South Sea Islands—Bertrand D'Astorg replies:

> First the certainty—and how deeply rooted it is!—that the wind of Eros blows into the sails, and that the kingdom arrived at truly will be known only through the wedding of the sailor and the king's daughter, substituting for the queen herself. ... The European travel narrative is at its origin an epithalamium, that is, a nuptial song. It translates a desire for exogamy. ... What we seek in the Orient is to cross the 'Great Wall of China' of our immurement in order to reach the friendly spaces of the steppes. It is its spices to relieve the insipidity of our existence, its fabrics to veil the misery of our nudity, the shades of its groves to still or hide the impatience of illicit desires. (D'Astorg, 1980: 12–13, 15, translation mine.)

The image so eloquently conjured by d'Astorg corresponds to another trope of xenological discourse, that of xenotopia as sensuous paradise and sexual idyll.

---

[9] The context of this comment is the following: "We know less about the sexual life of little girls than of boys. But we need not feel ashamed of this distinction; after all, the sexual life of adult women is a 'dark continent' for psychology." It is important to note that the words "dark continent" appeared in English in the original German text, underscoring the fact that Freud was fully conscious of the colonial connotations of his wording. (Freud, 1953–74: 20: 212.) See also Brantlinger, 1988; Doane, 1991: chapter 11.

This theme was applied especially to the South Sea Islands, following the reports of early explorers that described boatloads of nude native women welcoming their ships and offering their bodies to the sailors as tokens of hospitality or (doubtless more often) in exchange for trinkets such as iron nails. Already in 1769, Philibert Commerson, a botanist who had accompanied the explorer Louis-Antoine de Bougainville, had dubbed Tahiti the "New Cythera," after Aphrodite's island. Starting with James Cook's several expeditions (1769–80), travelers' accounts created the image of an unspoiled terrestrial paradise, a population somehow unaffected by the Fall, for whom existence meant harmony with nature, and nature was synonymous with sexuality. In his *Voyage autour du monde* [A voyage round the world] (1771), Bougainville wrote that "the very air which the people breathe, their songs, their dances, almost constantly attended with lascivious postures, all conspire to call to mind the sweets of love, all engage to give themselves up to them." (Bougainville, 1772: 1: 228.)[10] The famous "Supplément au *Voyage* de Bougainville" [Supplement to the *Voyage* of Bougainville] (written in 1772, published in 1796) by Denis Diderot, who, incidentally, had never been to Tahiti, added to the mystique.[11] "Thanks to the narratives of travelers," write Yvonne Knibiehler and Régine Goutalier, "the Westerner could thus believe that countries overseas would offer him an abundance of women who were compliant, loving, and completely naked. The myth of the good [female] savage transformed in advance all the colonies into sexual paradise." (Knibiehler and Goutalier, 1985: 29, translation mine.)

Elaborated and embellished during the late eighteenth century,[12] this image was subsequently popularized by the likes of Paul Gauguin and his posthumous promoter Victor Segalen.[13] Thus, the barebreasted, nubile, ever-loving *vahine* effectively came to function as a

[10] The translator has "indecent" for the original *lascives*. See the French edition of 1771: 220.
[11] On Diderot's anthropological views, see Duchet, 1971: part 2, chapter 5.
[12] See for instance Porter, 1990; in particular, see 120–21 on the differences between the British and French attitudes towards Tahiti. Also, Douthwaite, 1992: chapter 3.
[13] For example, Segalen, 1907; Segalen, 1975. Also, Solomon-Godeau, 1989; for an interesting defence of the subversive/critical contents of Gauguin's work, see Brooks, 1993: chapter 6.

metonym for the South Sea Islands, as Maori culture was "massively coded as feminine, and glossed by constant reference to the languor, gentleness, lassitude and seductiveness of 'native life'—an extension of which is the importance in Polynesian culture of bathing, grooming, perfuming, etc." (Solomon-Godeau, 1989: 124.) (As discussed later in this volume, bathing and personal care was a leitmotif of orientalist literature as well.) Frenchmen felt irresistibly attracted to what they perceived as a haven from the sexually repressive bourgeois Europe, and while few actually packed up and moved to the tropics, many supported the colonial policies that appropriated and exploited them. In their imagination, in other words, they let France do with the territories what they would have wished to do with its women.

Although the South Sea Islands represent perhaps its apotheosis, the trope of xenotopia as sexual idyll was also applied to other parts of the world, notably the Orient. From Loti and Gautier to Flaubert and Burton, many writers/travelers were led to the East by sexuality. It would indeed not be an exaggeration to say that this literature treated the Orient as if it were the harem of the West, that the traveler entered an imaginary harem upon setting foot there. (Kabbani, 1986: 67; Knibiehler and Goutalier, 1985: 21.)[14]

But the idea of a remote sexual topos was not limited to the European exploration of Asia, Africa, or the New World: many seventeenth-century French novels featured the image of a gallant, amorous Greek society, and Greek women often embodied sexual desire in those works as courtesans or slaves. (Douthwaite, 1992: 45–6.)[15] Likewise, in the nineteenth century, Europe was mapped on an imaginary "grid of sexual difference, the Alps often serving as the boundary between masculine North and feminine South." This imagined polarity derived in large part from the growing popularity of continental travel—the "Grand Tour" as it became known from the eighteenth century onward—coupled with the fact that such trips were often a source of

[14] On sexuality and the Orient in the works of Hugo and Nerval, see Taha-Hussein, 1962; on Flaubert, see Porter, 1991: chapter 6; and Said, 1979: 182–90. See also De Groot, 1989.

[15] I might mention that Greek women continued to be viewed as sexually desirable in the multi-ethnic İstanbul of my youth.

sexual experience for privileged British young men. Thus, Italy, for example, was generally depicted as feminine in the works of authors like Henry James. (Buzard, 1993: 130–36.)[16]

In short, colonial discourse represents only one strand in the long-standing practice of gendering and sexualizing geography. During the nineteenth and twentieth centuries, French colonial writers wrote abundantly of the sexual lives of French soldiers and colonial administrators stationed in remote parts of the world. "As they moved from colony to colony," writes Hugh Ridley, "their experience of the various races increased and the Grand Tour took on an almost gastronomic quality. French colonial fiction devoted much of its attention to demonstrating the particular qualities of the various races as lovers, with a relish and a delight in voluptuous descriptions which only the most hard-bitten reader . . . could fail to respond to." (Ridley, 1983: 80.)[17]

While sexuality was hardly the *driving force* of colonialism, as some have been known to argue, it was thus without doubt an important means for its representation and legitimation, as well as for the interpellation of metropolitan subjects. As Ronald Hyam writes, "the expansion of Europe was not only a matter of 'Christianity and commerce,' it was also a matter of copulation and concubinage." Certain cities specialized in the sex industry, catering to colonial cadres: "Port Said, Singapore and Macao were intercontinental sex capitals and initiation centers for whites new to empire. Before 1914 a young man's first experience of the East might well be in a brothel in one of these cities." (Hyam, 1990: 2, 108.)[18]

Needless to say, such experiences found their way into erotic works.

[16] Buzard goes on to discuss the "sex change" undergone by Italy after it managed to put its political house in order, united, and thus became more "masculine" in the eyes of British men. That Italy is, in present-day Anglo-Saxon popular culture, identified primarily with machismo bears eloquent testimony to the fact that it is in the nature of stereotypes to retain their form even when their contents change fundamentally. On the "continental grand tour" in the late eighteenth century, see also Porter, 1991: chapter 1. On the sexualization of the North-South divide, see also Mosse, 1985: 20.

[17] A particularly unadulterated example of this genre is Pétrus Durel's *La Femme dans les colonies françaises*. For an interesting survey of the representation of African women as colonial consorts, see Martinkus-Zemp, 1973.

[18] An effusive description of an Algiers brothel frequented by French officials is in Gauthier-Villars and Prille, 1926: 57–60.

Vénus in India; or, Love Adventures in Hindustan (1889) was published under the pseudonym "Captain C. Devereaux" and purported to narrate a British militaryman's exploits in India.[19] A later novel, *Kama Houri* (1956), published under the pseudonym "Ataullah Mardaan,"[20] tells of the sexual adventures of the daughter of a British colonel in northern colonial India, and of the tragic consequences of her unsuppressed lust for a Pathan servant. Another account of sexual doings abroad is *Darkest Orient* (1937), supposedly the record of travels in Port Said, İstanbul, Ankara, Bombay, Calcutta, and other cities of the East. Though ostensibly written by a certain "Riza Bey," a butler in the employ of an unnamed gentleman referred to only as "the Khan," there is nothing in the text that would suggest that the author was anything but a Westerner, and much of the narrative draws upon well-established clichés. In a similar vein, a series of guides to "night life" in major cities published during the late 1960s and early 1970s includes *Istanbul After Dark* (1970) in addition to books on various European, Asian, and American cities. In all these works, the sexualization of xenotopia came into sharper focus, as libidinized spaces of otherness acquired names.

It is worth noting paranthetically that the pattern continues today: Southeast Asian countries, especially Thailand and the Philippines, have become the new "sex capitals" to which Europeans and Americans flock—not to find a less inhibited, more "natural" society than their

[19] Patrick J. Kearney notes that this work has been ascribed to a Dan Harding, and may have been published in Amsterdam by Auguste Brancart. (Kearney, 1981: nos. 571–2.) There also exist what appear to be later imitations of this book: see Anon./*Amorous Memoirs*, 1982; Anon./*Nights of the Rajah*, 1983.

[20] Maurice Girodias, who, with his father, directed the Olympia Press, writes: "*Kama Houri* was written by a Pakistani girl who lived in Paris during Olympia's flourishing fifties. She was married to a Dutch photographer, had been educated at Columbia University, was the daughter of a distinguished Pakistani psychiatrist, and like everyone else in Paris needed money. We enjoyed her irregular trips to our office when she would deliver her latest chapters for our approval. She always wore flowing silk saris, her hair, thick and braided had never been cut or coiffed, she was modest, beautiful, patient, polite, and draped in veils as she handed us the not so innocent product of her cultivated mind. She was, in every way, what my father and I had dreamed a pornographer should be." (Girodias, 1967: 297.) I cannot vouch for the exoticism of the author (the name "Robert Desmond" appears without explanation on the title page), but I must say this is an unusually *literate* piece of erotica. It is also, among all the works I have read, the one that sets up most starkly the equation of racial other with sexual other.

own, but rather to use the strength of the dollar or the Deutschmark to purchase partners with whom to indulge in pedophilia and other illicit practices. The degree to which sexual tourism has become institutionalized can be surmised from Bill Bronson's *Sexual Paradises of Earth: A Single Man's Guide to International Travel* (1993), a book over 200 pages long covering Thailand, Jamaica, and the Dominican Republic in detail, and several other countries (the Philippines, India, Egypt, Mexico, Brazil, the Netherlands) more briefly. Emphasizing the "otherness" of the East and the sexual availability and submissiveness of its women, the discourse of sex tourism is, according to Thanh-Dam Truong, aimed first at "creating a distinct national identity to attract consumers," and secondly at "legitimizing oppressive practices by relegating them to the culture of a particular ethnic group and thereby helping to ease the conscience of the customers." (Truong, 1990: 199–200.)[21] Truong's first point is particularly apt, testifying to the contemporary shift from traditional imperialism to neo-colonialism, from military conquest to economic domination, from occupying armies to consuming tourists. In other respects, however, this discourse is squarely within the tradition of sexualized geography.

The Omnisexual "Other"

In a passage typical of what is most offensive about his writing, Sir Richard F. Burton declared that "the Chinese, as far as we know them in the great cities, are omnivorous and omnifutuentes: they are the chosen people of debauchery and their systematic bestiality with ducks, goats, and other animals is equalled only by their pederasty." (Burton/ *Arabian Nights*, n.d.: 10: 238.)[22] This image of the "Other" as omnisexual, prone to engage in sexual relations with anyone or anything, animate or inanimate, is common in xenological discourse. It was associated primarily with the climate and with the supposed "indolence" of Eastern

[21] See also Hall, 1992. For an interesting discussion of Dennis O'Rourke's film *The Good Woman of Bangkok*, and of the spirited controversy it engendered, see Berry, 1994.
[22] For a nice analysis of the relations between food and sexuality in Victorian society and "harem literature," see Melman, 1992: 122–30.

life, as heat and boredom were believed to arouse sexual desire. Translations of "oriental" works included numerous tales about bestiality, as for instance in the stories "Wardan the Butcher: His Adventure with the Lady and the Bear" and "The King's Daughter and the Ape" in the *Thousand and One Nights* (Burton/*Arabian Nights*, n.d.: 4: 293–9),[23] or "The Thirty-Eighth Vezir's Story" in *The History of the Forty Vezirs* (1886),[24] and these were considered to be evidence of such practices there.

When people or animals were not available, masturbation was of course always an option—indeed, one in which the "other" was thought to indulge whenever the opportunity presented itself. Burton expressed the opinion that "in many Harems and girls' schools tallow-candles and similar succedania are vainly forbidden and bananas when detected are cut into four so as to be useless." (Burton/*Arabian Nights*, n.d.: 2: 234.) The significance, if not necessarily the frequency, of such references greatly increased in the eighteenth and nineteenth centuries, when masturbation became a virtual fixation for the European medical establishment, resulting in an all-out "war against onanism." For instance, the anonymous *Onania; or The Heinous Sin of Self-Pollution and its Frightful Consequences in Both Sexes Considered, with Spiritual and Physical Advice to those who have Already Injur'd Themselves by this Abominable Practice*, apparently authored by a certain Dr Balthazar Bekkers, was first published in 1708 and went through at least nineteen editions, selling nearly 38,000 copies. (Wagner, 1988: 17.) Dr Tissot's *L'Onanisme; ou dissertation physique sur les maladies produites par la masturbation* [Onanism; or physical dissertation on the illnesses produced by masturbation], first published in Latin as part of a larger work, appeared in French translation in 1760 and was reprinted countless times during the decades that followed, as well as being translated into several languages. By stressing the fact that women in the Orient systematically

---

[23] For an unscholarly, but nevertheless useful survey of bestiality and other manifestations of sexuality in the *Nights*, see Dehoï, 1963; also see Elisséeff, 1949, which presents a typology of the stories in the *Nights*.

[24] See Şeyhzâde, 1886: 353–4. I should note that E.J.W. Gibb, the editor and translator of this volume and a well-known historian of Ottoman literature, left this tale—which relates how a man forced his concubine to mate with an ape, then killed their offspring—untranslated; presumably the bestiality, the infanticide, or both, were too offensive for his delicate Victorian sensibilities.

engaged in masturbation, a connection was drawn between the alien and the pathological, an important link to which I will return.

An interesting point about these accounts is that they constitute the site of another inconsistency—or polyvalence—in sexualized xenological discourse: although the harem is often described, by present-day authors, as a monument to the male scopic desire, a phallocratic fantasy where a multiplicity of women exist only to sexually service a unique despot, it also harbors "the possibility of an erotic universe in which there are no men, a site of social and sexual practices that are not organized around the phallus or a central male authority." (Lowe, 1991: 48.)[25] True, the ape and the bear in the above stories are male, and the phallic significance of candles and bananas needs no elaboration; nevertheless, the woman is always firmly in control and it is her sexual needs and desires that take central stage, not a man's.

Not surprisingly, therefore, female homosexuality was also extremely central to these writings. Early travelers' accounts made sweeping claims about the prevalence of lesbianism in harems, as for instance George Sandys, who wrote in his *Relation of a Journey begun An. Dom. 1610* (1615) that "much unnaturall and filthie lust is said to be committed daily in the remote closets of these darkesome *Bannias*: yea women with women; a thing uncredible, if former times had not given thereunto both detection, and punishment." (Sandys, 1621: 69.)[26] Similarly, Jean Chardin declared in his *Voyages de Monsieur le Chevalier Chardin, en Perse, et autres lieux de l'Orient* (1711; first volume only published in 1686) [translated as *Sir John Chardin's Travels in Persia*] that "Oriental women have always passed for *Tribades*. I have heard it asserted so often, and by so many people, that they are so, & that they have ways of mutually satisfying their passions, that I hold it to be quite certain. They try to prevent them as best they can, because they claim that this diminishes their lure, & renders them less sensible to the love of men." (Chardin, 1711: 2: 280, translation mine.)[27]

[25] On the harem as a female social space parallel to and autonomous from male-dominated public life, see for example Ahmed, 1982.

[26] The word *bannia* is a corruption of the Italian *bagno*, meaning bath.

[27] The chapter containing this passage, concerning "the palace of the wives of the king," appears not to have been included in English translations of this work.

Sexual depravity was, then, pictured as an endemic condition in the East, and lesbianism, like masturbation and bestiality, was viewed as merely another facet of oriental pathology and decadence. A striking court case from nineteenth-century Scotland is indicative of this attitude: when a charge of lesbianism was leveled against two mistresses of a boarding school, the judges pronounced the women innocent by virtue of the simple fact that they were "incapable of committing a sin that did not exist in Britain." Indeed, the girl who had brought the charges was accused of having an overdeveloped sexual curiosity most probably acquired from "her lewd Indian nurses, who were, in contrast to British women, entirely capable of obscene chatter on such subjects." (Kabbani, 1986: 53.)[28]

In other words, oriental women were liable to engage in any kind of "perversion," so infused were they with sexuality, and so unable to control their bestial urges. They were seen as "at once passive and insatiable, oppressed and duplicitous, lascivious heterosexuals and sly homosexuals." (Douthwaite, 1992: 96.) It was not an accident that this conflicted personality was ascribed to them: women were believed to engage in lesbianism not out of choice or predisposition but merely in order to satisfy their general lust when men happened to be absent. Thus, Habesci wrote in his *Present State of the Ottoman Empire* that "the most infamous lasciviousness is likewise common in the chambers of the girls. Nor is it at all astonishing that handsome girls, well fed, undergoing neither fatigue nor vexation; girls that have nothing to do but to prepare themselves for sensual pleasures, and who think of nothing but Venus and her son, should give way to unnatural lasciviousness for want of the proper means of gratifying their amorous inclinations." (Habesci, 1784: 171.) Likewise, Charles Nicholas Sigisbert Sonnini de Manoncourt wrote in his *Voyage dans la haute et basse Égypte* (1798) [translated as *Travels in Upper and Lower Egypt*]:

---

[28] On the relations between European concerns about child sexuality and colonial concerns about native women servants' sexual transgressions, see Stoler, 1995: chapter 5. On the view of interracial lesbianism as a pathology all to itself, see Baker, 1992. On contemporary representations of lesbianism and the elision of racial difference, see Hart, 1994: chapter 6.

Nature, whose powerful voice, which is too often unheeded by those whom she calls to submit to her laws, as well as to enjoy her pleasures, stirs up their passions: every thing, in short, contributes to direct their burning imagination, their desires, their discourse, towards an end which they are not at liberty to attain. They amuse themselves in their parties by completely changing their dresses, and putting on each other's clothes. This sort of disguise is only the prelude and the pretext of less innocent diversions; the particulars of which Sappho is thought to have both practiced and taught. Skilled in the art of eluding and not of quenching the ardor that consumes them, the same ungovernable desire still follows them into retirement; sad resources, feeble solace for a privation, which, under an atmosphere equally hot and dry, seems very difficult, and especially for ardent minds, to support. (Sonnini, 1800: 167.)

Like masturbation, lesbianism too was thus seen merely as an outlet for these orientals who cared not a whit if the means of satisfying their desires were male or female, animate or inanimate. Gustave Flaubert epitomized this view when he wrote, in an 1853 letter:

The oriental woman is a machine, and nothing more; she does not differentiate between one man and another. Smoking, going to the baths, painting her eyelids, and drinking coffee, such is the circle of occupations around which turns her existence. . . . It is we who think of her, but she hardly thinks of us. (Flaubert, 1922–25: 2: 15, 17, translation mine.)[29]

Burton too wrote that "while thousands of Europeans have cohabited for years with and have had families by 'native women,' they are never loved by them." Ever insightful, Burton attributed this to the fact that Europeans "ignor[e] the science and practice" of prolonging coition, while "Hindu women . . . cannot be satisfied, such is their natural coldness, increased doubtless by vegetable diet and unuse of stimulants, with less than twenty minutes." (Burton/*Arabian Nights*, n.d.: 5: 77.) Kabbani comments: "Perhaps it never occurred to Burton, at ease within the patriarchal values of the colonial enterprise, that the native woman might not have felt attachment for the European for different— and more complex—reasons than those he chose as explanation. The European, after all, had occupied her land, oppressed her people, and

---

[29] This letter is included in Flaubert, 1980: 1: 181, but the translation there is less literal.

imposed his personal will upon her. Her emotional detachment was her only defence—feeble as it was—against total victimisation." (Kabbani, 1986: 47–8.)[30]

Likewise, in his *Chair noire* [Black flesh] (1889), Vigné d'Octon declared that "the black woman has neither the same qualities, nor the feelings nor the same experiences as a woman of the Caucasian race. Between her and the white man there is no possibility that love—in any psychological sense—might exist." (Cited in Ridley, 1983: 84.) Little wonder that in *The Citizen of the World* (1762), an amusing satire of orientalist discourse from the pen of a "Chinese philosopher residing in London," Oliver Goldsmith had a young Englishman declare: "a seraglio, my dear creature, wipes off every inconvenience in the world. Besides, I am told, your Asiatic beauties are the most convenient women alive, for they have no souls." (Goldsmith, 1891: 2: 185.)

Asiatic or African, as the sexuality of the female "other" was emphasized, she was simultaneously deprived of a self. "Black women seldom have names, for they are not so much people as presences," writes Abena Busia. "The black woman remains an unvoiced object, most often to be found prone, legs spread, lurking in the shadows of a bedroom. It is required of black women not only that they be sexual, but above all that they be silent." (Busia, 1986: 364–5.)[31] In fact, this is another point of instability in colonial discourse: while the female other was portrayed as "naturally" exuding sensuality, she was also often depicted as sexually passive in interracial contexts. As Martinkus-Zemp puts it, "the *mousso* serving the white man, maximally eroticized as to her physical aspect, has her sensuality denied when it comes to her sexual behavior. ... [T]he white man feels he has been duped: the African woman's sensuality is nothing but a lure." (Martinkus-Zemp, 1973: 79.) The sexuality of the female "other" is manifest, and yet, it is

---

[30] See also Knibiehler and Goutelier, 1985: 37; Marshall and Williams, 1982: 145–6. It is worth noting that this view was not universally held in xenological discourse: there are many instances of trans-cultural romance, such as the seventeenth-century story of Captain John Smith and the Native American princess Pocahontas. I will return to this point.

[31] On the colonial silencing of black women, see also Busia, 1989–90.

beyond the white man's reach. Hence, she can be no more than the passive recipient of the colonizer's lust.

It is worth noting that omnisexuality was not limited to women in xenological discourse; for example, the British generally believed Indians to be more lascivious by nature than they were themselves, and took child marriage and polygamy as proof. This view was manifested in metropolitan concerns with the contents of school textbooks, since officials believed that "books that are innocuous to the comparatively pure and healthy morals of English boys may not be so to the more inflammable minds of Indian boys." (Ballhatchet, 1980: 5.) The licentiousness attributed to the Indian male was viewed as "one facet of a general pattern of moral shortcomings, and as a reflection of the presence of a diffuse but debilitating sexuality that permeated Indian society." By contrast, the British regarded themselves as "the incarnation of austerity, courage, and self-control; natives were caricatured to an increasing extent as their emotional opposites, and as captives of a constitutional weakness for emotional excess and moral depravity. Such moral shortcomings were said to reflect the inroads of centuries of breeding and climate, and were not amenable to simple legislative or educational remedies." (Wurgaft, 1983: 10, 49.) Thus, sexuality was again used as a distinguishing feature between colonizer and colonized, one that led directly to the conclusion that colonial rule was necessary and inevitable.

The Female "Other" as Threat

Like the land itself, represented now as inviting and virginal, now as wild and threatening, the female "other" too was sometimes depicted as a great danger to the European explorer. For example, Peter Hulme has identified two images of America's sexuality, one "manageable and invitingly erotic," the other "fully Amazonic, threateningly self-sufficient." (Hulme, 1985: 2: 17.)[32] The image of the female "other" as

---

[32] On the theme of amazons, see also Montrose, 1992: 171–4; and Brown, 1993: chapter 5, as well as the references cited therein.

threat runs through the colonial literature, at times replacing her representation as an enticing object of desire, and at times coexisting alongside it. Women and natives (the categories often overlapped) were viewed both as passive, child-like, and in need of stewardship, and as "outside society, dangerous, treacherous, emotional, inconstant, wild, threatening, fickle, sexually aberrant, irrational, near animal, lascivious, disruptive, evil, unpredictable." (Carr, 1985: 50.)[33]

These conflicting images derived from a singular conflation of racial and gender stereotypes, and were intimately related to the character ascribed to the land. As Busia notes, "the promiscuous nature of the continent in her luscious and uncontrollable fertility affect[ed] the Europeans, the men in particular, and they [gave] way to whatever temptations cross[ed] their paths, a weakness which always [led] to social ostracism and often self-destruction." Thus, the imperial response to African women was complicated by the sexuality of the continent itself. (Busia, 1986: 364.) The female "other" was depicted as a dangerous temptress who preyed on the white man and could, if his vigilance failed him, lead him astray just as her frightful continent would. In Kabbani's words, "Eastern women were described as objects that promised endless congress and provoked endless contempt." (Kabbani, 1986: 59.)

The motif of the native woman as threat occurs throughout Rudyard Kipling's works, where Indian women play key roles in cautionary tales. John McBratney has argued that Kipling's native women carry out three principal functions: they represent dangerous hybridization, the epistemological limits of British colonialism, and finally the Indian's alterity incarnate. Of these, the first refers to the threat of miscegenation: the Indian woman was "the potential bearer of the greatest danger to British prestige: the Eurasian child. . . . [A]s soon as [she] bids to join a Briton in procreating a child, she threatens the genetic encoding that assures Anglo-Saxon racial purity." Thus, "it is no accident that none of Kipling's tales of interracial love results in the birth of a child who survives." (McBratney, 1988: 49, 51.) Not all colonial authors killed the fictional offspring of their characters' miscegenation, but even when

---

[33] See also D'Astorg, 1980: 14–15.

they allowed them to live, they generally portrayed them as morally corrupt—"villainous, treacherous, manipulative degenerates who, contrary to genetic laws of breeding, manage[d] to inherit both the most repulsive physical and spiritual traits of their parents." (Busia, 1986: 367.) In short, interracial marriage was often depicted as a transgression, its participants generally suffered the consequences, and any children born to such unions either died or should have.

Concern with miscegenation was of course a common theme in colonial literature, although there are major differences between the treatment of this subject by German, French, and British colonial writers. (Ridley, 1983: chapter 4.)[34] These differences, however, were related not only to the nationalities of the authors, but also to the status of the individuals concerned as well as the political balance within a given colony. British authorities, for instance, treated enlisted men and colonial administrators very differently, providing facilities for sexual relations between the former and native women, while strongly discouraging the latter from pursuing such relations. Ballhatchet explains this distinction in terms of an anxiety to preserve the structures of power: "In the one case the soldiers' virile energies had to be maintained. In the other case the social distance between the official elite and the people had to be preserved." Eurasians, therefore, "came to be regarded with uneasy disfavor, as threatening to bridge the social distance between the ruling race and the people." (Ballhatchet, 1980: 4, 164.) Similarly, relations between British men and native prostitutes were tolerated in Africa precisely because they did not threaten the social order; as Busia puts it, the implicit understanding was: "If you wish to sleep with a black woman you may do so, so long as she remains a prostitute, so long as you don't want to bring her to the club, and so long as you don't spread the disease that she is almost certainly going to give you." (Busia, 1986: 367.)

This last point about prostitution and venereal disease was viewed as particularly important, and a three-way debate raged throughout the nineteenth century in India among colonial administrators anxious to

[34] On the highly romanticized depiction of Southeast Asian women in French literature, for example, see Malleret, 1934: part 3, chapter 3.

curb expenditures, military authorities trying to safeguard the health of their men while allowing them to satisfy their "natural" cravings, and clergymen unwilling to allow the mitigation of the "wages of sin." British conservatives, reformers, Quakers, and nonconformists, not to mention Indians and Eurasians, locked horns over hospitals for venereal diseases, regimental brothels known as the *lal bazaar* ("red bazaar," after the color of British troops' uniforms), the Contagious Diseases Acts, and various other policies that attempted—with wildly varying success—to control sexual relations between the colonizers and the colonized. The urgency of these debates is well illustrated by the fact that during the Governor-General's Legislative Council debates in 1895, Sir Griffith Evans qualified syphilis as a subject "of national importance," arguing that "the disease strikes at *the vitality of the race.*" (Ballhatchet, 1980: 86, italics mine.)[35]

Seen from this viewpoint, Kipling's strictures to whites never to go "Beyond the Pale" carried multiple layers of meaning. His story bearing this title began with "A man should, whatever happens, keep to his own caste, race and breed. Let the White go to the White and the Black to the Black" (Kipling, 1899: 189–98)—and predictably went on to tell a tragic tale of transgression and punishment. Sex became metonymic, "with miscegenation standing on the lowest rung of the metaphoric ladder of values and behavioral norms by which all characters are judged. . . . The combination of the two factors of sex and race serves to make miscegenation the ultimate taboo, abrogating unto itself the suggestion of taintedness or evil." Sex, in other words, provided an important boundary between the "ruling race" and the natives; it became "deeply symbolic, with miscegenation the *bête noire* of a deep,

---

[35] This is, of course, rather ironic since the British, along with the French and other Western colonizers, were the propagators, not the victims, of syphilis and other diseases hitherto unknown outside Europe. Thus, syphilis was aptly known in the Ottoman Empire as *frengî*, or "Frankish." Ballhatchet provides a detailed description of the debates surrounding prostitution and venereal disease; see also Levine, 1994, which explores "how India could be metastasised into a definitional organism of uncleanliness through womanhood." On the relationship between health care and empire, and the hegemonic practices of colonial medicine, see Arnold, 1993; while very interesting, however, this book is only marginally concerned with venereal disease.

dark colonial nightmare always threatening to raise not so much her head, as her tail." (Busia, 1986: 363, 366, 369–70.)

Indeed, McBratney's second category—that of epistemological limits—refers to the symbolic role of the Indian woman as the boundary that the British official may not transgress; she "powerfully condenses and concretizes what Kipling calls 'the powers of darkness'—that general enveloping menace, that abstract threat, to British imperial prestige." (McBratney, 1988: 50, 52.) Native women attracted and repelled, their bodies were sources of fascination and fear, their seclusion elicited both a desire to transgress and an unmistakable warning not to enter the dark abyss that lay beyond—in every sense of the term. Lewis Wurgaft suggests that the women's quarters, with its locked doors, "symbolized the barrier between Anglo-Indian society and the unsettling mysteries of native life." But if the gates of the gynaeceum epitomized the chasm between the British and their Indian subjects, the Indian woman herself "embodied what was unknown and inscrutable in Indian life. And for the Englishman in India, himself trained and educated in a male culture, this mystery was charged with the emotional appeal of power, and the threat of a destructive sexuality." Thus, Wurgaft concludes, "the British would never feel comfortable in India until they could see its women." (Wurgaft, 1983: 51–3.) And that day would never come.

The third category of Kipling's representations of the Indian woman stems from her perceived connection with the Indian powers-that-be "as either their metonymy, expression, or instrument." She was, according to McBratney, "*the* sign of the 'other,' *the* marker of what is different from (and therefore both inferior and yet threatening to) the British." Although Kipling's misogyny also extended to Englishwomen, whom he viewed as tending to domesticate men, draining male energies better spent on military affairs and government, the fact that they shared the Englishman's racial and national identity placed them above the Indian woman, who presented "the direst possible threat to the homosocial solidarity of district officer, soldier, and intelligence agent." (McBratney, 1988: 50, 52–4.)[36] The paranoid view of Indian women

---

[36] On the elision of male heterosexual desire in Kipling and other colonial writers, and

as agents of dark and oppositional forces was not limited to Kipling. The subservience of women to men in India and other British colonies suggested to the administrators that they would inevitably use their charms to further the interests of male family members. Thus, for example, although Burmese women were viewed as attractive, sexually free, and "willing to comfort English officials doing their imperial duty in lonely places," they were considered especially threatening because of Burma's particular social structure; colonial officials believed that power networks there were such that British men marrying Burmese women would constantly run the risk of being influenced by local special interests. (Ballhatchet, 1980: 145–55.)

There are numerous other examples of the representation of the female "other" as threat, whether in novels or in political discourse. In Henry Rider Haggard's *She* (1887), for instance, an immortal Persian priestess named Ayesha brutally rules over savage cannibals in the heart of Africa while awaiting the reincarnation of her lover as an urbane, Cambridge-educated Englishman. In Richard Marsh's *The Beetle* (1897), an Egyptian priestess portrayed as possessing "an aggressive and fearsome femininity that explodes cultural roles, and an Eastern mentality that is utterly foreign: alien, inexplicable, inimical" to that of the English, a woman embodying "a devouring force which emasculates its male object and literally dehumanizes the sexualized female" (Hurley, 1993: 195, 213),[37] goes to Britain seeking vengeance. In Charlotte Brontë's *Jane Eyre* (1847), Bertha Mason, Rochester's West Indian Creole first wife and "the monstrous embodiment of unchecked female rebelliousness and sexuality," blurs the boundary between human and animal. (Sharpe, 1993: 45; Spivak, 1986: 266, 268.) In British accounts of the so-called Indian "Mutiny" of 1857, the Rani of Jhansi, said to have been one of the most vicious leaders of the revolt, is alleged to

---

the literary construction of the homosocial world of empire, see Bristow, 1991: 80–89; also Low, 1993a.

[37] Hurley recognizes that this character "is presented more consistently as a threat, a devouring and engulfing force. In the novel, the oriental female, or the feminized orient, is far from being characterized by any womanly 'penetrability' or 'malleability.'" (Hurley, 1993: 198.) However, she does not extend this observation to a more general critique of the traditional identification of Europe with masculinity, and its colonies with femininity.

have "order[ed] her men to rape, humiliate, and torture their female victims"; indeed, Jenny Sharpe states that the "colonial constructions of the Rani, particularly those that describe her cruelty and lasciviousness, cast her in a decidedly masculine role," underscoring the fluidity of gendered identification in colonial discourse. (Sharpe, 1993: 73–6.) Instances of this trope can also be found in the romantic myths woven around such characters as Salomé, Helen, and, of course, Cleopatra— described by Mario Praz as "one of the first Romantic incarnations of the type of the Fatal Woman," combining "a fabulous Oriental background with a taste for algolagnia, which . . . seemed to be in the very air of the Romantic period." (Praz, 1970: 214–15.)[38]

Still, one of the most striking (and strangest) instances of this trope is a passage from Frederick Millingen's *Wild Life among the Koords* (1870), which, although lengthy, well deserves to be quoted in its entirety:

Amongst the many acts of brigandage of which the Koords make themselves guilty, a peculiar kind of highway robbery must here be stated, which is probably unparalleled. The culprits—the brigands—are in this case young women, who set out on plundering pursuits, in order to turn a dishonest penny. A troop of fair bandits take up a station at the side of the road, there patiently to wait for the arrival of the doomed traveler. As soon as the *vedettes* announce his approach, the fair troop starts off to meet him, welcoming him with dances and with fiery glances of irresistible power. He is compelled to stop, as a matter of course, and the fair maids then politely request him to alight from his horse. No sooner than the bewildered victim, unconscious of his fate, puts his foot on the ground that he finds himself at close quarters with the whole troop. Immediately he is stripped of all he has on his back, and is left in that primitive state in which Adam was at one time. Then begins a series of dances and fascinating gestures in the style of those performed by the maids at the Lupercalian festival, the object of which is to make the

[38] Praz discusses at some length the romantic motif of woman as threat, and its connections to the exotic, in chapter 4. See also Showalter, 1990: chapter 8, where connections are made between the motif of the oriental veil and the trope of woman as threat; Azim, 1993: chapter 7; and Dijkstra, 1986. On the persona of Cleopatra, see Hughes-Hallett, 1990; on her role in preserving the sexual purity of the Englishwoman by being endowed with "everything that is (literally) outlandish and foreign and necessarily repugnant to a decent young woman," see Miller, 1990: 111.

unfortunate lose his self-control. An attempt, however, on the part of the victim to reciprocate the advances of his alluring tyrants becomes instantly fatal, as the troop get hold of him in a summary way, declare him to have made attempts on the virtue of one of the fair maids, and condemn him to be pricked with thorns on a very sensitive part of his person. These dances, and the flagellations which serve as *entr'actes*, are repeated several times over, till the sufferer, exhausted and bleeding, is nearly in a fainting condition. Then the female troop of bandits drags the wretched traveler before a court of matrons, which holds its sittings somewhere in the neighborhood. There a charge of attempting a criminal assault is brought against the pretended culprit, who not only receives a good dose of upbraiding, but is also condemned to pay the fine stipulated by the court. (Millingen, 1870: 243–5.)[39]

This passage was incongruously inserted into Fred Burnaby's *On Horseback through Asia Minor* (1877) as Appendix XIII, between a report to the British government by a certain Mr Taylor concerning "the corruption of Armenian officials in the Erzeroum [Erzurum] district" and a turgid disquisition by Burnaby himself on the strategic routes between the Anatolian highlands and Syria. (Burnaby, 1877: 2: 366–7.) It is by no means the only reference in the orientalist literature to Kurdish women as strong, independent, and war-like—that was a recurrent theme.[40] What is most amazing about this particular passage, though, is that what is essentially a masochistic fantasy staged in the Orient was included in a relatively "serious" book on Asia Minor as merely another neutral bit of information, not unlike a report on public administration or a study of communications and transportation in the region. It seems to me that the role of eroticism as a technology of place is particularly starkly underscored by this inclusion: *this*, the reader is told, is the kind of place Asia Minor is.

---

[39] Born in İstanbul to a British doctor and his Levantine wife (who later gained notoriety as Melek Hanım, the author of memoirs on life in a Turkish harem), Major Millingen (a.k.a. Osman Bey, a.k.a. Vladimir Andrejevich) also wrote books on Ottoman women, dervishes, and Turkey under Sultan Abdülaziz, as well as one on "the Jewish conspiracy to take over the world" which went through numerous editions in English, French, Italian, German, and Russian.

[40] A nice example is in Gourdault, 1882: 47–52.

The Male "Other" as Effeminate

To the end of his translation of the *Thousand and One Nights* (1884–86), Richard Burton appended an essay which, though excluded from subsequent editions, has been widely reprinted elsewhere. In that essay, Burton advanced a theory on the global distribution of homosexuality:

[E]nquiries in many and distant countries enabled me to arrive at the following conclusions:

1. There exists what I shall call a Sotadic Zone, bounded westwards by the northern shores of the Mediterranean (N. Lat. 43°) and by the southern (N. Lat. 30°). Thus the depth would be 780 to 800 miles including meridional France, the Iberian Peninsula, Italy and Greece, with the coast-regions of Africa from Morocco to Egypt.
2. Running eastward the Sotadic Zone narrows, embracing Asia Minor, Mesopotamia and Chaldæa, Afghanistan, Sind, the Punjab and Kashmir.
3. In Indo-China the belt begins to broaden, enfolding China, Japan and Turkistan.
4. It then embraces the South Sea Islands and the New World where, at the time of its discovery, Sotadic love was, with some exceptions, an established racial institution.
5. Within the Sotadic Zone the Vice is popular and endemic, held at the worst to be a mere peccadillo, whilst the races to the North and South of the limits here defined practice it only sporadically amid the opprobrium of their fellows who, as a rule, are physically incapable of performing the operation and look upon it with the liveliest disgust.

(Burton, 1964: 174–5.)[41]

After this bizarre introduction, Burton embarked on a rambling discussion, replete as usual with references to an astounding number of literary and historical sources, concerning the causes and manifestations of male homosexuality in diverse parts of the world.

Whether or not there is any truth to the notion that the incidence of male homosexuality is geographically determined, Burton's theory fits right in with a long-standing belief that male "Others" were somehow

[41] This essay was also reprinted in book form, under the title *The Sotadic Zone*.

"less manly" than Europeans.[42] This notion too goes back at least to Hippocrates, who suggested in his *Airs Waters Places* that "with regard to the lack of spirit and of courage among the inhabitants, the chief reason why Asiatics are less warlike and more gentle in character than Europeans is the uniformity of the seasons, which show no violent changes either towards heat or towards cold, but are equable." (Hippocrates, 1923–28: 1: 115, 133.) In *A Complete System of Geography* (1744–47), a work largely based on the fourth edition of Herman Moll's *The Compleat Geographer* (first published in 1701), it is written that those Asians "who have escaped the *Turkish* Tyranny are still in a high flourishing Condition, and more so, in a great measure, thro' the Richness of their Soil, than the Industry of their Inhabitants, who are justly blamed for their natural Indolence, Effeminacy and Luxury." The text goes on to argue that:

> this Effeminacy is chiefly owing to the Warmth of the Climate, tho' perhaps heighten'd by Custom and Education, and is consequently more or less rife, as they are seated nearer or farther from the North. For it is plain, that the southern Climates produce not such robust Natures as the Northern ones; from which we may infer that these *Asiatics*, who live near the same Latitude with us, cannot be much inferior to us in this respect." (Moll, 1744–47: 2: 67.)

In 1767 Adam Ferguson voiced his belief that "under extremes of heat and cold, the active range of the human soul appears to be limited; . . . in both the spirit is prepared for servitude." He went on to claim that extreme heat makes men "feverish in their passions, weak in their judgements, and addicted by temperament to animal pleasure." (Ferguson, 1966: 112.)[43] It is indeed hard to miss the exact correspondence between these "effects of heat" and the characteristics traditionally attributed to the female gender. Similarly, Robert Orme concluded his 1782 study *Historical Fragments of the Mogul Empire, of the Morattoes, and of*

---

[42] On the attribution of effeminacy to the enemy, see Trexler, 1995. On the political dimensions of this trope in the context of India, see Sinha, 1995.

[43] Susan J. Wolfson discusses the issue of effeminacy in the context of Byron's *Sardanapalus* (1821), William Hazlitt's "On Effeminacy of Character" (1822), and other such works published in the early part of the nineteenth century; see Wolfson, 1991.

the English Concerns in Indoostan with the assertion that "breathing in the softest of climates; having so few real wants; and receiving even the luxuries of other nations with little labor, from the fertility of their own soil; the Indian must become the most effeminate inhabitants of the globe; and this is the very point at which we now see him." (Orme, 1805: 472.)

The eunuch was a ubiquitous and extremely powerful symbol in gendered orientalist discourse, personifying at once the arbitrary power, the pathology, the racial difference, and the lack of masculinity that supposedly characterized the Orient. I will not dwell on this theme here, primarily because it deserves a book-length study of its own; however, I do want to relate a rather amusing passage from a late seventeenth-century description of the imperial seraglio by Albert Bobovi (or Bobowski), a Polish convert to Islam also known as Ali Ufkî Bey. He writes that the eunuchs often took part in harem intrigues, and:

> when successful, they are given the most important posts of the Empire. While they are properly speaking only half-men, this does not alter the fact that they are often at the heads of the armies, and have governed the greatest of the provinces. One sees by this that the jobs are not always given to those with the most merit, or those who are the most capable of possessing them. (Bobovi, 1985: 22.)

This does make one wonder in precisely what part of the male anatomy leadership ability was thought to reside!

The way in which the supposed effeminacy of non-Europeans was explained varied with the times, largely reflecting the *Zeitgeist*. During the seventeenth and part of the eighteenth centuries, Europeans had been concerned with reconciling the tremendous human variability revealed by the Age of Exploration with the Biblical doctrine of monogenesis. Climate provided a good (though hardly original) explanation.[44] More than a century later, Burton still held "pederasty . . . to

---

[44] On the doctrine of monogenesis and the use of environmental factors to explain the differences observed among different peoples, see Marshall and Williams, 1982: 136–8; Hodgen, 1964: 207–53.

be geographical and climatic, not racial" (Burton, 1964: 175),[45] but by then, monogenesis was out of fashion and "scientific" racism (or, to be more precise, racialism) was in full swing. Piet de Rooy argues that "in the development from popular ethnocentrism to natural-scientific racism during the first half of the nineteenth century, the sexual factor looms large indeed." (Rooy, 1990: 21.)

Racialist thinking in the nineteenth century was frequently expressed in sexual terms, notably in the case of Gobineau, author of *Essai sur l'inégalité des races humaines* [Essay on the inequality of the human races] (1853–1855) and the "father of racist ideology."[46] Using gendered metaphors to characterize the races, he referred to blacks and Jews as the "feminine populations of Ham and of Shem," and considered them sensually oriented but lacking in essential "male" qualities such as linguistic skills and scientific reasoning.[47] Ham and Shem are, of course, two of Noah's three sons according to Biblical tradition, and Genesis 9 relates that the former's progeny were cursed and con-demned to eternal servitude because he saw his drunken father naked. In addition, a spurious Jewish haggadic tradition, subsequently taken up by both Christian and Muslim commentators, held that Ham's sin had been to engage in carnal relations with his wife aboard the Ark, despite his father's interdiction, and to have thus conceived in lust a son in order to ensure that his progeny, as the first-born after the flood, would inherit the earth. In both cases, and in a number of other traditions as well, Ham—whose name has been etymologically linked to both heat and blackness—is depicted as having committed a sin of lust; since he is generally held to be the ancestor of the black race, the association of blackness and lustfulness may have its origins in this myth. (Perbal, 1940.) I shall return to this point.

Whether ascribed to environmental or racial factors, the effeminacy

[45] On the supposed relationships between climate, race, and character, see also Living-stone, 1994: 132–54.

[46] This characterization is due to Michael D. Biddiss; see Biddiss, 1970.

[47] See for instance Miller, 1985: 122; also Mosse, 1985: 36; and Green, 1979, which cites the following hierarchization of masculinity from Thomas Babington Macaulay's "Essay on Warren Hastings" (1841): "What the Italian is to the Englishman, what the Hindoo is to the Italian, what the Bengalee is to other Hindoos, that was [the Brahmin] Nuncomar to other Bengalees." (32.)

of the male "other" was interpreted as implying his unfitness for self-government, and therefore as a justification for colonialism. An important factor in the perceived "weakness" of the male "other" was the precocious sexuality attributed to children in xenotopia. The British, for instance, believed that the creative energies of young Indians were "eroded by the physical and moral ravages of too early sexual intimacy. The ultimate product of this imbroglio was the physical and moral weakling who had lost the taste or capacity for vigorous leadership." It was widely believed that the cause of this decadence was the harem system, and writers decried the "evil consequences of the princely courts, where sexual depravity and the overcharged environment of the prince's harem were . . . deadly to the human spirit." The vitality of the Indian ruling class was sapped by this feminine/sexual atmosphere, the British claimed, since "the young prince's life in the female-dominated seraglio inevitably reduced him to impotence and degeneracy. As a ruler such a man could never control himself or his subjects." (Wurgaft, 1983: 51.)

The theme of precocious sexuality recurs frequently in the colonial and travel literature. For instance, Mrs John Elijah Blunt wrote in her memoirs of life in the Ottoman Empire that "in those early years spent at home, when the child ought to have instilled into him some germ of those principles of conduct by which men must walk in the world if they are to hold up their heads among civilized nations, the Turkish child is only taught the first steps towards those vicious habits of mind and body which have made his race what it is." (Blunt, 1878: 2: 153–4.) Edith Wharton was more specific, stating that while children did receive much love in their homes, "ignorance, unhealthiness and a precocious sexual initiation prevail in all classes." (Wharton, 1920: 194.) And such observations extended to girls as well: Bayle St John described two ten-year-old apprentice dancers in Egypt, adding that "whilst the Arabs assembled swore with admiration and grunted out lascivious sighs, we could not help feeling saddened by beholding childhood thus profaned." (St John, 1853: 1: 18.)

It is necessary to place this concern with early sexuality into its proper context: Foucault has noted that "the sex of children and adolescents has become, since the eighteenth century, an important area of contention around which innumerable institutional devices and discursive strategies have been deployed." Indeed, he argues that one of the "four great strategic unities" that constituted mechanisms of knowledge and power centered on sexuality was "a pedagogization of children's sex: a double assertion that practically all children indulge or are prone to indulge in sexual activity; and that, being unwarranted, at the same time 'natural' and 'contrary to nature,' this sexual activity posed physical and moral, individual and collective dangers." Foucault goes on to point out that "the sexualization of children was accomplished in the form of a campaign for the health of the race," since "precocious sexuality was presented from the eighteenth century to the end of the nineteenth as an epidemic menace that risked compromising not only the future health of adults but the future of the entire society and species." (Foucault, 1978–85: 1: 27–31, 30, 41–2, 103–4, 98–9, 146.)[48]

Thus, deeply concerned with the protection of their children from the harmful effects of early sexuality, Europeans projected their anxieties onto xenotopia; in doing so, they both marked it as different and provided justification for the rule of its corrupted and weakened peoples by an external authority untouched by such vices. Indeed, the British sought to raise the age of consent for Indian girls from ten to twelve through the Age of Consent Act of 1891, an undertaking that sparked lively debate. (Sinha, 1995: chapter 4.)

The harem was also believed to lead to homosexuality by quelling men's appetite for women. In 1902, Lord Curzon, Viceroy of India, attributed homosexuality "largely to early marriage. A boy gets tired of his wife, or of women, at an early age, and wants the stimulus of some more novel or exciting sensation." (Ballhatchet, 1980: 120.) Similarly, Pinhas ben Nahum wrote that "the existence of polygamy quickly brings about in the man the satiety for natural intercourse. This results in pederastic love not merely in Turkey but throughout Oriental Mohammedanism. . . . Every student of anthropology must be aware that polygamy incites to amorous abnormality because normal sexuality very

---

[48] An interesting recent study of the representation of child sexuality and the othering of pedophilia is Kincaid, 1992.

early in life becomes cloyed and satiated." (Pinhas, 1933: 87, 161.) It is ironic that the very institution that was seen as embodying oriental patriarchy was, by a discursive sleight of hand, summarily transformed into the cause of effeminacy. I shall return to this seeming paradox when discussing the trope of oriental despotism.

An instance where the trope of the effeminacy of oriental men is used against the grain involves, not coincidentally, a woman, the French-Indochinese novelist Marguerite Duras. In an interesting comparative study of her *Un barrage contre le Pacifique* (1950) [translated as *The Sea Wall*] and *L'Amant* [The lover] (1984), Suzanne Chester uncovers certain significant differences in the novels' respective treatment of the male "other":

> as a lower-class woman in the patriarchal society of French colonial Indochina, Duras was *already* in the position of Other. Her subordinate status as object of both prostitution and the male gaze is clearly represented in *The Sea Wall*. In *The Lover*, Duras establishes a female subjectivity through the appropriation of the masculine position of the observer, through the construction of an active relationship to desire, and by recourse to a variety of Orientalist topoi—the eroticization of the exotic, the feminization of the Asian lover, and the representation of an unchanging Oriental essence.

In this manner, she *"reinscribes* a variety of Orientalist/colonialist themes in order to transform her own marginalized position as Other and to achieve a position of power and dominance in relation to her Chinese lover." (Chester, 1992: 452.) Thus, sexualized international relations were mobilized by Duras to combat gender imbalances in European colonial society, as she used the "effeminacy" of the Asian male to center the European female.

Duras is not unique in this regard, nor particularly innovative. In early seventeenth-century British literature, women writers used the dark/light dichotomy in their efforts to establish a subject position from which to write. According to Kim F. Hall, these writers "demonstrate a heightened sensitivity to difference and to the cultural implications of their own investment in the language of racial difference," and "use the arbitrariness of this aesthetic to strengthen their own rhetorical and social positions at the expense of more marginalized groups."

Thus, she suggests, women "borrow from patriarchal categories in order to empower themselves as white women," trying "to avoid the strictures of gender by borrowing authority from other categories reified by patriarchal structures: class, whiteness, and 'Englishness.'" (Hall, 1994: 179–80, 336.) These two examples seem to confirm the hypothesis put forward by those who argue that women travelers' accounts were inherently different from men's due to their marginal positions in metropolitan or colonial societies—in other words, because of their capacity to mobilize their own alterity in various ways. While this may well be true in certain cases, however, it is by no means universal.

The Male "Other" as Rapist

Contrasting with the depiction of the male "other" as weak and effeminate, another streak in xenological discourse painted him as dangerously oversexed, vicious, and particularly threatening to white women. Examples of this range from narratives of captivity on the Barbary Coast and in North America, through British colonial discourse on India following the "Mutiny" of 1857, to the charge of raping a white woman that often preceded the lynching of black men in the United States during the late nineteenth and early twentieth centuries.[49]

Concern with the protection of white women's sexual propriety took different forms in different contexts. For the most part, it was regarded as inconceivable that European women would willingly engage in sexual relations with native men; hence, when the subject did come up, it was more often than not related to rape. In her powerful study of the trope of rape in British colonial discourse, Sharpe observes that references to the Indian male as a rapist of white women do not occur in Anglo-Indian fiction and colonial records prior to the 1857 revolt. When the revolt took place, and for some months fundamentally

---

[49] See for instance Baughman, 1966; also Hodes, 1993, and other contributions to that Special Issue on "African American Culture and Sexuality"; and Carby, 1986.

challenged British authority in India, the crisis was, according to her, *"managed through the circulation of the violated bodies of English women as a sign for the violation of colonialism.* ... Thus propagating fantasies of Oriental men desiring white flesh, Mutiny fiction enhance[d] the sexual coding of anti-colonial insurgency that is latent in the historical narratives." Sharpe's assertion that a crisis in British colonial rule was represented and "managed" through the motif of natives raping white women is significant in that it points to a new way in which sexuality was deployed in accordance with the exigencies of the political situation. Natives heretofore depicted as weak and effeminate suddenly became brutal rapists, as a heretofore acquiescent India rose up against the invaders. In this way, the anti-colonial struggle was reduced to savage brutality, and the repressive measures taken against it were legitimated as British masculinity defending its womenfolk's honor and safety: "The binarism of Western civilization and Eastern barbarism is difficult to maintain when the colonizer is an agent of torture and massacre. A discourse of rape—that is, the violent representation of gender roles that positions the Englishwomen as innocent victims and English men as their avengers—permits strategies of counterinsurgency to be recorded as the restoration of moral order." (Sharpe, 1993: 3–4, 6, 86, italics mine.)[50]

If Anglo-Indian fiction and colonial records did not refer to male "others" as rapists prior to 1857, certainly other cultural productions that accompanied European forays into distant and often hostile lands did.[51] Among these, a fascinating genre is that of first-person narratives of captivity at the hands of Barbary Coast pirates and North American Indians, not to mention China Sea pirates, Australian aborigines, and Turks. Although many of these were read as fact when first published, it is, for our purposes, much more interesting to view them as discursive

[50] See also Paxton, 1992.

[51] The rhetoric of "sexual fear" and the imposition of sexual sanctions along racial lines has been discussed in several studies, notably Ingilis, 1975; Callaway, 1987: 235–8; Stoler, 1991; Ware, 1992: 38–44; Gouda, 1993; JanMohamed, 1992. The precise role (or instrumentality) of white women in the changing relations between the races has been the subject of considerable revisionist (in the positive sense of the word) historiography in recent years. In addition to the above, see for example Strobel, 1991; also some of the contributions to Chaudhuri and Strobel, 1992; and to Callan and Ardener, 1984.

tools with which Europe's spaces of otherness were constructed and sexualized. Thus Kay Schaffer analyzes the popular shipwreck and captivity story of Eliza Fraser "not as a historical event but as a foundational fiction aligned to the maintenance of a colonial empire and to the making of the Australian nation." (Schaffer, 1994: 102.)

By most accounts, Eliza Fraser was apparently not raped by her captors—although the best-known published relation of her captivity does describe with some relish the loss of her clothes and even features two engravings of her naked.[52] In fact, many captivity narratives included sexual content, and it is fairly clear that their eroticism was intentional. According to June Namias, the American Indian captivity literature extended the possibilities of sexual encounters across racial, ethnic, and cultural lines; titillation and eroticism were apparent, the distinction between "fact" and "fiction" was blurred, Indian "brutality" was portrayed as especially targeted at white women, and violence against Indians was sanctioned as necessary acts of retaliation. (Namias, 1993: 97.)[53] In general, the sexually charged portions of captivity tales followed a fairly standard scenario: women were invariably stripped naked, often before a large assembly of their captors, after which they were sexually abused, raped, and tortured. It is interesting to note, incidentally, that while tales of rape and sexual abuse were abundant especially among men's accounts of women's captivities, those written by the women captives themselves generally painted a much more benign picture.[54] Indeed, some former captives went to great lengths to reassure their readers that they had been treated perfectly "honorably"; of course it is difficult to know for certain, and their assertions may have been due as much to their reluctance to face white society's

---

[52] See Curtis, 1838: 140, 143; the illustrations are opposite 147, 163.

[53] On the portrayal of Indian resistance as the rape of "virgin" whites, see also Hulme, 1985. The literature about American Indian captivity narratives is huge; on their use in the construction of whites as true Americans and the concomitant marginalization of Natives as well as Americans of African and Hispanic descent, see especially Smith-Rosenberg, 1993. For an interesting comparison between the rape of white settlers by Indians, and the rape of black slaves by plantation owners, see Brownmiller, 1975: 140–70.

[54] See, for instance, Derounian-Stodola, Zabelle, and Levernier, 1993: 3–4, 66–7, 127–30. For a comparison between men's and women's writings pertaining to the female "other," see Douthwaite, 1992: 17, 187.

reaction or to their unwillingness to provide male readers with titillation at their own expense, as to the fact that the abuse and rape never took place.

Like native Americans, the Barbary Coast pirates also occasionally kidnapped Europeans, either selling them into slavery or holding them for ransom; some of those who escaped or were redeemed returned to Europe to write of their sufferings.[55] As with Indian captivity tales, some Barbary Coast narratives were evidently fictitious, for example the anonymous *Voyages and Adventures of Captain Robert Boyle in Several Parts of the World, intermix'd with the Story of Mrs Villars, an English Lady with whom he made his Surprizing Escape from Barbary* (1726), once thought to be the work of Daniel Defoe but now generally attributed to William Rufus Chetwood. (Gove, 1961: 251.) It tells of the capture of an Englishman by Moorish pirates led by an Irish renegade, of his confinement in the latter's house in Morocco and his encounter there with a beautiful countrywoman whom he helps escape and marries in an impromptu ceremony, and of their tragic separation and eventual reunion—with details of harems, eunuchs, voyeurism, adultery, betrayal, and a good deal of sex and violence thrown in for good measure. Also set in North Africa were the well-known anonymous erotic classic *The Lustful Turk* and a similar anonymous work brought out by Ernest Leroux, a Parisian publisher partial to exotic erotica, entitled *Marché aux esclaves et harem: Épisode inédit de la piraterie barbaresque au XVIIIe siècle* [Slave market and harem: a hitherto unpublished episode of Barbary Coast piratry in the eighteenth century] (1875). Both told of the capture of European women by pirates, of their sale into slavery, and of their internment in harems where they were subjected to all manner of indignities.

The suggestively titled *La Femme et son maître* (1902) [translated first as *Woman and her master* and later as *Black Lust*] appeared under the pseudonym Jean de Villiot, and describes the misadventures of an Englishwoman captured by Mahdist rebels in the Sudan, also providing an exotic setting for tales of flagellation and violation. Paul Little's *Turkish Delights* (1973), published under the pseudonym A. de

---

[55] See for example Vovard, 1959; Clissold, 1977.

Granamour, likewise describes the torture and violation of English and Greek women at the hands of an Ottoman officer (as well as an unscrupulous Greek spymaster) around the time of the Dardanelles invasion by the Allied forces in 1915; it is only one of many later works in this genre. In Ataullah Mardaan's *Kama Houri*, a young English virgin in colonial India lusts after a Pathan servant and is brutally raped by him. They then become lovers and, willingly abandoning the society of her racial equals, she follows him into the threatening countryside only to be abused, forced to have sex with other men, and finally sold into prostitution. Sexual aggression against her is invariably couched in racial/political language. She is eventually instrumental in his arrest and execution, and is killed in revenge by his blood brother; it is difficult not to see her death as punishment for both having transgressed the racial/sexual sanctions upon which colonialism depends for its very existence, and having so enjoyed her mistreatment at the hands of all those brown men.[56]

Next to these frankly pornographic works, there were also those that might perhaps better be described as romances (though the distinction is admittedly fuzzy), such as E.M. Hull's *The Sheik* (1921)—on which Rudolph Valentino's wildly popular film was based—and Vere Lockwood's *Son of the Turk* (1930). Both told of the abduction of Englishwomen by dark and sinister foreigners, the former by an Arab chieftain and the latter by a Turkish Bey. The incessant, obsessive repetitions of the "fair girl/dark man" dichotomy that punctuate *Son of the Turk* almost like a religious incantation leave no doubt as to the impulses animating the story.[57] Indeed, the general tenor of these works is well

---

[56] As mentioned earlier, this book may have been written in the 1950s by a Pakistani, and one might therefore question its interpretation as a colonial morality tale; I think, however, that the important point is not so much its authorship as its plausibility for a Western readership.

[57] It is worth pointing out that E.M. Hull and Vere Lockwood were both women, as, of course, is Barbara Cartland, who "condensed" *Son of the Turk* and published it in 1980 in her "Library of Love" series. Cartland introduced her own version of the novel as follows: "This dramatic, exciting story of the East was very popular at the time it was written. Young women dreamt of being abducted by dark-eyed, passionate Sheiks, Rajahs, and Beys." (Lockwood, 1980.) She is no doubt right, as evidenced by the phenomenal following that Valentino's *The Sheik* elicited among women during the 1920s. This is not the place to dwell on that issue at any length, but I think it noteworthy to stress that there

condensed by the Bey of Tunis in *The Lustful Turk*, who boasts that his British victim:

> not only screamed but struggled; however I was safely in her; another thrust finished the job, it was done, and nobly done, by Mahomet! Europa was never half so well unvirgined, although love might have had the strength of a bull. (Anon./*Lustful Turk*, 1984: 99–100.)

Of all the tales of violation in classical mythology—and there are many—this particular choice makes amply clear the symbolic meaning attached to this story: it was Europe itself that was being raped by the barbaric "other." (Equally significant, I must add, is the fact that the novel ends with the castration of the Dey of Algiers by one of his many victims; no longer having any use for his two English captives, he sets them free, giving each a part of his genitals in a jar! Evidently, even the most pornographic work can have a strong didactic, programmatic component.)

Narratives of captivity were enormously popular in their own day, some attaining genuine bestseller status. They served diverse functions—a few were pornographic; others purely propagandistic, exhorting the metropoles to support efforts to drive away the Indians or decisively defeat the Barbary pirates who hindered free navigation in the Mediterranean; many were strongly religious, describing the power of faith in the face of adversity, miraculous signs, and providential deliverance. Still others, much like the epistolary texts discussed later in this study, occasioned social criticism; as Mary Louise Pratt writes, "survival literature furnished a 'safe' context for staging alternate, relativizing, and taboo configurations of intercultural contact: Europeans enslaved by non-Europeans, Europeans assimilating to non-European societies, and Europeans cofounding new transracial social orders." The context was "safe" for transgressive plots because "the very

---

is a long tradition of books *written by women* that tell of a woman's loss of control, of her discovery of "the joys of total submission to a man." While they are no doubt the by-product of a society characterized by power differentials (including, but not limited to, those based on gender), I think it would be simplistic to dismiss them outright as simply the fruit of some sort of "false consciousness." But this is a topic for further research. On the role of rape in romantic/erotic fiction written by and targeted at women, see Radway, 1984: 71–7, 141–4.

existence of a text presupposed the imperially correct outcome: the survivor survived, and sought reintegration into the home society. The tale was always told from the viewpoint of the European who returned." (Pratt: 1992: 87.) Speaking of transgressive plots and transracial social orders, a fascinating appropriation of Barbary Coast captivities by an American is Charles Sumner's *White Slavery in the Barbary States* (1847), in which an abolitionist case is made by invoking the sufferings of fellow white men at the hands of captors of a different race; and this is not an isolated example.

Sexualized xenological discourse thus constructed spaces of alterity, both as the locus of a threat to the white man's most precious "possession," his woman, and as a site of non-conformity or transgression. In the Eliza Fraser narrative, for example, the victim/heroine:

> becomes a figure of display for an imperial/colonial audience and her story *a myth by which the popular imagination understood the civilized world by means of its difference from the savage "others" at its margins.* In terms of the construction of social space, Mrs Fraser's captivity narrative provided for a widespread Western colonial audience the justification for control by the West over the rest of the world. ... Not Mrs Fraser, but her story in its various guises provides the white, male Western hero of progress *the space in which to perform a "rescue" operation through which he marks the boundaries between colonizer and colonized, man and his "others"*—an operation that protects the idea of "a people" through the exclusion of native inhabitants on an alien, yet-to-be-claimed, physical, psychic, and mythically constructed landscape. (Schaffer, 1994: 107, 110, italics mine.)

Of course the threat of miscegenation, of the "desecration" of white femininity by black masculinity, also occurs in forms other than rape. Othello and Desdemona were certainly a consenting couple, and yet for their transgression of the entire racial/sexual system of their day (*Othello* was first performed in 1604, and first published in 1622), their union was cursed, and the lovers punished by tragedy. Iago's inflammatory words to Brabantio, "an old black ram is tupping your white ewe," and "your daughter covered with a Barbary horse" (1.1.88–9 and 111–12), provide some insight as to the manner in which an interracial union would be seen in Elizabethan England.[58] Of a much more mundane nature were the grave concerns voiced in the nineteenth century about Indian royalty having sexual intercourse with European women—both by seducing British ladies visiting India, and by *being* seduced by working-class Englishwomen during their travels to Britain. (Ballhatchet, 1980: 116–120, 165.) The class-specificity of each concern needs no elaboration.

Although these examples could be multiplied, consensual interracial sexual unions involving white women and non-white men tend to be relatively rare as compared to those involving white men and non-white women. Indeed, in colonial literature during the period of high imperialism, one gets the impression that such unions were simply unthinkable, and only rape could explain such a violation of the "laws of nature."

The Female "Other" as Rape Victim

Although the trope of rape in colonial discourse has been widely discussed in the contexts of legitimating the Western takeover of foreign lands and justifying counter-insurgency measures against natives, relatively little attention has been paid to a third form it sometimes took: descriptions of the rape of native women intended to provoke revulsion in the metropole and incite the public to action.

For example, Samuel Purchas wrote in his *Pilgrimage* (1613), "let us draw neerer the Sunne to New-Britaine, whose Virgin soyle not yet polluted with Spaniards lust ... was justly called *Virginia*." (Purchas, 1626: 828.) Indeed, a theme frequently used by the British to legitimate their own efforts to colonize the New World was precisely the "rape" of America by Spaniards, whose enslavement of native American men was, according to Louis Montrose, asserted in part by their sexual abuse of

---

[58] For an interesting discussion of *Othello* from this viewpoint, see Newman, 1991: chapter 5. For a contemporary story of miscegenation, complete with elements of lustful abandon, cruelty, and venereal disease, see Legh-Jones, 1975; the jacket describes it as "The poignant story of love faced with the ultimate impossibility of combining two utterly divergent civilisations into a single pattern of life."

native American women. As colonists like Sir Walter Ralegh admiringly portrayed the Indians as innocent and trusting, they simultaneously "displace[d] on to the Spaniards the implicit betrayal of that trust which [was] at the heart of the English enterprise." Ralegh exhorted his countrymen to rise up and free the Indians from the yoke of Spanish oppression, while at the same time inciting them to replace the Spaniards and plunder Guiana for the British crown. The violence committed by the Spaniards against women was thus used to fabricate an emergency by means of which to legitimate intervention. But it was also a means of defining the Englishness of the English: "In this intolerable situation, in which the Other is always threatening to collapse into the Same, feminine figures must be textually deployed in an attempt to keep Spaniards and Englishmen apart," writes Montrose. In this fashion, native women were reduced to markers of difference among men, a common pattern in patriarchal discourse. (Montrose, 1992: 163, 166, 169.)[59] In nineteenth-century racialism, this issue mutated into accounts of widespread miscegenation in Spain's South American colonies, taken up as prime examples of the alleged degenerative effects of racial hybridization. (Young, 1995: 175–7.)

Another noteworthy occurrence of this trope was in the impeachment trial of Warren Hastings, Governor-General of Bengal. Lasting from 1786 to 1794, the trial was essentially but one episode in Edmund Burke's crusade to bring some accountability to the East India Company and curb its abuses of power—and more generally to oppose the evil of colonialism.[60] Interestingly, one of the main accusations against Hastings was the so-called "Begums Charges," having to do with his extortion of payments from the widow and mother of the late Nawab of Oudh in 1781. What is most significant about this case is that its pleading foreshadowed the Mutiny reports some 70 years later: Burke mesmerized the proceedings with horrific stories relating how

[59] See also Lavrin, 1989; and Douthwaite, 1992: 111, who discusses images of the Spanish "rape" of Peru in eighteenth-century French literature.
[60] Much was written about this trial, both in its own day and subsequently. For a useful recent discussion, see Suleri, 1992: chapters 2 and 3. On Hastings and other "sexual episodes" of British rule in India, see Edwardes, 1966; this work should be consulted more for entertainment than for historical edification.

Hastings's troops had ransacked the Begums' estate, dragged out the women, stripped them naked in public view, raped them in the Court of Justice where they had taken refuge, tore off their nipples, and so on. The narrative gave Burke and others ample opportunity for rhetorical prowess, and Richard Brinsley Sheridan's speech on this charge in the House of Commons, also dwelling at length on that violation of a female sanctuary, was later celebrated by Lord Byron as "the very best Oration . . . ever conceived or heard in this country." (Byron, 1813: 3: 239.) The nation, needless to say, was duly scandalized. But while it was once again the sexualized and violated bodies of women that provided the language for mobilizing British public opinion, this time the instrument of that mobilization was the circulation of the violated bodies of *Indian,* not English, women. The parallels between the "Begums Charges" and tales about the Cawnpore (Kanpur) massacre and other horror stories that gained prominence during and after the 1857 Mutiny are of course not incidental—nor, for that matter, is it entirely coincidental that the East India Company was finally abolished in 1858, immediately following the Mutiny. These attest to the extraordinarily compelling power wielded by sexualized images of female bodies in the political imagination of the times, to the centrality of gendering and sexualization in colonial discourse, and to the unity—despite the wide variety of forms it could take—of the sexual dimension of xenological discourse.

In fact, Burke's case was not unique: it was not unusual for criticism of the British imperial presence in India to take sexual form, and be voiced in terms of a threat posed by British troops to the native population and particularly to native women. Thus, Maurice Gregory appealed to his nonconformist readers in the *Banner of Asia* by arguing that "respectable Native shopkeepers and residents" were threatened with "the very possible debauchery of their daughters by English officers"; and in 1888, the Hindi weekly *Almora Akhbar* opposed Alfred Dyer's campaign to purge British garrisons in India of their resident prostitutes by arguing that "not to provide women for European soldiers who are drunk and mad with lust would be like letting loose beasts of prey." True, such concerns were not necessarily idle; British military authorities themselves "predicted that there would be unpleasant 'incidents' if the soldiers' energies had no outlet," and assaults on Indians by British soldiers, including some violence against women, came to attract growing attention towards the end of the century. The stereotype of the oversexed British soldier was thus deployed both in Britain and in India to criticize British colonial rule. (Ballhatchet, 1980: 64, 66, 140.)

A fascinating subject that, as far as I know, remains to be studied concerns the links between the struggle for, and imposition of, sexual sanctions in the colonies, and parallel actions in the metropoles—such as the Purity Campaign, the Eugenics movement, the campaign for sexual hygiene including the widespread practice of circumcision, and the war against masturbation. (Young, 1995: 116.)

An important question arises from the juxtaposition of the various examples discussed so far: is it meaningful—or, for that matter, fair— to group together Ralegh's aggressive colonialism and what was ulti- mately (despite Burke's quirks and personal vendettas) a principled moral stance against imperialism? Insofar as their use of sexual tropol- ogy is concerned, I think the answer must be *yes*. The fact is that even the most committed opponents of colonialism, down to Frantz Fanon and Jawaharlal Nehru, frequently appropriated the colonial trope of rape, and regardless of how noble the cause, it is important not to lose sight of the role played by this trope in the reproduction of *gender*. As Sharpe notes, "the *representation* of rape [in Mutiny narratives] violently appropriates English women as 'the sex.' This appropriation takes place through an objectification of the women as eroticized and ravaged bodies." But such discursive strategies have profound social implications: the stories of rape "violently reproduce gender roles in the demonstration that women's bodies can be sexually appropriated. In this regard, the meaning of rape cannot be disassociated from its discursive production." (Sharpe, 1993: 66–7, 120.) It is therefore necessary to be very conscious of the ways in which the category of rape was historically produced within the context of a system of colonial relations, and of the significational practices accruing from it.

Indeed, as Derrida and others have shown, meaning is never simply given; it exists within and through language, it is fluid, it is discursively produced and reproduced. To quote Derrida's well-known aphorism, "*there's no racism without a language.* The point is not that acts of racial violence are only words but rather that they have to have a word. . . . Racism always betrays the perversion of a man, the 'talking animal.'" (Derrida, 1986: 331.) As I argued in chapter 1, it is especially important to bear this in mind when politically confronting a significational system such as that of colonialism. To consider but one example, Peter Hulme has pointed to the irreducible connections between the term "cannibalism" and its discursive production, stressing that the process of signification cannot be viewed outside specific discursive networks, and arguing that "it is not a question of a discourse employing a particular word whose meaning is already given: *the discourse constitutes signification.* 'Cannibalism' is a term that has no application outside the discourse of European colonialism: it is never available as a 'neutral' word." (Hulme, 1992: 84.)

And neither is rape. There is no rape without a language; this word is trapped within a complex of discursive networks, and acquires meaning only in the context of discourse. Stories that recount the rape of white women by natives not only bolster racism and reaffirm a hierarchical anthropology that places Europeans at the apex of the human pyramid, but they also reproduce gender by objectifying women and portraying them as natural targets of violation. As Nancy Paxton writes, "the colonial rape narrative performed double duty," in that it "naturalized British colonizers' dominance by asserting the lawlessness of Indian men and, at the same time, shored up traditional gender roles by assigning to British women the role of victim, countering British feminist demands for women's greater political and social equality." (Paxton, 1992: 6.) And this is no less true of rape narratives where the victims are native women.

Clearly, the same can be said of what would pass for "progressive" uses of the trope of rape: the metaphorical application of sexual violence in anti-imperialist discourse sanctions the deployment of rape as a metaphor for imperialism; and while there is arguably good reason to utilize this metaphor, particularly in representations that "authorize a European claim of ownership through a feminization of the colonial body" (Sharpe, 1993: 137), it brings along its own set of problems. The representation of land ownership as the appropriation of female bodies takes for granted the implicit premise that female bodies are subject to appropriation. It is not possible to dissociate the use of the trope from the trope itself; whether the woman who is raped is white, brown, or black, and whether she is raped by a white, brown, or black man, ultimately the trope reproduces women as objects. In the words of Suleri, "the anxieties of empire are only obscured by a critically unquestioning recuperation of the metaphor of rape, in which colonized territory is rendered dubiously coterminus with the stereotype of a precultural and female geography." (Suleri, 1992: 16–17.)

The Male "Other" as Despotic Oppressor of Women

One of the main defences offered by Warren Hastings during his impeachment trial was that arbitrary power was a necessity in India since its people were accustomed only to unconditional servitude to an absolute ruler. Although Edmund Burke argued against this claim— pointing out that Islamic law had, for centuries, imposed a particular system and order in India, and that its government had therefore been anything but arbitrary—this was an uphill battle, for Hastings's plea conformed perfectly to an established Western belief in "Asiatic absolutism" going back at least to Aristotle, and revived in the seventeenth and eighteenth centuries as the discourse of "oriental despotism."

In his interesting study *Structure du sérail* [Structure of the seraglio] (1979), Alain Grosrichard has suggested that the notion of oriental despotism was fundamentally sexualized, and that the sultan's seraglio as prisonhouse of women, seen as "a site of absolute power so completely invested by sexuality," served as a central trope in this discourse:

> It must be recognized that oriental despotism is essentially linked to a certain type of gender relation, a certain sexual economy, in which power is rooted and within which it is exercised as an insurpassable natural necessity. More fundamental than its military origin or even its complicity with the Mohammedan religion—which is only the expression of that same necessity—this is perhaps the ultimate explanation of the power of the oriental despot, simultaneously the source of fear and of passionate love. . . . The limitless

sexual gratification granted to him as an exclusive right is also the means of his absolute power and the deep explanation of the form taken by that power. . . . It is into the domain of sexuality, where it is rooted, that oriental despotism must be placed back in order to grasp its true nature and to assess the strength of the fascination it elicits. Likewise, the heart of oriental despotic power, which rules over immense empires, hides within the very place where the despot exercises his *domestic* power: in that enclosed space forbidden to the gaze, saturated and structured by sex—the seraglio.

According to Grosrichard, this state of affairs only proved the effeminacy of the male "other," as the subservience of women became a paradigm for subjugation to the despot. In other words, the harem was a microcosm of the despotic state, and oriental men were to the absolute ruler as oriental women were to their husbands and masters: "On the one hand despotic society presents itself as a chain of domestic despots (the men) all reigning absolutely over their little subject peoples of slaves (the women); on the other, those men themselves are nothing before the One: they vanish before his law, and worship his person to which their imagination bequeaths all sorts of prestige." Thus, oriental men "show themselves to be women: that is, in fact, what the climate of Asia has destined them to be, giving to men there all the traits that in Europe characterize femininity." (Grosrichard, 1979: 147–9, 156, translation mine.)

The best-known example of this kind of identification between despotism and the harem is no doubt Montesquieu's *Lettres persanes* [Persian letters] (1721),[61] but the theme was in common use from early on. A bizarre passage from the journal of Sir George Courthop, who traveled to İstanbul during the late 1630s, provides a striking example of the eroticization of the arbitrary power and cruelty of the "oriental despot":

[The sultan has] a pond made all porphyry stone, that is in the middle of a grove all beset with trees, on which he hangeth carpets: that none can see into it, or dare approach near it. Here he putteth in his Concubines stark naked and shooteth at them with certain pelletts that stick upon them without any damage to their bodies. And sometimes he lets the water in such

---

[61] For an interesting recent study of this work, see Schaub, 1995.

abundance upon them (for he can let what quantity of water he will in) that being above their heights they all bob up and down for life; and when his pleasure is satisfied with the sport, he lets down the water, and calls the Eunuchs who wait upon his women, to fetch them out if alive. (Courthop, 1907: 123).

What is one to make of a passage like this? To be sure, Sir George had a vivid imagination, and his sexual fantasies were, at the very least, interesting; but what is most noteworthy about such accounts is that the line between fantasy and reality is never quite clear in them. And while Courthop's memoirs remained unpublished until this century, other fantastic descriptions of oriental sexuality—like Millingen's story about Kurdish female brigands, for instance—were often taken as fact. As Patrick Brantlinger writes of British descriptions of India, even at its most positive, the East was represented as "only a false Eden, a sensual paradise of luxury, tyranny, and erotic decadence." (Brantlinger, 1988: 85.)

By the nineteenth century, descriptions of the sufferings of women in the East had become a commonplace of xenological discourse. In religious tracts, the trope was used with great efficacy to garner support for missionary work. (Başcı, 1998.) In the writings of feminists such as Charlotte Brontë and Mary Wollstonecraft, it provided a handy tool with which both to mark the oppression of women as fundamentally alien to civilized Europe, and to render feminism less threatening by displacing its target to distant lands. (Zonana, 1993.) In the hands of anti-feminists, by contrast, the debased status of oriental women was used to the exact opposite effect, as a cautionary tale of what might happen to European women if they were granted greater freedom. For example, claiming that the movement for women's emancipation in Europe was inspired by a desire for sexual liberation, Flora A. Steel purported to show "in her Indian stories the degrading effects which their obsession with sex had brought upon the women of India. In strident reaction against the Victorian New Woman, Mrs Steel proclaimed marriage as 'a duty to the race.'" (Ridley, 1983: 74.) With delicious irony, anti-feminists thus pointed to xenotopia—precisely the site where women were believed to be hopelessly enslaved—as epitomizing the consequences of the uncontrolled female sexuality that was likely to result from women's liberation in Europe.

Erotic works made use of the trope as well: Hendrik de Leeuw's *Cities of Sin* (1934) set out to describe "the shocking story of vice in the ancient cities of the East," chiefly sexual slavery, and to "lift the veil from the romantic falsehoods told in novels."[62] An anonymous pamphlet published several times around the turn of the century under slightly different titles and formats, *Traffic in Women, including Detailed Descriptions of the Customs and Manners of the White Women Slaves and Wives of Asia, Turkey, Egypt, etc.*, also capitalized on the subject, offering what purported to be an eyewitness account of the interior of a harem as well as sordid descriptions of concubinage and the slave trade. And thrillers too used a conflation of sexual oppression and foreignness: for example, a novel set in the Ottoman Empire in the turbulent years of 1908–9, Elliot Tokson's *Harem Games* (1984), constantly invokes themes like circumcision, eunuchs, rape, and concubines, using sexuality as the principal signifier of alterity. Upon returning to İstanbul, the protagonist—whose sister has apparently been imprisoned in the imperial harem—reflects that "tonight the City struck me as a sepulcher for women," an image that constructs space as sexual otherness itself. Sultan Abdülhamid's supposed mistreatment of his harem is made into a clear metaphor for tyranny, and the hero's final act is to shoot the now deposed sultan in the crotch so that "he would never father another child on a young girl again"! (Tokson, 1984: 204, 293.)[63]

Colonial politics also capitalized on this motif. In 1883, when Courtenay Ilbert, law member of the Governor-General's Legislative Council, proposed a bill that would enable Indian judges to try European subjects on criminal charges, a significant part of the opposition was expressed in the language of gender and sexuality: thus, a letter to the

[62] Quote taken from the dust jacket of De Leeuw, 1953. The words "Eastern" and "ancient" were apparently thought synonymous by the author, since he discusses altogether modern urban centers like Port Said and Hong Kong alongside older (but equally colonial) places such as Macao and Singapore. For a discussion of sex in port cities, see also Schidrowitz, 1927.

[63] Similarly, sex is used as a technology of alterity in Dennis Wheatley's *The Eunuch of Stamboul* (1935), a spy thriller set in the immediate aftermath of the Kemalist revolution. On sexual violence in thrillers set in the Middle East, see Simon, 1989: 103–7.

Englishman assailed "Mr Ilbert's proposal to subject civilized women to the jurisdiction of men who have done little or nothing to redeem the women of their own races." As Ballhatchet notes, "English womanhood [was] readily seen as at risk when the structure of British power and authority [was] threatened." (Ballhatchet, 1980: 6–7.)[64] The oppression of women in the East became evidence of despotism, and therefore proof of the East's inhospitability to the rule of law.

The trope of the female other as victim was invoked particularly intensely in the debates surrounding the abolition of *sati* (widow immolation) in India in 1829. Indeed, it was an important element in colonial discourse and policy: "The degeneration of Hindu civilization," writes Uma Chakravarti, "and the abject position of Hindu women, requiring the 'protection' and 'intervention' of the colonial state, were two aspects of colonial politics. The third aspect was the 'effeminacy' of the Hindu men who were unfit to rule themselves. On all these counts British rule in India could be justified on grounds of moral superiority." (Chakravarti, 1989: 35–6.)[65] Thus the oppression of women and the effeminacy of men, twin constituents of the trope of oriental despotism, provided a rationale for colonization. That the "Orient" had historically been ruled by despotism, combined with the thesis that oriental states were moribund and decadent, suggested a need for the imposition of rational government from without—and who better to do that than the West?

The oppression of women thus supplied colonialism with an alibi: it created a scenario, in Gayatri Chakravorty Spivak's well-known wry formulation, of "white men saving brown women from brown men." (Spivak, 1988: 297.) From the sexual subjugation of oriental women, to the political subjugation of oriental men, xenotopia needed Western masters. In his *Les Fastes de l'amour et de la volupté*, Alfred de Theille explicitly linked the trope of oriental despotism to the imperative for Western control, which, without a trace of self-consciousness, he

---

[64] On the Ilbert Bill, see also Sinha, 1995: chapter 1.
[65] The literature on *sati* is large; for recent contributions, see for example Spivak, 1988; Mani, 1985; Mani, 1989; Das, 1986; Sunder Rajan, 1993: chapters 1 and 2; and Hawley, 1994.

conjured up with obviously sexual metaphors—railroads-cum-progress penetrating the Orient:

> The foolish vizir who thinks himself loved and lovable, because he tosses an absolute handkerchief to the unfortunate—who, by higher authority and facing imminent punishment, surrenders to him her person while withholding her soul; for her soul, her will, her feelings, her tenderness ... the foolish vizir has none of all that! It is a *beautiful cadaver* whom he violates, the barbarian ... [B]ut let us hope that thanks to railroads, progress will one day penetrate the Orient, and woman, a slave in those parts, will recover the rank to which her grace and virtues entitle her in the civilized world! (Theille, 1839: 1: 239–40, translation mine.)

More than two centuries ago, Voltaire professed to hate Turks as "tyrants of women and enemies of the arts." (Voltaire, 1877–85: 20: 21, translation mine.)[66] Today, political capital continues to be made of the sufferings, whether systematic or isolated, of non-European women, and issues like child prostitution, *sati*, veiling/reveiling, and genital mutilation receive a great deal of coverage—a good deal of it sensationalistic—in the Western media.[67] To be sure, neither indifference, nor abject relativism would be the correct response to such realities; nevertheless, it is necessary to bear in mind the geopolitical matrix within which these images of victimized oriental women circulate. The monolithic persona of the "Third World Woman" becomes, in such representations, the overdetermined symbol both of universal patriarchy and of specifically non-European social and religious practices (Sunder Rajan, 1993: 15); and we have seen that gendered and sexualized symbols are routinely deployed in the service of both international and gender hegemony. As Shohat asks rhetorically, "is it a coincidence that stories of the sexual violence committed against 'Third World' women are relatively privileged over those of violence

---

[66] It is worth noting that the context of this statement is a passage in which Voltaire refutes the common imputation of sensuality to the Muslim faith.

[67] Kadiatu Kanneh draws interesting parallels between colonial efforts to remove the veil, missionary efforts to cover the breasts, and feminist discourse focused on genital mutilation, in "The Difficult Politics of Wigs and Veils: Feminism and the Colonial Body," a paper presented at the Conference on Gender and Colonialism, University College, Galway, May 1992. Passages from this essay appear in Ashcroft, Griffiths, and Tiffin, 1995: 346–8.

toward 'Third World' men, including sexual violence?" (Shohat, 1991a: 57.) It is not, of course.

That Homosocial/Sexual Business of Empire

Like the society in which they were conducted, studies focusing on the sexual dimension of Europe's confrontation with the rest of the world have generally tended to be strongly heterosexist, emphasizing the white male explorer's conquest of a feminized land or of native women, the dark-skinned native man's rape of European women, and other heterosexual tropes. Yet, the very nature of human sexuality would suggest that there must have been more to the confrontation than that—indeed, that the overwhelmingly heterosexual models that have been proposed for the colonial experience can only have been obtained through the active suppression, whether deliberate or subconscious, of its homosexual dimension. (Boone, 1989.)[68] For instance, much has been written about Gustave Flaubert's frolics with the Egyptian courtesan Kuchuk Hanem ("*küçük hanım*" means "little lady" in Turkish), but very little about his fascination with the transvestite dancer Hasan el-Belbeissi or his many references to sexual experimentation with boys. In one letter, he wrote:

> Here it is quite accepted. One admits one's sodomy, and it is spoken of at table in the hotel. Sometimes you do a bit of denying, and then everybody teases you and you end up confessing. Traveling as we are for educational purposes, and charged with a mission by the government, we have considered it our duty to indulge in this form of ejaculation. So far the occasion has not presented itself. We continue to seek it, however. (Flaubert, 1972: 84.)[69]

[68] On gender indeterminacy, transvestism, and homosexuality in orientalist discourse, see Garber, 1992: chapter 12; on the question of transvestism as it pertains to Western women travelers disguised as men (such as Isabelle Eberhardt), see also Behdad, 1994: chapter 6.
[69] Though his reference in the present context to the educational purposes of his trip and to his governmental mission is, of course, facetious, his interest in the male sex apparently was genuine; for homosexual motifs in Flaubert's correspondence, see Flaubert, 1972: 83–5. On Flaubert's sexual tourism, see also Porter, 1991: chapter 6.

Egypt—the "here" to which Flaubert refers, and the "there" relative to his native France—is transformed in these playful lines into a locus of sexual alterity, a place where the European traveler can give free rein to his hidden impulses, where he can be "himself" without fear of censure. Significantly, this "true nature" aching to be set free was homosexual, a point often overlooked nowadays.

Drawing attention to "the marked homoeroticism of the narratives of colonial encounter," Sara Suleri sets out to reread themes like the romance between Kim and his lama in Kipling's *Kim* (1901), and the unresolved friendship between Fielding and Aziz in E. M. Forster's *A Passage to India* (1924), in the light of a colonial erotic. She suggests that the politics and narratives of British India are "fraught with a deferred homosexual decorum that lends a retroactive significance" to Kipling's well-known claim in "The Ballad of East and West," that the cultural difference of East, West, Border, Breed, and Birth will only vanish when "two strong men stand face to face, though they come from the ends of the earth"; indeed, she goes as far as to argue that "the colonial encounter depends upon a disembodied homoeroticism *rather than* on the traditional metaphor of ravishment and possession." I hope I have established that such categorical statements are not much help, since in fact the colonial encounter was represented by a wide range of erotic imagery; nevertheless, it is certainly true that the motif of male homosexuality is present in a number of works of colonial literature. For example, the latent homoeroticism of the relationship between Fielding and Aziz, so central to Forster's novel, can, Suleri suggests, more fruitfully be explained by reference to the author's political project than to autobiographical details such as his homosexuality or his deceased Egyptian lover. Thus, "in place of the Orientalist paradigm in which the colonizing presence is as irredeemably male as the colonized territory is female, *A Passage to India* presents an alternative colonial model: the most urgent cross-cultural invitations occur between male and male, with racial difference serving as a substitute for gender." (Suleri, 1992: 16–17, 77, 133, italics mine.) As Joseph Boone writes, for many colonial writers the "quest for sexual identity cannot escape a continual negotiation of the homoerotic, in the guise of foreign otherness" (Boone, 1989: 83); *homo*sexuality, in other words, was made *hetero*typical by the injection of racial difference into sexual identity.

In his psychohistorical study of Kipling's work, Wurgaft has similarly underscored the author's "fantasies of destructive female sexuality," arguing that "the male-dominated life of frontier fighting, where women were altogether absent, and where Englishmen and Pathan confronted each other in open warfare, allowed the most unconflicted expression of male aggressiveness." By contrast, he suggests, "the 'stink' of the plains which Kipling described was constituted, at least partially, of the contaminating 'odor' of female sexuality." (Wurgaft, 1983: 50.)

Homosexuality was also a central organizing theme in the life and writing of T.E. Lawrence (a.k.a. Lawrence of Arabia). Analyzing his *Seven Pillars of Wisdom: A Triumph* (1926) and *The Mint* (1935) against the backdrop of his life and correspondence, Kaja Silverman has suggested that Lawrence's works "oblige us to approach history always through the refractions of desire and identification, and to read race and class insistently in relation to sexuality." She argues that his participation in the Arab nationalist struggle was "in large part because his particular homosexuality promotes an erotic identification both with its leaders and its servants." Showing that Arab nationalism is "intimately linked to the male body" in Lawrence's discourse, she writes that his "imaginary alignment with a series of Bedouin figures is made possible . . . by the fact that each of them is at some point displayed for him within a libidinal configuration which conforms to his 'own' fantasmatic." (Silverman, 1989: 4, 10, 20, 22.)[70] Thus, T.E. Lawrence's involvement in the colonial effort, and his activities during the Arab revolt (which were not always in perfect harmony with British interests), had nothing to do with the trope of the Orient as a woman; the connection was entirely homoerotic.

Burton's promising military career in British India almost came to an abrupt end—and arguably never quite recovered from the shock—after a report he had filed in 1845, detailing the results of "research"

---

[70] Although most of this essay is included in the Silverman, 1992, I am citing the earlier version (with apologies) because some of the passages I found pertinent were left out or modified in the later edition. On the relationship between Lawrence's homosexuality and his view of the Arab struggle, see also Mosse, 1985: 120–22; and Garber, 1992: 304–9.

he had conducted in the male brothels of Karachi, resurfaced. Though his sexual leanings remain uncertain to this day, it is impossible to miss the fascination with which he wrote of the boys and eunuchs he encountered there.[71] Lord Byron and Lawrence Durrell had recourse to homoerotic motifs in their depictions of the Orient, and the list goes on. Indeed, if Peter Hulme is to be believed, "the true romance in *Robinson Crusoe* is between Crusoe and Friday," for "Crusoe's description of Friday is certainly tinged with erotic delight." (Hulme, 1992: 212.) Inter-racial homosexuality was, without doubt, an important element in sexualized xenological discourse.

In his *Empire and Sexuality: The British Experience* (1990), Ronald Hyam offers a gossipy and somewhat rambling survey of the sexual proclivities of various British colonial officials—ranging from asexual to heterosexual, homosexual, bisexual, pedophilic, and sadomasochistic. By saying so much, he ends up saying little, save that they were of all tastes and persuasions, just like the rest of the population from which they were drawn. Nevertheless, this polymorphism bears emphasizing, because it fundamentally destabilizes the facile binarism that ceaselessly equates Europe with masculinity and xenotopia with femininity. True, mainstream colonial discourse by and large used heterosexual imagery, in which the female "other" was deflowered, seduced, conquered, ravished, raped, penetrated, appropriated, and so forth by the male European; but the mainstream is not the whole, and this heterosexual tropology was by no means unanimous.

One last point: as with the trope of rape, that of homosexuality too has been put to (highly problematical) use in anti-imperialist rhetoric, notably by Fanon. (Fuss, 1994.) But a liberation movement cannot afford to become a force of oppression itself: the struggle against colonialism is not truly emancipatory if it draws munition from homophobia (or from any other ideology of hatred), a point sometimes lost in an amoral grope for political expediency.

---

[71] Burton describes this in his "Terminal Essay"; see also Brodie, 1967: 66, 69.

"Going Native"

From fairly early on, xenological discourse was peppered (pun intended!) with accounts of Europeans and Americans who had "turned Turk" or "gone native." Why particular individuals may have chosen to turn their backs on their societies of origin and start their lives anew in foreign lands and among foreign peoples does not concern us here; rather, it is the narrative reconstruction of their defection that I wish to discuss. As Brantlinger writes, "Europeans found their savage impulses were never far from their civilized surfaces; the potential for being 'defiled,' for going native, led them again and again to displace these impulses onto Africans, as well as onto other nonwhite peoples." Thus, "the myth of the Dark Continent contains the submerged fear of falling out of the light into the abyss of social and moral regression." (Brantlinger, 1988: 194.) This fear of losing oneself among the natives, of falling into an abyss of regression, had a profoundly sexual dimension.

To the British in India, for instance, the country itself was threateningly libidinized, and the colonists' hostility towards the natives derived in part from a deep fear of its seductive and mysterious qualities. (Wurgaft, 1983: 49.) To be sure, attitudes were not constant throughout the colonial literature; German authors were almost fanatical in their rejection of miscegenation, while French colonial literature contains many sincere accounts of the temptations of that "dropping out" from European civilization which the Germans so feared. (Ridley, 1983: 80.) Nevertheless, whether viewed with apprehension or with fascination, "going native" was a ubiquitous and highly sexually-charged theme in colonial literature. So much so, in fact, that Jean E. Howard has interpreted the castration of Clem in Heywood's *The Fair Maid of the West* in this light: "In the land of the Moors he, an Englishman, wears a version of Moroccan attire and for doing so seems to get a grotesquely hideous warning of the dangers of 'going native.' The idea seems to be that if the white European gives himself to the customs of Barbary, his manhood may be lost." (Howard, 1994: 115.)

Frequently, the wages of transgressing the boundaries between European and "other" were not the loss of manhood but rather its affirmation, for one of the most telling indicators that a man had "gone native" was his relationship with native women. But the allure of inter-racial romance in the colonies has surely been vastly exaggerated: many commentators have pointed out the dreariness of colonial posts and the importance of local women in mitigating it, but also their role as symbols of the final act of surrender to alterity. Knibiehler and Goutalier, for instance, write that the colonizers had to "endure all the hardships of exile in the tropics: the devastating climate, recurring fevers, boredom, sometimes alcohol or drugs. A relationship with a colored girl [was] the last stage of their degradation." (Knibiehler and Goutalier, 1985: 46, translation mine.) Similarly, Hyam writes that:

> running the Victorian empire would probably have been intolerable without resort to sexual relaxation. The historian has to remember the *misery* of empire: the heat and the dust, the incessant rain and monotonous food, the inertia and the loneliness, the lack of amusement and intellectual stimulus. . . . Language barriers and other cultural impediments to relationships sometimes led Europeans into sexual intimacy with non-Europeans almost as an act of baffled despair. (Hyam, 1990: 89–90.)

Degradation, baffled despair—these are words that rather diminish the glamor of colonial service, and of the much-heralded sexual liberties it was supposed to provide.[72]

Thus, when Jean Peyral, the white protagonist of Pierre Loti's *Le Roman d'un spahi* [The romance of a spahi (colonial cavalryman)] (1881), first has sexual relations with his Senegalese lover Fatou-Gaye, "it seemed to him that he was about to step over a fatal threshold, to sign with that black race a sort of deathly compact"; afterwards, he feels that "his 'white man's' dignity . . . had been soiled by contact with that black flesh." (Loti, 1930: 93, 199.)[73] The theme was drawn to its absurd

---

[72] For another perspective on inter-racial sex and colonialism, this time from the point-of-view of the colonized African, see Fanon, 1967: chapters 2 and 3; also Busia, 1986.
[73] For an interesting analysis of Loti's female characters as points along a continuum stretching from nature/animal/desire to culture/human/knowledge, see Maccagnani, 1978. The differences among Loti's various novels with respect to sexual liaisons with native women are also discussed in Bongie, 1991: 91–106; Todorov, 1993: 308–23; and Szyliowicz, 1988.

extreme in Johann Gottfried Schnabel's tale of shipwreck and adventure, *Die Insel Felsenburg* (1731) [roughly, "The Isle of Cliff Castle"], where the lone survivor recalls: "my three remaining compatriots had tamed three female apes for some months past, with which they indulged day and night in the most shameful obscenities." The three men eventually kill one another over a favorite ape. (Ridley, 1983: 9.)

How different those accounts are from the effusive description given by Theille:

> A superb negress ... adorned with diamonds and pearls, looks like a beautiful night sprinkled with stars. The vivid incarnadine of her lips of roses, the enamel of her teeth, the brightness of her eyes, are also capable of inspiring love. More than one white man has tasted happiness in the arms of an African beauty! Does the imagination not relish strong contrasts? (Theille, 1839: 1: 228, translation mine.)

Indeed, "going native" did not always carry a stigma; many travel books featured a frontispiece showing the author in oriental garb, thus providing some form of authentication for their accounts. Of course these were "safe" images in the sense described by Pratt, since they accompanied accounts written by travelers who had "returned" and rejoined the fold; still, the image of the European man or woman in Ottoman, Persian, or Indian costume evidently aroused interest, rather than horror or ridicule, in these cases.[74] Authors like Pierre Loti, who spent various lengths of time living in the exotic locations they described in their works, made much (usually way too much) of their integration into native society, not only acquiring the status of unimpeachable informants through their books but also becoming expert advisors to new arrivals and travelers.[75] For example, Claude-Alexandre, Comte de Bonneval (a.k.a. Humbaracı Ahmed Paşa), who voluntarily "turned Turk" in 1730, shows up in Giacomo Casanova's autobiography (written from 1789 onward, published in various versions at different

[74] On this kind of "cross-dressing," see Low, 1993b. Also see some of the contributions to Pollig, Schlichtenmayer, and Baur-Burkarth, 1987, a very interesting catalog published in conjunction with an exhibition held during 1988–89.
[75] Still, Loti was, as is well known, plagued until his final days by the suspicion that he had been duped by the "Turkish" heroines of his *Les Désenchantées* [*The Disenchanted*] (1906). See, for instance, Szyliowicz, 1988: chapter 6.

dates) as an old sage well versed in Turkish matters, who disabuses the author of some of his misconceptions concerning Ottoman women. "The most reserved of Turkish women wears her modesty only on her face," he tells him knowingly; "as soon as that is covered, she is sure she will blush at nothing." (Casanova, 1966–68: 2: 99.)[76] That de Bonneval was unlikely to have met many local women was not relevant: in his contemporaries' eyes, his residence as a "Turk" in Turkey endowed him with deep knowledge of Turkish women, knowledge that any reader would take for granted and none would question—even though it obviously contradicted the sexual segregation practiced by Muslims that Westerners equally took for granted.

One of the best known Europeans to have "gone native" is, of course, Paul Gauguin. His decision to abandon a humdrum existence in France for the unspoiled idyll of Tahiti, and the numerous scantily clad native women he painted (and slept with), are the stuff of legends. As is so often the case, however, there was considerably less to the story than meets the eye: in a sharp critique of the mystique surrounding the painter's life, Abigail Solomon-Godeau has pointed out that despite his claims to the contrary, Gauguin never learned the language spoken by the natives; that far from living off the earth, he survived on canned goods from the local trade store; and that for him, integration into native society meant little more than copulating with younger and younger girls. This, she argues, was the true background of the gendered discourse of primitivism, which grew out of the French colonial enterprise and in turn supported it. Setting out to uncover the constituent elements of that discourse, notably "the dense interweave of racial and sexual fantasies and power—both colonial and patriarchal—that provides its raison d'être," she argues that the quest for the primitive became increasingly sexualized, and that "from 1889 on, there is an explicit linkage of the natural and Edenic culture of the tropics to the sensual and the carnal—nature's plenitude reflected in the desirability and compliance of 'savage women.'" Gauguin's life, Solomon-Godeau maintains, "provides the paradigm for primitivism as a white, Western and preponderantly male quest for an elusive object whose very

---

[76] This is, incidentally, a common assertion in the travel literature, as I discuss later.

condition of desirability resides in some form of distance and differ-ence, whether temporal or geographical." (Solomon-Godeau, 1989: 120, 123.)

The case of Gauguin brings me to my final example of sexualized xenological discourse, the image of the "primitive."

Sex and the "Primitive"

The trope of the sexuality of "primitives" or "savages" had two separate but strongly interrelated components: race and pathology.

In the first instance, race was a profoundly gendered category—a connection evident, for instance, in Gobineau's discourse on the "effeminacy" of Africans and Jews. This kind of intertextuality is not unusual: alteritisms routinely traverse each other, mutually constituting, if never actually reducible to, one another. As Lowe writes, "the discursive representations of gender have social determinants—includ-ing the organization of the family, the construction of sexuality, medical practices—which are distinctly different from the conditions that produce discourses about cultural and racial differences; *yet these diverse means of inscription traverse one another.*" (Lowe, 1991: 3, italics mine.)[77]

The discourse of anatomical science viewed both women and "prim-itives" as representative of lower forms of humanity: in an interesting study of early anatomical illustrations, Londa Schiebinger writes that as the nineteenth century progressed, "some anatomists came to believe that differences between male and female bodies were so vast that women's development had been arrested at a lower stage of evolution. . . . Neither in the development of the species nor in the development of the individual were women thought to attain the full 'human' maturity exemplified by the white male. In terms of both physical and

---

[77] See also Higginbotham, 1993; David, 1992; De Groot, 1989; Ferguson, 1993; Herzog, 1983; Ware, 1992; Young, 1995; and the contributions to Hendricks and Parker, 1994. It is worth noting that these attitudes were not limited to non-European races: the Irish—Carlyle's "white negroes"—were sexualized in both Irish and English discourse. See Jones and Stallybrass, 1992; Glover, 1995.

social development, these anatomists classified women with children and 'primitive' peoples." (Schiebinger, 1987: 63.)[78] It is significant, for instance, that in a 1907 essay entitled "The Mind of Woman and the Lower Races," William Isaac Thomas used the nature *vs.* nurture argument to refute theories that posited the biological inferiority of both women and the dark-skinned races. (Thomas, 1907: 251–314.) Sexism and racism thus bolstered each other, the subaltern positions of women in patriarchal society and non-whites in the colonial enterprise each providing a model and a fount of metaphors for describing (and deprecating) the other; native women, of course, were doubly demeaned, being neither white nor male. (Kabbani, 1986: 7.)

This attitude essentially stemmed from the social composition of the scientific community, that is, from the unquestioning reflexivity of the white male scientists' outlook: those who practiced science—in other words, enjoyed a monopoly over the actual means of conducting scientific research and disseminating its results—took themselves to be the norm, and viewed those who diverged from that norm as inferior. In women, blacks, or the working class, they found evidence of imperfection, signs of stunted evolution. In this respect, race and gender as social constructs had much in common with each other. Yet, as Ware cautions, "blackness and whiteness are both gendered categories whose meanings are historically derived, always in relation to each other *but rarely in a simple binary pattern of opposites.*" (Ware, 1992: xvii, italics mine.) It is important, then, to dig a little deeper: rather than simply accepting an unchanging feminine identity for the "other," one must try to see in what ways gendered subjects are racialized, and vice versa. Women and non-whites may have shared, in the eighteenth- and nineteenth-century imagination, certain common characteristics, but neither group was reducible to the other.

More than gender, the underlying theme was sexuality; indeed, pointing out that nineteenth-century debates on race were largely centered on the question of hybridity, that is, inter-racial sexuality, Young has argued that "theories of race were . . . also covert theories of

---

[78] On the conflation of primitivity and womanhood, see also Tiffany and Adams, 1985.

desire." (Young, 1995: 9.)[79] The racial "other" was also a sexual "other."
As Kabbani puts it, Europeans viewed non-whites as their inferiors,
"lower down on the great scale of being (how low depending on how
dark they were). And since they were lower down on that chimerical
scale, they shared many qualities with animals, of which unbridled
sexual ardor was one." (Kabbani, 1986: 7–8.)[80] Dark-skinned peoples
were believed to have a ravenous sexual appetite, as evidenced by the
practice of polygamy—believed to serve the dual purpose of providing
men with the means of fulfilling their needs while simultaneously
keeping those of women under check. African women were even
reputed to engage in sexual relations with apes. (Marshall and Williams,
1982: 239.) This was one of the most powerful and enduring motifs of
sexualized xenological discourse: not only was the "other" omnisexual,
but in addition the darker his or her skin, the more "primitive" and
hence the more "animalistic" were his or her passions.

In *Das Unbehagen in der Kultur* (1930) [translated as *Civilization and
Its Discontents*] and elsewhere, Freud held that while civilization arose
to protect humans from uncontrolled sexuality and aggression, it did
so at the cost of repression. But as Torgovnick incisively remarks, "the
flip side of this theory was a widely shared, unexamined belief that
'uncivilized' people—that is, primitives and certain marginal members
of the lower classes—are exempt from the repression of sexuality and
control of aggression." (Torgovnick, 1990: 228.) Viewing civilization as
a function of the degree of control exercised by a society over the
sexuality of its members—that is, deploying sexuality as a technology of
identity and alterity—thus simultaneously marked the "other" as sexually different: uncontrolled, unbridled, frightening, but also attractive,
fascinating.

While the psychological apparatus needed to cast the issue in these

---

[79] This is a powerful book and Young constructs an extremely compelling argument, but
his totally seamless articulation of sex and reproduction is to my mind problematical. As
Freud might have said, sometimes a hybrid is just a hybrid; reading sexual desire into
every discussion of procreation—whether inter-racial or not—tends to overstate the case.
[80] On the sexual dimension of race and images of black sexuality, see for example Young,
1995; Stember, 1976; Nederveen Pieterse, 1992: chapter 12; Staples, 1982: chapter 5;
Gilman, 1985: chapter 4; Jordan, 1968; Hernton, 1965; Kuoh-Moukoury, 1973; Henriques,
1974; Roberts, 1994; Fredrickson, 1972.

precise terms may be due to Freud, the sexually saturated representation of the "primitive" is much older. The "nakedness" of African,
American, or Pacific natives—a state which, to the European explorer
first confronted by them, necessarily implied a strong preoccupation
with sex—was a key element in the formation of this image. For
example, Benjamin ben Jonah, the celebrated "wandering rabbi" of
Tudela who traveled in the Eastern Mediterranean during 1160–73,
wrote of a people south of Egypt who "go about naked and have not
the intelligence of ordinary men. They cohabit with their sisters and
any one they find"; these he identified as "the Black slaves, the sons of
Ham." (Benjamin, 1907: 68.) Such associations deepened beginning
with the eighteenth century, when, as Foucault has argued, pressures
mounted for defining normality and formulating criteria of social
exclusion—among which the sexuality of the margins took a central
position:

> The nineteenth century and our own have been . . . the age of multiplication:
> a dispersion of sexualities, a strengthening of their disparate forms, a
> multiple implantation of "perversions." Our epoch has initiated sexual
> heterogeneities. . . . *The machinery of power that focused on this whole alien strain
> [the perverts] did not aim to suppress it, but rather to give it an analytical, visible,
> and permanent reality*: it was implanted in bodies, slipped in beneath modes of
> conduct, made into a principle of classification and intelligibility, established
> as a *raison d'être* and a natural order of disorder. *Not the exclusion of these
> thousand aberrant sexualities, but the specification, the regional solidification of each
> one of them.* The strategy behind this dissemination was to strew reality with
> them and incorporate them into the individual.

I think the connection with the discourse on "primitive sexuality" is
clear: the analogue of Foucault's notion of the "psychiatrization of
perverse pleasure" was the anthropologization of "foreign" pleasure.
(Foucault, 1978–85: 1: 37, 44, 105, italics mine.)[81]

This goes a long way towards explaining the surge in the number of
books on sexuality overseas printed during those years: although some-

---

[81] On the need to augment Foucault's objects of sexual knowledge—the child, the woman,
the procreative couple, the pervert—with imperial subjects—"the savage, the primitive,
the colonized"—see Stoler, 1995: 6–7.

thing that could be called "sexual anthropology" existed earlier,[82] the field underwent unprecedented growth during the late nineteenth and early twentieth centuries. Roger Goodland's *A Bibliography of Sex Rites and Customs*, published in 1931, contains some nine thousand items, and is still by no means exhaustive. Authors like Bronislaw Malinowski, Hans Fehlinger, Henry T. Finck, Alfred Ernest Crawley, and Margaret Mead may have had widely differing outlooks on their subject matter, but they were united in their view of the "sexuality of the primitive" as a coherent object of knowledge. Even those with the best intentions, such as Mead, had an essentially dichotomous perspective in which the "primitives" were defined, whether or not to their advantage, in terms of the contrast they provided with "civilized," that is, Euro-American, society.

Thus, Sally Price is certainly justified in asserting that in this period, sexuality was "the vehicle par excellence for the expression of deviance from mainstream cultural norms, and Primitives [were], from a Western perspective, culturally deviant. . . . Ideas about Primitive eroticism [were] complemented by undercurrents of popular evolutionism in the depiction of non-Western peoples as uncivilized savages." (Price, 1989: 47.)[83] This perspective led to an interesting ambivalence, whereby the "other" was both sexualized and rendered untouchable: the uncontrolled sexuality attributed to "primitives," though strangely alluring, simultaneously functioned as a motive for rejecting them as mired in a developmental stage that is past, and to which "modern man" must never return. (Nederveen Pieterse, 1992: 172.)

As Price notes, at the root of this ambivalence was the often-made, fallacious identification of ontogeny with philogeny, that is, the tendency to project analytical models drawn from the psychosocial development of individuals to the evolutionary development of the human species. Being at an "earlier" stage of evolution, "primitives" were thus viewed as akin to children, not yet socialized, their natural impulses untamed—in short, candidates for the always difficult process of

---

[82] See, for instance, Flaherty, 1990: 261–80. For early examples of the juxtaposition of erotic and naturalist discourse, see Dufrenoy, 1946–7, I: chapter 6.
[83] On the "deviance" of the racial "other," see also Manganyi, 1985.

maturation. Like an infant whose life activity is limited to natural processes, "primitives" were seen as lacking any significant form of social organization. It was their natural bodies that characterized them, not history or culture, a body social or a body politic. (Price, 1989: 47.) In other words, the "savage" was a body pan-sexualized, saturated with sexuality, indeed homologous with it. Note, incidentally, that I say "pan-sexualized" rather than using Foucault's "hysterized," as is often done (e.g. JanMohamed, 1992: 104–5): by that term, Foucault denoted "a threefold process whereby the feminine body was analyzed—qualified and disqualified—as being thoroughly saturated with sexuality; whereby it was integrated into the sphere of medical practices, by reason of a pathology intrinsic to it; whereby, finally, it was placed in organic communication with the social body ... and the life of children." (Foucault, 1978–85: 1: 1040.) I have a narrower definition in mind, corresponding more or less to Foucault's first process.

The "other" was pathological, then, because he or she was unlike the European, and, in turn, unlike the European because he or she was pathological. A case in point is B. J. F. Laubscher's *Sex, Custom and Psychopathology: A Study of South African Pagan Natives* (1937), which covers such topics as mental illness and suicide, theft and murder, and sexual behavior. Although the medicalization of sexuality does, of course, have deep roots in modern Western culture, it is nevertheless not immediately obvious that all the subjects discussed by Laubscher have anything in common; until, that is, one realizes that from a particular viewpoint, the social, mental, and physiological pathologies of "primitive" peoples explicitly included their sexual practices. This is, not incidentally, a property "primitives" were believed to share with women.

In another telling example, Berthold Schidlof wrote in his *Das Sexualleben der Australier und Ozeanier* [The sexual life of the Australian and Oceanian] (1908) that "cunnilingus is wide-spread among all primitive peoples and ... even the children are already prepared for this aberration. The same is probably true of *coitus in os. Coitus inter mammas* has been demonstrated in a great number of Australian tribes. ... No doubt, sexual imagination bears strange fruit among primitive peoples also and gives rise to hypererotic tendencies."[84] No doubt, indeed. What Diana Fuss has called an "epidemiology of sexuality" (Fuss, 1994: 35) was thus deployed in colonial discourse, not only to give spatiality to sexual pathology, but also, by the same token, to help construct spatiality itself.

Interestingly, some authors claimed that blacks do not know sexual perversions since they are of nature and hence ignorant of the evil born to civilization; (Martinkus-Zemp, 1973: 75–6.) Others, notably Iwan Bloch, went to great lengths to disprove this. (Bloch, 1933; Bloch, 1935.) Needless to say, those seeking unanimity in sexualized xenological discourse are bound to be disappointed.

Some of the most elaborate discussions of the conflation of alterity and pathology, particularly in the domain of sexuality, are due to Sander L. Gilman, whose analysis of the tragic story of Saartje Baartman has made these connections amply explicit. Dubbed the "Hottentot Venus," Baartman was widely exhibited in Europe, died aged 25 in Paris in 1815, and was subsequently subjected to the final indignity of having her genitals put on display at the Musée de l'Homme in Paris. (Gilman, 1989: 274–81, 287–97; Gilman, 1992.)[85] The sources of Baartman's fascination for Europeans were her steatopygia and highly developed labia; as Anita Levy has emphasized, in the process of using women to secure racial boundaries, the prevailing discourse "produce[d] a standard of 'femaleness' from which the 'primitive' female deviates not from a *lack* of female features, but from an *excess* of them." (Levy, 1991: 71.)

It goes without saying that these various tropes did not surface randomly in xenological discourse. Some were part of what Kay Schaffer

---

[84] Schidloff, 1935: 289–90. For those whose Latin is rusty, *coitus in os* means fellatio, and *coitus inter mammas* is nowadays referred to as "tit-fucking."

[85] Shohat calls it the "final patriarchal irony" that the genitals of the "Hottentot Venus" were displayed at the Musée de l'Homme [Museum of Man] (Shohat, 1991a: 69), which is of course true. Yet, it is also the act of putting on display that is on display there, and in that sense, this is indeed a Museum of "Man." On the intersection of racial and sexual modes of "Othering" as applied to blacks and Jews, see also Mosse, 1985: chapter 7.

has called a "liminal narrative, that is, a narrative arising from first contact between Europeans and the indigenous people, Europeans and the foreign land occurring in an alien situation that has no predetermined meaning." (Schaffer, 1994: 114.) Others appeared in what— following Schaffer's example—we might 'term a settler-colonial narrative, that is, a narrative arising from prolonged contact between Europeans and indigenous peoples within an unequal relation of power, one in which the Europeans' rule over the foreign land is legitimated by a host of discursive devices that evolved over a period of time and were overdetermined by the colonial situation itself. Some were the product of unchallenged European hegemony, others of times when Europeans were or believed themselves to be under threat. Some reflected the explorer's wanderlust and adventurousness, others the colonial administrator's bureaucratic concern with safeguarding law and order and maintaining clear lines of demarcation between the rulers and the ruled. The class, gender, and sexuality of the author was another factor in the choice of trope. Establishing precise correlations between each motif and the socio-cultural milieu in which it arose is beyond the scope of this study. Suffice it to say that the deployment of gender and sexuality in xenological discourse was much more complex and variable than is usually acknowledged.

The sexual tropes enumerated above, and many more that I have no doubt overlooked, were produced and reproduced by and through narrative. Ranging from travelogues to novels, from colonialist tracts to pornography, from captivity tales to military reports, from ethnographic studies to court records, this vast literature, whether explicitly fictional or not, worked to construct the "East" in a particular way—to reinvent its *genius loci* in sexualized form. Through stereotyping, repeated borrowing, selective representation, and other devices, gendered and sexualized discourse *constructed* xenotopia, the "other" place. In so doing, it both defined the "rest of the world" in a way that resonated with Euro-American imperialism, and, more importantly perhaps, it helped form Western Europe's and North America's self-identity and sense of home.

Part III

Harem Women in Western Erotica

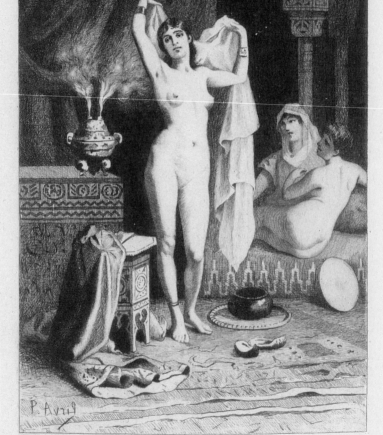

The Book
of
Exposition

5

Harvesting Clichés

In 1704, Antoine Galland began publishing his *Les Mille et une nuits: contes arabes* [The thousand and one nights: Arabic tales], a project that was only completed in 1717 with the posthumous publication of the last two of twelve volumes. In 1710, François Pétis ·de la Croix began publishing his *Les Mille et un jours: contes persans* [The Thousand and one days: Persian tales], whose fifth and final volume appeared in 1712. Both works aroused enormous interest, and were quickly translated into many languages.[1] The symmetry in the titles seems almost too good to be true, and indeed it is: although the former was for the most part the translation of an Arabic work, as advertised, the latter turned out to be nothing more than a fabrication based on a pastiche of Middle Eastern and mostly Turkish tales—not surprising, since the story-teller in that case was a nurse by the name of Sutlumemé ("*sütlü memé*" means "lactating breast" in Turkish). It had evidently been compiled with the sole purpose of capitalizing on the immense popularity enjoyed by Galland's work. Why a highly respected scholar like Pétis de la Croix would stoop to such a scam is another matter, but the fact is that for many years, readers had no way of knowing that *Les Mille et un jours* was not "authentic," which is precisely the first point I wish to make in this section.[2]

---

[1] For translations of the *Thousand and One Nights*, see Borges, 1953; Gerhardt, 1963: chapter 3. For translations of the *Thousand and One Days*, see the notes by Paul Sebag in the French edition of 1980. The latter was also translated several times from the French into Turkish, and published under the titles *Elfü'n-Nehâr ve'n-Nehâr* (1285–7/1867–70, 1290/1873) and *Bin Bir Gün* (1339/1341/1923). (Özege, 1971–9: no. 4740–41.)

[2] It is worth noting that this formula was used repeatedly by Thomas-Simon Gueullette,

The motif of translation was frequently used by European writers starting in the late seventeenth century, often in epistolary form, and dozens of such works were published, ranging from Giovanni Paolo Marana's *L'Esploratore Turco* (1684) [translated as *Letters Writ by a Turkish Spy*] to Montesquieu's *Lettres persanes*.[3] Some of these works focused on the failings of European society, choosing to present their critique through the pen of a fictitious foreigner in order to evade official censure; others were merely commercial ventures, feeding upon the Western public's seemingly insatiable appetite for material concerning the Orient. Their subjects spanned a broad range, from the imaginative, through the moralistic and philosophical, to the satirical.[4] Whatever reasons may have led to their genesis, and whatever their subjects, the fact is that it had become increasingly difficult, by the end of the eighteenth century, to distinguish between genuine translations and Western imitations of Middle Eastern works. Thus, in the appendix to his translation of the *Thousand and One Nights*, Sir Richard Burton, who had some experience of his own faking Eastern texts, classified the fairly large corpus of so-called "Oriental Tales" in Western European languages into seven groups: "satires on the Nights themselves, satires in an Oriental garb, moral tales in an Oriental garb, fantastic tales with nothing Oriental about them but the name, imitations pure and simple, imitations more or less founded on genuine Oriental sources, and genuine Oriental tales." (Burton/*Arabian Nights*, n.d.: 10: 507–13.)[5]

Some imitations came equipped with all the paraphernalia of authenticity, including copious footnotes, glosses, discussions of philological nuances, and comparisons among different manuscripts—all, of course,

---

who successively published *Les Mille et un quarts-d'heure: contes tartares* (1715) [The thousand and one quarters of an hour: Tartar tales], *Les Mille et une soirées: contes mogols* [The thousand and one evenings: Moghul tales; first published as *Les Sultanes de Guzerate* (1732)], and *Les Mille et une heures: contes péruviens* (1733) [The thousand and one hours: Peruvian tales; subsequently published in English translation with an additional third volume by John Kelly]. See Dufrenoy, 1946–7, I : 46–8.

[3] See Weisshaupt, 1979: 1: 145–7, I ; and Dufrenoy, 1946–7, I: parts 3 and 4.

[4] See Conant, 1908, which analyzes more than ninety works of "oriental and pseudo-oriental fiction" produced in England. Dufrenoy, 1946–7, provides a comprehensive list of "oriental tales" from eighteenth-century France.

[5] See also Mannsåker, 1990: 175–95; and Martino, 1906: 154–7, which discusses the public demand for translations of Oriental works and the resulting forgeries.

fictitious; Aleister Crowley's homoerotic masterpiece *The Scented Garden of Abdullah the Satirist of Shiraz* (1910) is a good example.[6] Indeed, like the screens, rugs, pillows, water-pipes, and braziers that gave nineteenth-century studio photographs an authentic cachet, footnotes played an important role in legitimating this literature. Of course, they also allowed authors so inclined to indulge at will in titillating sexual digressions. An anonymous letter published in the *Pall Mall Gazette* in 1887 gives some indication of their centrality to this discourse: criticizing the half-million-strong British colonial cadres for their low standards of morality, the author assailed them for "think[ing] like Burton and his appalling footnotes." (Cited in Hyam, 1990: 91.)[7]

It is in this context, and bearing in mind the fact that the average reader was not equipped with Burton's familiarity with original sources and could therefore not help being far less discriminating than he, that I wish to discuss the role of translation in the development of a gendered and sexualized geographical discourse.

In *Le Miroir d'Hérodote: Essai sur la représentation de l'autre* (1980) [translated as *The Mirror of Herodotus: The Representation of the Other in the Writing of History*], François Hartog writes that "[a] rhetoric of otherness is basically an operation of translation." (Hartog, 1988: 237.) In many ways, the converse is just as true: translation is essentially a rhetoric of otherness. It is based upon assimilation, upon subsuming the other in the same. At the root of the act of translating is the implicit assumption of translatability; yet, the validity of this assumption is far from universally evident, and the effect of making it is anything but value-neutral. In his study of translation and imperialism, Eric Cheyfitz has shown that following a certain "pattern of transfiguring the domestic and the foreign in terms of one another, so that, ironically, the differential connections between them are repressed in a particular ideological representation of the foreign, the romance of racial, or national,

[6] This is a very interesting publication, whose Arabic typography, though largely incorrect, exudes an aura of scholarship. Though its first edition is exceedingly rare, owing to the fact that most copies were impounded and destroyed, a facsimile edition has recently been issued.

[7] Some of Burton's racier footnotes (as well as other sexually explicit material) have been collected in Leigh, 1966.

identity . . . is inevitably a romance of translation, in which . . . *the other is translated into the terms of the self in order to be alienated from those terms.*" (Cheyfitz, 1991: 15, italics mine.)[8]

The etymological roots of the word notwithstanding, translation is thus hardly ever mere transposition; rather, it usually involves both an act of epistemological appropriation/violence, and a praxis, conscious or otherwise, whereby material is selected, paraphrased, and restated. In other words, not only must one be concerned about any new meanings with which a text may have been infused in the process of rendering it into a different language, but one must also problematize the very choice of text to be translated.

The Sexual Politics of Translation

Take, for instance, the case of Jean-Adolphe Decourdemanche, a French orientalist who published myriad books of translations from the Turkish. Generally speaking, Decourdemanche leaned towards popular works, including fables, proverbs, and the humorous tales of Nasreddin Hoca. More interesting, however, at least for my purposes, is his translation of Enderunlu Fâzıl Bey's *Zenânnâme* [The book of women, translated as *Le Livre des femmes* (1879)], a whimsical and often racy description in verse of the women of all nations. For all his wit and clever figures of speech, Fâzıl Bey was by far not one of the greatest Ottoman poets, and the question that perhaps first comes to mind is why anyone would choose to translate his work, at a time when Ottoman poetry was all but unknown to the Western reading public. Decourdemanche answers that question in his Preface, where he writes, first, that Fâzıl was one of the rare Ottomans whose poetry is not so opaque nor his imagery so contrived as to turn a Western reader off; and second, that he selected this work "especially in view of the subject it treats, which is precisely in line with the kinds of ideas—women and harems—that most excite our western attention when there is question of the Turks. To make known the opinion of a Turk on the women of

---

[8] On translation and colonization, see also Rafael, 1988.

each country seemed to us something altogether titillating." (Fâzıl, 1879: 3, translation mine.)[9]

The translator makes no mention of the fact that the Turk in question was not only a male homosexual with (by his own admission) no interest in the female sex outside the realm of poetry, but also an avowed misogynist; presumably, that bit of information would not have done much to boost sales. Indeed, he even translates Fâzıl's prefatory account of being charged by his lover with the task of writing the *Zenânnâme* so as to make the latter into a woman.[10] By contrast, he takes care not to leave out the juicy detail that the book had once been banned in the Ottoman Empire—a ban, incidentally, prompted not by the erotic nature of the poetry, but by its strongly articulated hostility towards the institution of marriage. (Bardakçı, 1992: 122.)

Decourdemanche also translated an anonymous collection of tales entitled *Mekr-i Zenân*, [The wiles of women, translated as *Les Ruses des femmes* (1896)], as well as another book bearing the suggestive title of *La Morale musulmane; ou, L'Akhlaqi-Hamidé* (1888) [The Muslim morality; or, the *Ahlâk-ı Hamîde*]. The former is an exemplar of a rather common genre about which I will say more later. The latter, on the other hand, was a translation of Mehmed Sa'id Efendi's *Ahlâk-ı Hamîde* [The praiseworthy morality], a book published several times in the Ottoman Empire;[11] despite its title, sexuality is not one of its major themes—it is actually a composite of moralistic works by Ahmadu'd-dīn 'Abdu'r-rahman ibn Ahmad and Imām Muhammad Ghazzālī, a commentary by Taşköprüzâde Ahmed bin Mustafa on the former, and Mehmet Sa'id Efendi's own observations.

---

[9] This work was included in English translation in the voluminous anthology *Eastern Love*, edited and translated from French sources by E. Powys Mathers—the very same to whom Malinowski dedicated *The Sexual Life of Savages*. I might mention that Fâzıl Bey's other well-known work, *Hubânnâme* [The book of handsome men] was also translated, some decades later; this suggests that it was oriental sexuality, rather than oriental women *per se*, that attracted the Western public.

[10] Despite the ambiguity in the original (owing to the fact that the Turkish language is ungendered), it is known from the introduction to the *Hubânnâme* that the lover was indeed a man.

[11] Özege lists four editions, with dates ranging from 1297/1880 to 1324/1908. (Özege, 1971–9: no. 244.) The title may be a pun on the name of Sultan Abdülhamid II, who reigned between 1876 and 1909.

By the end of the nineteenth century, translations of Eastern erotica had become big business. In 1882 or 1883, Sir Richard F. Burton and his friend F. F. Arbuthnot founded the Kāma Shāstra Society, primarily for the purpose of printing erotic works. Henry Spencer Ashbee, the nineteenth-century bibliographer of erotica, writes that Burton and Arbuthnot had attempted to publish a book entitled *Káma-Shástra, or the Hindoo Art of Love (Ars Amoris Indica)* in 1873–74, but that the printer had refused to go through with the job once he saw the contents of the book. (Ashbee, 1877: 282–99.) It is possible that this experience led them to set up their own publishing house. According to the authoritative bibliography of Norman M. Penzer, the Society only lasted until Burton's death in 1890, and published five books including two Indian works—the well-known *Kāma Sūtra* of Vatsyāyana (1883) and the *Ananga Ranga* of Kalyāna Mall (1885)—and *al-Rawdu'l-ʿāṭir fī nuzhati'l-khāṭir* [translated as *The Perfumed Garden*] of ʿUmar ibn Muḥammad an-Nafzāwī (1886). (Penzer, 1923: 161–2.)[12]

For legal reasons, many of these works were printed on the continent, mostly in Belgium and France, where another notorious publisher of erotica, Charles Carrington, also practiced his trade: Carrington issued translations of *Kitāb Rudjūʿ ash-Shaykh ilā Ṣabāh fī'l-Quwwah ʿalā'l-Bāh* [translated as *The Old Man Young Again, or Age-Rejuvenescence in the Power of Concupiscence* (1898)], generally (though not uncontroversially) attributed to the Ottoman scholar Kemâl Paşa Zâde Şemseddin Ahmed bin Süleyman (also known as İbn-i Kemâl Paşa) and possibly translated by him from a work due to Tīfāshī; and *Kitābu'l-Izāh fī ʿIlmi'n-Nikāh* [translated as *The Book of Exposition* (1896)], attributed to the highly prolific Egyptian scholar Djalālu'd-dīn as-Suyūṭī.[13] Both books had been translated by "an English bohemian." While the latter is mostly composed of erotic tales, the former is a how-

---

[12] A book purporting to contain parts excluded from the original translation of *The Perfumed Garden*, including passages dealing with homosexuality, has since been published as *The Glory of the Perfumed Garden: The Missing Flowers* (1975).

[13] For another, more recently translated, erotic work by Suyūṭī, see *Nuits de noces, ou comment humer le doux breuvage de la magie licite* (1972) [Wedding nights, or how to inhale the sweet liquor of licit magic]. As the title (added by the translator) might suggest, this is a very amusing work in which men of different professions describe their wedding nights, always using the idioms and terminology of their own profession.

to manual not unlike *The Perfumed Garden*, but with considerably greater emphasis on aphrodisiacs.[14] Jules Gay, another well-known publisher and bibliographer of erotica, issued *Le Livre de volupté (Bah Nameh)* (ca. 1878–79) [The book of voluptuousness (*Bahnâme*)], translated from the Turkish by a certain Abdul-Haqq Effendi and also attributed to İbn-i Kemâl Paşa.[15]

Le Divan d'amour du Chérif Soliman [The love poetry of the S͟harīf Sulaimān] (1911), supposedly translated into French from a "unique manuscript" by Iskandar-al-Maghribi, tells of the amatory adventures of a late-nineteenth-century Algerian womanizer in the course of his travels through North Africa. The differences between this French edition and a Spanish translation published in 1921 are substantial enough to have led one researcher to conclude that they were based on two different manuscript variants of a genuine Arabic work. (Wood, 1992b: 7.) The identities of the author and translators, however, remain uncertain.

And then there is the intriguing case of Paul de Régla's *El Ktab des lois secrètes de l'amour d'après le Khôdja Omer Haleby, Abou Othman* [*al-Kitāb* (the book) of the secret laws of love according to Khôdja Omer Haleby, Abou Othman] (1893). De Régla, who had several books to his credit treating the underbelly of Ottoman society, claimed in his introduction to have translated a manuscript given to him by an old scholar he had met in İstanbul, a certain "Omer Haleby." Already this name raises some questions, since it includes the toponymic "Ḥalebī" (or "of Aleppo") even though the man was supposed to have been born in Algiers of a Turkish father and a Moorish mother; the fact that

---

[14] For a review of Arabic aphrodisiacs culled from works translated into European languages, see Walton, 1958: chapter 2.

[15] The attribution of this book to Jules Gay is due to Pia, who suggests that it may be a translation of İbn-i Kemâl Paşa's *Kitāb Rud͟jū ͨ ash-S͟hayk͟h ilā Sabāh fī'l-Quwwah ͨalā'l-Bāh* (Pia, 1978: cols. 106–7, 395–6), and later printings of the French translation make this latter claim explicit; however, while I have admittedly not compared these works in detail, there is at first glance no indication that they are one and the same. The copy of *Le Livre de volupté* at the Bibliothèque Nationale, incidentally, includes a series of illustrations which, I believe, were added later; though fairly crude, they depict some interesting as well as quite amusing scenes of men and women in late Ottoman garb in the throes of sexual intercourse. Sections from what appears to be the original Turkish version of *Le Livre de volupté* are reproduced in Bardakçı, 1992: 58–77.

Pétis de la Croix had likewise claimed to have received the manuscript of *Les Mille et un jours* from some old dervish he had met during his travels to Persia gives another reason to be cautious. Be that as it may, the book became enormously popular: according to the Preface to the second (cheap) edition, the first edition sold more than 21,000 copies, which sounds plausible in view of the fact that many subsequent authors of pseudo-scholarly books on sexuality in the Middle East refer to it frequently.[16]

Similarly, *Abdeker; ou L'art de conserver la beauté* (1748) [translated as *Abdeker, or The Art of Preserving Beauty*], apparently written by Antoine Le Camus and published anonymously, claimed to be "a Translation of an *Arabian* Manuscript, which Diamantes Utasto, Physician to the Turkish Ambassador, brought to Paris in the Year 1740." (Le Camus, 1754: v.) It is an interesting mixture of cosmetic prescriptions and a passionate love story between an Arab physician and the Georgian beauty Fatima.

Next to Ernest Leroux, who published much of Decourdemanche's work, a number of other publishers also joined the fray. Isidore Liseux printed French translations of several works published in English by the Kāma Shāstra Society. Gustave Ficker initiated a series entitled "Contributions au folklore érotique: contes, chansons, usages, etc. recueillis aux sources orales" [Contributions to erotic folklore: tales, songs, customs, etc. gathered from oral sources] with *Contes licencieux de Constantinople et de l'Asie Mineure* (1906) [Ribald tales of Constantinople and Asia Minor]—a book containing numerous and highly entertaining Greek and Turkish erotic folk tales compiled by Jean Nicolaidés,[17] who had already published two collections of folklore from İstanbul and Anatolia. The newspaper and book publishers Société du Mercure de France brought out a series of anthologies of

---

[16] An English translation of this work was prepared but never printed: *El Ktab: the Book of the Secret Laws of Love according to The Khôdja Omer Haleby Abou Othmân*. The translator, Adolph F. Niemoeller, was a prolific author of erotica, and a microfilm of the corrected galley proofs (with the imprint "New York: Panurge Press, 1935") is preserved at the New York Public Library. The influence of this work continues to this day: Malek Chebel treats it as an authentic source in his *Encyclopédie de l'amour en Islam* [Encyclopedia of love in Islam] (1995).

[17] *Within* the book, the name is spelled "Nicolaïdes."

love poetry, including *Anthologie de l'amour turc* [Anthology of Turkish love] (1905), edited by Edmond Fazy and Abdul-Halim Memdouh; *Anthologie de l'amour asiatique* [Anthology of Asian love] (1907), edited by Adolphe Thalasso, a well-known Ottoman intellectual and the author of books on painting and theater as well as plays and poetry; and *Anthologie de l'amour arabe* [Anthology of Arabic love] (1902), edited by Ferdinando de Martino and Abdel-Khalek Bey Saroit. These are actually quite tame, leaning more towards the romantic than the erotic. The anonymous *The Arabian Droll Stories* (1929), published by The Lotus Society, is another entertaining collection of erotic tales, as is *Liebesgeschichten des Orients* [Love stories of the Orient] (1922); the compiler of this latter volume, Franz Blei, subsequently published *Der persische Dekameron* [The Persian *Decameron*] (1927), a collection of ostensibly Persian erotic tales. Another such work is Hermann Scharfenberg's *Persische Liebesgeschichten* [Persian love stories] (1924).

There were also some surveys of a somewhat more general nature. E. Powys Mathers's *Eastern Love* (1927–30) is a voluminous anthology containing tales translated not only from the Arabic, Persian, and Turkish, but also from countries as diverse as Japan, China, Cambodia, and India. *Le Livre d'amour de l'Orient* [The book of love of the Orient] (1910–21)—edited by Raoul Vèze under the pseudonym "B. de Ville-neuve"[18] and published in the series "Les Maîtres de l'amour" [The masters of love] by the prolific Bibliothèque des Curieux—brought together reprints of erotica translated from Arabic, Persian, Turkish, as well as Sanskrit. The survey *L'Art d'aimer à travers les âges et les littératures* [The art of love through the ages and the literatures] (ca. 1920) began with a volume entitled *En Orient: Anthologie des maîtres de la littérature orientale* [In the Orient: anthology of the masters of oriental literature], treating primarily India and the Middle East.

Another interesting—and more focused—anthology was Gustave Le Rouge's *Turquie: mariage, adultère, prostitution, psychologie de l'eunuchisme. Anthologie* [Turkey: marriage, adultery, prostitution, psychology of eunuchism. Anthology] (1912), published in the series "Encyclopédie de l'amour" [Encyclopedia of love]; as with the others, this book drew

---

[18] For the identification of B. de Villeneuve with Raoul Vèze, see Pia, 1978: cols. 56–7.

heavily upon previously published works, recycling excerpts from such books as Decourdemanche's translation of the *Zenânnâme* and the *Anthologie de l'amour turc.* Indeed, there is generally tremendous overlap among these various titles, and most of the material in any given anthology is likely to be a translation or reprint of previously published works.

Georges Grandjean's *L'Amour en Islam* [Love in Islam] (1931), published in the series "L'Amour autour du monde" [Love around the world], is a collection of tales and anecdotes purportedly illustrative of love in Muslim lands. The second volume of the expansive and interesting collection *Mille et un contes, récits, & légendes arabes* [Thousand and one Arabic tales, stories, and legends] (1924–27), edited by René Basset, is entitled *Contes sur les femmes et l'amour, contes divers* [Tales on women and love, miscellaneous tales]; in contrast to other such compilations, this book contains copious (and apparently genuine) footnotes, making it possible to trace individual tales to original sources.

Collections of some of the more "juicy" tales in the *Thousand and One Nights* were also published. For instance, *Die Liebesgeschichten des Orients: Aus den tausend Nächten und der einen Nacht* [The love stories of the Orient: from the *Thousand Nights and One Night*] (ca. 1913), featuring engravings by the celebrated erotic artist Wilhelm Franz, Marquis von Bayros, sold more than 40,000 copies.[19] Other such compilations include *Arabian Nights Love Tales* (1926); *Arabian Love Tales: Being Romances Drawn from the Book of the Thousand Nights and One Night* (1949), selected from the translation by E. Powys Mathers; *Eastern Love Stories: Classic Tales of Oriental Love* (1951), which also contains some tales from China; and *Geschichten der Liebe aus den tausendundein Nächten* [Love stories from the *Thousand and One Nights*] (1953).

---

[19] The printing I examined was marked "41. bis 45. Tausend" [41 to 45 thousand]. It included a preface dated 1913, presumably present in the original printing, and an additional preface dated 1917 apparently written at the occasion of the 21 to 25 thousand printing.

The Rules of Evidence

As we have seen, a large number of translations of "oriental" erotic works were published from the eighteenth century onward. These works provided entertainment for a reading public increasingly conscious of the world lying beyond the shores of Europe, as well as providing material for European writers of xenological erotica to embroider upon. What is most noteworthy, however, is not only the number of translations, or their wide dissemination, but their reception in the West.

Foucault has distinguished "two great procedures for producing the truth on sex," which he termed *ars erotica* and *scientia sexualis*. The former, found according to him in Southern and Eastern Asia, the Muslim world, and Ancient Rome, was "understood as a practice and accumulated as experience [. . . and] deflected back into the sexual practice itself, in order to shape it as though from within and amplify its effects." The latter, on the other hand, only emerged in post-Enlightenment Western European society, and consisted of "procedures for telling the truth of sex which are geared to a form of knowledge-power strictly opposed to the art of initiations and the masterful secret," namely the confession. In other words, Western society has, according to Foucault, inscribed sex "not only in an economy of pleasure but [also] in an ordered system of knowledge," striving to produce "true discourses concerning sex" by adapting the practice of confession to the rules of scientific discourse. (Foucault, 1978–85: 1: 57–8, 67–8, 69.)[20] In contrast to the Western emphasis

---

[20] Ali Behdad criticizes this binary scheme as reflecting traditional orientalist stereotypes—after which he goes on to explain these latter with colorful stereotypes of his own: "Europe's own sexual repressions, erotic fantasies, and desire of domination . . . the European's own frustration with the obstacle in the way of his voyeurism . . . the 'scopic desire' of the European subject . . the European's own obsession with 'deflowering' " and so on and so forth. (Behdad, 1989: 110, 114, 118. But *who is* this archetypal "European"?) The fact is, however, that there do appear to be certain discernible differences between erotic writings originating in Western Europe and those originating, say, in the Muslim Middle East, and proving the contrary requires considerably more than the mere invocation of the evil specter of orientalism.

on the production of "truth" about sex, *ars erotica* "consists not of rules, laws, or norms, but of methods. Instead of forbidding or permitting, or distinguishing and naming, it evaluates pleasure, its intensity, its duration, and its qualities. This erotic art is not attained by surveillance or inquiry, but by initiation into a body of lore that leads to a mastery of its secrets." (Shumway, 1989: 145.)

Foucault's fairly reasonable taxonomy sheds new light on the translations mentioned above, casting them as works of *ars erotica* appropriated by Europeans as raw material or "data" for their *scientia sexualis*. In other words, what had originally been written as part instructional manual, part philosophical disquisition on the art of love, became "evidence" pertaining to the ways in which sexuality is actually practiced in xenotopia. Burton made this clear in the terminal essay to his translation of the *Thousand and One Nights*, where he offered a political justification for his study of foreign sexual practices: "I also maintain that the free treatment of topics usually taboo'd and held to be 'alekta'—unknown and unfitted for publicity—will be a national benefit to an 'Empire of Opinion,' whose very basis and buttresses are a thorough knowledge by the rulers of the ruled." (Burton/*Arabian Nights*, n.d.: 10: 301.) Needless to say, anything Burton has said or written should be taken with a grain of salt; nevertheless, whether or not he believed this himself, he clearly expected his readership to do so, and that is the key.

Tales about Arabian women engaging in sexual intercourse with, say, bears or monkeys, not to mention each other, were thus viewed not as humorous, or allegorical, or didactic, or whatever their original audiences might have thought of them, but as true accounts of sex in the Orient. It was not hyperbole, then, for Gobineau to state that "with every step one takes in Asia, one understands better that the truest, most exact, most complete book on the kingdoms of this part of the world is the *Thousand and One Nights*." (Gobineau, 1859: 170, translation mine.)[21] In this respect, translations of Eastern erotica served a

---

[21] For many other such statements, see Mabro, 1991: chapter 1. In *Arabesque: Narrative Structure and the Aesthetics of Repetition in the "1001 Nights"* (1991), Sandra Naddaff has proposed a reading against the grain of an erotic story from the *Nights*, interpreting it as the construction of a female voice and a female space. Though there is always the danger

dual purpose: they provided some of the basis upon which European authors built their own erotic tales staged in the Orient; and they were a technology of place which constructed the Orient as a particular kind of location, namely one in which people copulate often and in ways quite shocking to European bourgeois mores.

Filling in the Blanks

Sometimes, too, it was an *absence* in a translation that spoke most eloquently, because it allowed the Western reader to cathect the text at will. Consider again the example of *Les Mille et un jours*: at the beginning of the fifth and last volume, perhaps as an afterthought, Pétis de la Croix wrote a notice that was subsequently paraphrased and incorporated into the preface of the English translation of the work, published two years later. The latter version goes as follows:

> There are many of his Stories so licentious and extravagant, that it would have been an Imposition on Reason and good Sense, to have render'd them: For if the Manners and Religion of the Eastern People will bear them, they cannot by any Means be accommodated to the Purity of ours. So that the Translator was oblig'd to vary from his Original, still taking Care that he pursued the Thread of his Tales. (Pétis de la Croix, 1714: 1: unpaginated preface.)

This tantalizing, hypocritically prudish passage acquires an entirely new dimension when it is recalled that there was no "Original" to begin with, and that here, Pétis de la Croix was only *pretending* to be refraining from translating the "licentious" stories just as he was only *pretending* to be translating the rest! In a similar vein, we find in *Abdeker, ou L'art de conserver la beauté* the note "Here there was a great Chasm in the Manuscript." (Le Camus, 1754: 185.)

I wonder if it would be stretching it to see in this wording a metaphor for the veil, which was experienced by many Western men as both a

---

of presentism, I think there is a great deal of promise in such unorthodox interpretations of what the likes of Burton have generally taken to be naturalistic descriptions of the sexual practices of "orientals."

forbidding barrier, and a symbol of the erotic treasures hidden behind it.[22] In other words, Pétis de la Croix in effect presented to his readers a body of stories wrapped, as it were, in a veil that simultaneously testified to its alluring sexuality while shielding it from sight. To be sure, this practice neither started nor ended with him: in the preface to his translation of the *Thousand and One Nights*, for example, Galland had asserted that he had only deviated from the original when forced to do so by "modesty," prompting two centuries of excited speculation and increasingly "unexpurgated" translations.[23]

That this pattern was not limited to translations can be seen in Annie Reichardt's *Girl-Life in the Harem: A True Account of Girl-Life in Oriental Climes* (1908), which begins with a note stating: "The Publishers respectfully beg to intimate that there is not a single line in this book that the most scrupulous person may not read. There is absolutely no objectionable matter whatever, though the account is replete with thrilling incidents." (Reichardt, 1908: 8.) Here too, it would seem that these assurances were intended less to comfort potential readers weary of encountering objectionable material, than to remind them that a significant part of what is "thrilling" about life in "oriental climes" is precisely the ever-present threat/promise of sexual impropriety.

The practice, of course, has continued well into the present, eventually turning into the little black bars in newspaper photographs that do less to conceal body parts than to highlight them.

Often, the self-censorship exercised by translators reached the heights of silliness, even by the standards of Victorian morality. For instance, in his rendering of *Tarih-i Kırk Vezir* [translated as *The History of the Forty Vezirs*], E. J. W. Gibb not only left some tales untranslated (most of which were fairly tame and by no means explicit), but he also chose to censor some mildly off-color passages while at the same time making certain that the reader knows there is more to the story than meets the eye:

---

[22] See especially Frantz Fanon's well-known 1959 essay, "Algeria Unveiled" (Fanon, 1965: chapter 1); also Alloula, 1986; Fuss, 1994; Decker, 1990–91; Woodhull, 1991; and Moruzzi, 1993. For both literal and metaphorical examples of Western travelers' writings on the veil, see Mabro, 1991: chapter 4.

[23] For example, see Ali, 1981: 14–15.

Being productions of a more outspoken age, many of the following tales are, as was to be expected, of a character that is contrary to the taste of the present time. I have, however, omitted nothing in this book; but in the case of a few isolated passages and of three entire stories, the nature of which is such as to preclude the possibility of their publication in these days, I have been content to print the original transliterated into the Roman alphabet, but untranslated. (Şeyhzâde, 1886: xx–xxi.)

It is noteworthy that Gibb, who prided himself on his many acquaintances among Ottoman litterati, goes on to say: "All such matters, it should be added, are as offensive to the modern Ottoman as to the modern English reader." Primitive sexuality strikes again!

It seems to me that this practice of—to put it very crudely—cock-teasing[24] was also a technology of place: the "Orient" conjured by this veiled text was the locus of not only unseen, but also unspeakable pleasures. Of course this is hardly surprising: after all, showing Turkey as it truly was would hardly have resulted in the degree of mystification that could be achieved by concealing parts of it and letting the reader's imagination do the rest. Thus, the coyly advertised absence of sexually explicit text in these translations contributed to the construction of a particular image of xenotopia, paradoxically, as a sexual *topos*.

Clearly, then, Western erotica staged in non-Western settings did not, like Athena, spring forth fully formed from the head of Euro-American colonialism. Rather, it is a discourse constructed brick by brick from original as well as borrowed and reworked material, drawing upon a storehouse of images and themes accumulated over a fairly long period of time. Many of these images and themes can be traced to translations and pseudo-translations from Arabic, Persian, and Turkish, but their origins often antedate them and have roots in Western European cultures themselves. In other words, if translation provided Westerners with a window on the "Orient," then that window was at best quite foggy, and reflected back as much as it let through.

---

[24] Lest I be accused of phallocentricism, I hasten to point out that the intended audience of these works was predominantly male.

Fictitious Oriental Imprints

Lastly, it is worth noting that fictitious oriental imprints made their appearance on erotic works, especially from the eighteenth century onward.[25] For example, the *Histoire du Prince Apprius* [Story of Prince Apprius], supposedly translated from a Persian manuscript but generally attributed to Pierre-François Godart de Beauchamps, bears the imprint "Constantinople, 1728." (Reade, 1936: no. 2202 and 2205; Pia, 1978: cols. 593–4.) The "proper names" in this work are anagrams of sexually explicit terms, and some editions include a lengthy glossary to help the reader navigate through the cast of characters. For example, Apprius stands for Priapus, Brularnes for Branleurs (masturbators), Litocris for Clitoris, et cetera. Once the exotic-sounding names are decoded, there is nothing "oriental" about this tale; and this is generally true of the many books with fictitious oriental imprints.

Other examples include the anonymous *Histoire des cocus* [Story of cuckolds], marked "Constantinople, 1741" (Gay, 1894–1900, 2: 539); the anonymous *Les Passions charnelles, ou les joies de la luxure* [Carnal passions, or the joys of luxury], marked "Constantinople: Chez Mustapha, Libraire, à l'enseigne de l'Odalisque vérolée" [At Mustafa's, bookseller, at the sign of the poxy odalisque] (Perceau, 1930: no. 94); and *L'Odalisque* [The odalisque], a work allegedly translated from Turkish but in fact variously attributed to several authors including Voltaire, which carries the imprint "à Constantinople, chez Ibrahim Bectas, imprimeur du Grand Vizir, auprès de la Mosquée de Ste. Sophie. Avec privilège de sa Hautesse, & du Mufti, 1779" [In Constantinople, at İbrahim Bektaş's, printer to the Grand Vizier, near the Mosque of Hagia Sophia, under the licence granted by His Highness and the Müfti (the supreme religious authority)].[26] This novel, whose

---

[25] On false imprints, see Weller, 1864; Brunet, 1866; also the Appendix "Supercheries typographiques" [Typographical fakes] in Brunet, 1889. See also Erdem, 1995; this article, which appeared after the present text had been completed, contains a first attempt at compiling a bibliography of fake Constantinopolitan imprints.

[26] Although some editions bore Voltaire's name, Antoine-Alexandre Barbier's *Dictionnaire des ouvrages anonymes* [Dictionary of anonymous works] states quite categorically that "it is

narrator is a eunuch of the Ottoman imperial harem, is actually very interesting, and I shall have occasion to discuss it further.

Antoine-Alexandre Barbier mentions several books with the fake imprint of Constantinople, including two supposedly published by "Imprimerie du Mouphti" in 1750 and 1761 (apparently printed in Amsterdam), and one by "Imprimerie du Pacha" in 1788 (apparently printed in Switzerland). (Barbier, 1872–9: 75–6.) Similarly, *Le Livre de volupté (Bah Nameh)*, mentioned earlier, bears the imprint "Erzeroum: Chez Qizmich-Aga, Libraire-Éditeur" [Erzurum, at Kızmış Ağa's, book-seller and publisher], as do several other pornographic books of that period. Pascal Pia writes that the works bearing this imprint were published in Brussels by Jules Gay, "who enjoyed giving his clandestine products birthplaces that were at once very fantastic and very exotic." (Pia, 1978: cols. 106–7, 395–6, translation mine.)[27] *Le Bain d'amour* [The bath of love], published under the punning pseudonym "Le Bordelais," was marked "Smyrne: Athanassi et Economos, 1892." (Per-ceau, 1930: no. 118-1 and 118-2.) The anonymous *Le Passe-temps du Boudoir, ou Recueil nouveau des contes en vers* [The diversions of the boudoir, or new compilation of tales in verse] bore the imprint "à Galipoly: chez la veuve Turban, librairie rue du Ramasan, 1787" [Galli-poli: at the widow Turban's, bookshop on Ramadan Street]. (Goule-mot, 1991: 103–4.)

Fictitious oriental imprints were not limited to French publications; some German erotic books also bore such imprints as "Konstantinopel auf Kosten des Grossultanischen Serails, 1786" [Constantinople, (printed) at the expense of the great sultan's palace] and "Constantin-opel, Gedruckt in Sultan Solimans Hof-Druckerey, 1690" [Constanti-nople, printed in Sultan Süleyman's court press]. (Nay, 1875: 61–2.) While Gustave Brunet also mentions some Italian books with similar

---

surely not by Voltaire." (Barbier, 1872–9: 3: col. 644d, translation mine.) He mentions attributions to Pigeon de Saint-Paterne, Andréa de Nerciat, and Mayeur de Saint-Paul. See also Gay, 1894–1900: 3: 443–4.

[27] See also Apollinaire, Fleuret, and Perceau, 1913: no. 20–22. According to Perceau, who provides an extremely useful alphabetical table of imprints, five books (three titles) were issued under this imprint, starting around 1875. (Perceau, 1930: 327–64.) Other bibliog-raphers date this book to around 1878–9.

imprints, such as "Stambul: Ibrahim Achmet, stampatore del Divano, dell' Egira 122" [İstanbul: İbrahim Ahmed, printer of the *Divan* (court), (in the year) of the *Hidjrah* 122], actually printed in Florence in 1743, and "Constantinopoli: Mustafa Testadura, 1696" [Constantinople: Mustafa Testadura (hard-headed)], actually printed in Vicenza, these are not erotic works. (Brunet, 1866: 203, 229.)

Of course such imprints were usually designed to cover the tracks of the printers, as such books were often banned and their publishers prosecuted; nevertheless, they could not have failed to give their bearers a certain sexually suggestive legitimacy, as evidenced in part by the fact that the practice continued well into our century: *L'Apprentissage sensuel* [The sensual apprenticeship], published in Paris around 1960 under the pseudonym "Jean-Claude," is marked "Ankara." (Kearney, 1981: no. 111.) Thus, fictitious imprints not only further muddied the waters by making genuine translations and absolute fakes indistinguishable to the average reader, but they also contributed to the transformation of the Orient into a sexual *topos*.

6

Thinly Veiled References

In *A Full and Just Account of the Present State of the Ottoman Empire in All its Branches,* Aaron Hill makes the symptomatic statement that "in every Action of their Lives, the Turks oppose the European Customs." Even more symptomatic is the fact that this statement is immediately followed by two chapters, respectively entitled "Of their Wives, Concubines, Ways of Courtship, and Forms of Marriage," and "Of the Turkish Women, in General." Women, to whom Hill refers as "that *unintelligible sex,*" are one of the principal markers of alterity in xenological literature, and since—for many male authors—they are also fundamental signifiers of sexuality, the sexualized portrayal of women is a recurring theme. (Hill, 1709: 95, 97.)

As I have argued earlier, sexualized images of "other" peoples and places exhibit far too much variability to permit the sort of generalization that one often reads in the post-colonial studies literature nowadays. Thus, there is little point in extensively cataloging a huge repertory of often contradictory stereotypes developed over many centuries and referring to diverse groups viewed as "other." On the other hand, it is potentially instructive to focus in comparative fashion on particular subsets of this repertory, each of which is spatially and temporally delimited and hence relatively homogeneous.

I want to emphasize the word "relative": images of harem women in Western literature are by no means univocal, as can be seen, for instance, in Carroll McC. Pastner's analysis of the works of three British travel writers. (Pastner, 1978.) However, I believe that focusing on a somewhat more limited domain than I have surveyed so far will help crystallize matters, and highlight the many ways in which sexuality was used as a technology of place.

Accordingly, in this final chapter, I turn to the representation of harem women, particularly the women of Turkey, in sexually explicit writings produced by Europeans and Americans from the seventeenth century onward, in an effort to contribute to such an undertaking.

Denizens of the Harem

I say "the women of Turkey" rather than "Turkish women" not only out of political correctitude, but also because the women in tales about Turkish harems are seldom Turkish. From earliest times, Western travelers were fascinated by the ethnic and religious diversity they encountered in the course of their travels, and discussed at length the various "types" found in the Orient. Their descriptions of the harem, however, took the idea to its logical extreme, representing it as a virtual microcosm of Eastern human diversity.

In an account of the Ottoman seraglio written in 1608, Ottaviano Bon stated that:

> those which are kept up for their beauties, are all young virgins taken and stollen from forraign Nations; who after they have been instructed in good behavior, and can play upon instruments, sing, dance, and sew curiously; they are given to the *Grand Signor* as presents of great value: and the number of these encreaseth daily, as they are sent & presented by the *Tartars*, by the *Bashawes*, and other great men, to the King and Queen. (Bon, 1650: 39.)

Nearly three centuries later, William James Joseph Spry went into great detail in his *Life on the Bosphorus* (1895), conjuring a motley of oriental women inhabiting the Ottoman capital:

> What visions of lovely daughters of the Caucasus and the Archipelago, the mountain, the desert, and the sea! Mussulmans, Christians, Jews and others, won in battle by Pashas, presented by Princes, or stolen by corsairs, pass like shadows under those silvery domes. . . . Here are Circassians, whose fair skin and delicate colouring, blue-grey eyes, slightly arched noses, and almost golden-coloured hair go far to justify all I had from time to time heard of

the beauty of the Circassian women. Another beautiful woman passes. I am informed she is a Georgian. She is dark, with delicately-cut features, a lovely little mouth, and an ever-winning smile lighting up a charming face full of bright intelligence. A tall, blue-eyed, dark-haired girl is pointed out to me. I learn she is of Persian origin, captured, perhaps, when young, from some distant hill tribe. What lovely eyes and deep fringe of silken lashes! What a combination of charms! A lovely face so full of intelligence. She holds her head high, and walks with a queenly step, as one of great importance. Another, a moon-faced Turkish girl. I could not help noticing her well-formed figure was set off to perfection by the lovely draped costume she wore. Her bright eyes, long dark hair, the curved and pearly forehead and regular shaped nose, made a picture to dream of, and such hands— exquisitely small, soft and delicate. (Spry, 1895: 10, 151.)

To be sure, Spry's enticing oriental beauties could only add to the titillating mystique of Constantinople; yet, many other authors peopled their imaginary harems (Turkish or otherwise) with women more foreign to the locale in which they situated them, and more familiar to that of their Western readers.

Take, for instance, *A Night in a Moorish Harem* (ca. 1902), an erotic novel attributed to a Lord George Herbert. It purports to tell the tale of a British captain who, stranded in Morocco, is surreptitiously admitted into the harem of a local dignitary where he alternately listens to the stories of the "most interesting and voluptuous passage" from each inmate's life, and engages in sexual intercourse with them. The harem he describes is a true United Nations: there are nine women, of Spanish, Greek, Moorish, Italian, Circassian, Portuguese, Persian, Arabian, and French origin. The narrator observes that:

each one of them differed from all the others in the style of her charms. Some were large and some were small, some slender and some plump, some blonde and some brunette; but all were bewitchingly beautiful. Each, too, was the most lovely type of a different nationality; for war and shipwrecks and piracy enable the Moorish pashas to choose their darlings from all the flags that float on the Mediterranean. (Herbert, 1909: 9–10, 15.)[1]

---

[1] This edition has a prodigious number of typographical errors, and I have corrected any present in the quoted passages.

Similarly, the three women encountered in a Tunisian harem by the British heroine of *The Lustful Turk* are Italian, Greek, and French. In general, harem women in erotic novels are usually either Christian, for example Italian, French, Spanish, Georgian, or Greek, or, in those instances when they happen to be Muslim, often Circassian—a people obsessively described in orientalist writing and painting as extremely fair-skinned. Now it is true, of course, that the imperial harem contained many foreign women—some received as tribute, others captured as war booty—mainly due to the fact that the enslavement of Muslims was forbidden by Islamic law.[2] Understandably, this fact greatly captivated the Western imagination and much was written about some of the foreign-born consorts of Ottoman sultans like the Russian/Ruthenian Roxelana (Hürrem Sultan) in the sixteenth century, and the French Creole Martiniquaise Aimée Dubucq de Rivery (Nakşıdil Sultan) in the eighteenth. For example, Mlle de La Roche-Guilhem's sensationalistic *Histoire des favorites, contenant ce qui c'est passé de plus remarquable sous plusieurs régnes* [History of the favorites, containing the most remarkable events that occurred under several reigns] (1697) devotes no less than fifty pages to Roxelana.[3] However, the average Ottoman household was certainly not peopled with foreign captives, and it is important to interpret this apparent inconsistency correctly: it is not that this fiction was "inaccurate" and happened to represent "the wrong women"; rather, it pointedly represented the women occupying the Turkish space *as* non-Turkish. This is an interesting point worth thinking about: Pratt has pointed out that lovers in New World romances were "rarely 'pure' non-whites or 'real' slaves . . . [but] typically mulattoes or mestizos who already have European affiliations." (Pratt, 1992: 100, 101.) There as here, this no doubt served the important function of creating a fantasy of exogamy that was "safe" because its women were not *really* "other."

[2] See, for instance, Peirce, 1993: chapter 2.
[3] Sultan Süleyman the Magnificent and Roxelana are also prominently featured in Mouchet de Troyes' anonymously published biographical dictionary of great lovers. (Anon./*Dictionnaire*, 1811: 5: 301–7.) On Aimée Dubucq de Rivery, a popular topic of romantic speculation and the subject of a recent made-for-TV movie, see for instance Morton, 1923; Blanch, 1954: 205–82.

In fact, this device was used not only with foreign women but with foreign men as well: in Edgar Rice Burroughs's *Tarzan of the Apes* (1912), for example, the primitive/savage man of the jungle with whom Jane falls in love is *really* Lord Greystoke, a British aristocrat, who, though orphaned and raised by apes, has remained firmly in possession of all the elements of his racial and class superiority. Similarly, in E. M. Hull's *The Sheik*, the Arab chieftain who kidnaps and rapes the English heroine (much to her delight, as it turns out) is eventually revealed to be the son of a Spanish noblewoman and an English peer, adopted through a complex set of circumstances by the leader of a North African tribe. (Hull, 1921: 243–57.) And when the eponymous "son of the Turk" in Vere Lockwood's romance of captivity turns out to be not a Turk but an Englishman impersonating the long-absent son of the Bey in order to gain access to the latter's palace and save the English damsel in distress, she experiences nothing short of an epiphany: "There stood the real son of the Turk, and he beside her was the white man. Daphnne [*sic*] understood. . . . The barrier was down. What had been a cruel check upon her love was gone." She could, in other words, give free rein to her repressed love, now that she knew the object of her desire to be European. Later, when the hero asks her "Did you hate being kissed by the Turk's son? Did you hate—my kisses?" she replies "They hurt me a little, but—oh, I didn't hate them as I ought to have done!" (Lockwood, 1980: 134, 153.) Ought to, that is, had he been a real Turk.

Like so many fairytales and romantic stories in which class boundaries are suddenly dissolved when the poor lover is revealed to be a prince or a princess, it was possible in this fashion to write about what appeared to be interracial sexual intercourse without violating one of European society's greatest taboos, that against miscegenation.[4]

---

[4] For a discussion of the conflation of class, gender, and racial identities in the case of Daniel Defoe's *Roxana* (1724), see Azim, 1993: chapter 3.

The One and the Many

If the woman of Turkey was seldom Turkish, she was equally seldom *a* woman. Rather than an individual, the harem woman was always portrayed as a multiplicity, a *plurality* of women. This is true, of course, of all harem tales, not just those set in Turkey. A case in point is *A Night in a Moorish Harem*: there is at first sight very little in the book that establishes its "oriental" setting, except for precisely the multiplicity and national diversity of the women. In a fairly typical passage, the narrator recounts his exploits with a Spanish woman in the harem:

> I advanced and folded her in my embrace. Her soft arms were wound around me in response, and our lips met in a delicious and prolonged kiss, during which my shaft was imprisoned against her warm smooth belly. Then she raised herself on tiptoes, which brought its crest among the short thick hair where her belly terminated. With one hand I guided my shaft to the entrance, which welcomed it; with my other I held her plump buttocks toward me. Then she gradually settled on her feet again, and as she did so the entrance was slowly and delightfully effected in her moist, hot and swollen sheath. When she was on her feet again, I could feel her throbbing womb resting on my shaft. The other ladies gathered around us, their kisses rained on my neck and shoulders, and the pressure of their bosoms was against my back and sides; indeed, they so completely sustained Inez and myself that I seemed about to mingle my being with them all at once. I had stirred the womb of Inez with but a few thrusts when the rosy cheeks took on a deeper dye, her eyes swam, her lips parted, and I felt a delicious baptism of moisture on my shaft. Then her head sank on my shoulder and the gathered sperm of months gushed from my crest so profusely that I seemed completely transferred with the waves of rapture into the beautiful Spanish girl. Her sighs of pleasure were not only echoed by mine, but by all the ladies in sympathy gathered around us. They gently lowered us from their sustaining embrace to a pile of cushions. (Herbert, 1909: 12–13.)[5]

---

[5] See also the orgiastic conclusion, Herbert, 1909: 138–9. The motif of female ejaculation, incidentally, is extremely common in eighteenth- and nineteenth-century European erotica. On the elision of this theme in present-day pornography (interpreted, though not in so many words, as a technology of alterity), see Straayer, 1993: 168–74.

This account starkly illustrates the confluence of the one and the many, the representation of the harem woman as a multiplicity of women. It echoes William Beckford's *Vathek, an Arabian tale* (1786), where the Caliph, described as "much addicted to women and the pleasures of the table," counts among his palaces one, called "The Eternal or Unsatiating Banquet," in which there "were tables continually covered with the most exquisite dainties; which were supplied both by night and by day, according to their constant consumption"; and another, called "The Retreat of Mirth, or the Dangerous," which "was frequented by troops of young females, beautiful as the Houris, and not less seducing; who never failed to receive, with caresses, all whom the Caliph allowed to approach them and enjoy a few hours of their company." The numbers involved in these palaces can be surmised from the fact that later, when the Caliph was "in the most violent agitation" because of the appearance of a mysterious man at his court, "he sat down indeed to eat; but, of the three hundred dishes that were daily placed before him, he could taste of no more than thirty-two." (Beckford 1987: 151–2, 156.) A question that might, I would guess, cross a reader's mind is how many "young females" were "daily placed before him," and of how many of *those* "he could taste."

In the anonymous *Marché aux esclaves et harem*, an eighteen-year-old "young and charming Frenchwoman" is captured by pirates and sold into slavery. The narrator's closing reflections are indicative of the de-individualized nature of harem women in this literature:

> I was destined, they told me, to be an odalisque like them, to serve the pleasures, the scenes of love and debauchery that often took place in the harem where I was held; and finally, as a Christian slave purchased on the market, I would be obliged to carry the title and exercise the functions of a concubine of the master of the house. . . . I was locked up in such a place, entirely nude, and a slave for ever, as I submitted to the law of a barbaric country which made me nothing more than one among the white odalisques of its harems, no longer having a name nor ever belonging to myself. (Anon./*Marché*, 1875: 63, 70, translation mine.)

Becoming a harem woman, in other words, meant giving up one's selfhood and individuality, becoming just one among many, a nameless member of an undifferentiated plurality of women.

Mario Uchard's *Mon oncle Barbassou* (1877) [variously translated as *My uncle Barbassou, French and Oriental Love in a Harem*, and *A Frenchman in Mohammed's Harem*] provides an interesting and illuminating contrast: the novel tells of a young Frenchman who, upon the assumed death of his uncle (a captain who had "turned Turk") inherits not only a large fortune, but also a harem. The book recounts his efforts to introduce the four "Turkish" women in his harem to French, that is, "civilized" ways. Significantly, the women's civilization process is closely matched by their differentiation. Initially, the narrator notes: "I loved to overflowing these beautiful beings, without being able to separate one from another. So completely were they mingled in my fancy, they might have possessed but one soul between them. By reason of my certitude of equal possession, Kondjé-Gul, Hadidjé, Nazli, and Zouhra constituted in my imagination a single existence." (Uchard, 1935: 37.) Gradually, however, he comes to see them as individuals—particularly the beautiful Circassian Kondjé-Gul ("*gonce gül*" means "rosebud" in Turkish) whose greater access to European ideas, due to her knowledge of Italian and quick mastery of French, makes her "de-orientalize" fastest: she first becomes his favorite within the harem, then his mistress, and finally his wife, while the other three, who remain relatively undifferentiated to the bitter end, are sent away to Rhodes. The relation between each woman's level of individualization and the degree of her integration into Western society is unmistakable.

Another example of the plethoric representation of woman is Nicolas Fromaget's *Le Cousin de Mahomet, ou la folie salutaire* (1742) [translated as *The Prophet's Cousin* and *Eunuchs, Odalisques, and Love*], which tells of a young Frenchman who, in the course of fleeing his authoritarian family and trying to avoid punishment at school, is taken captive by pirates and sold into slavery in İstanbul. There are no scenes of group sex here, but the narrator is treated to a dizzying succession of women: during his eight years in captivity, he goes around like some priapic automaton, seducing the wives, sisters, daughters, and slaves of successive masters, always landing in trouble but apparently never losing his appetite nor his virility. In a far too generous Introduction to the English translation of the novel, Winifred Moroney writes that this forgotten work "belongs to top-shelf literature no less than the amorous adventures of the Venetian" Casanova, arguing that while the latter "pictures eighteenth-century Europe, Fromaget pictures eighteenth-century Turkey," and while "Casanova's memoirs are a portrait gallery of European women, Fromaget's novel is a portrait gallery of Eastern beauties." (Fromaget, 1932: 9.)[6] But how informative is this "portrait gallery," one might ask, and what exactly does it tell its readers about those "Eastern beauties"? The principal characteristic shared by the many women described by the narrator (beside their willingness to engage in sexual intercourse with him) is their undifferentiated plurality; indeed, the only woman who stands out from the pack eventually dies, and the narrator returns to France—with fond memories, but unburdened by any lasting attachments to foreign women.

It is informative to contrast this pattern of representation with the social reality to which it pretended to correspond. A statistical analysis of polygamy in Turkey, based upon a 5 per cent sample drawn from the 1885 and 1907 censuses for the five central districts of İstanbul, has revealed that only 2.29 per cent of all married men were polygynous; furthermore, among the polygynous households, the average number of wives was only 2.08. (Duben, 1991: 148–9.) In other words, the image of Turkish homes purveyed in the West, where one man ruled over innumerable women, simply did not correspond to the truth. Only in the imperial harem could one find large numbers of women, and even there, the majority of women at any given time were not necessarily consorts of the ruling Sultan. What, then, was the reason for the ubiquity of this motif?

Felicity Nussbaum has stressed the important role played by the trope of polygamy in the self-definition of early modern Britain, noting that "the domestic monogamous Englishwoman, an emblem of maternal womanhood, frequently contrasts to the wanton polygamous Other." Reviewing some of the debates that took place during the eighteenth century, she argues that "England's toying with and ultimate rejection

---

[6] Interestingly, even the otherwise skeptical Marie-Louise Dufrenoy cannot help being impressed by Fromaget's attention to detail and explanatory footnotes, commenting that the novel is very informative on the customs and mores of the Ottomans, and that it "evokes the voluptuous atmosphere of the Orient." (Dufrenoy, 1946–47, I: 70.)

of polygamy . . . is part of the nation's defining itself both as distinct from and morally superior to the polygamous Other. Monogamy is instituted as part of England's national definition, and whatever practices its explorers might find to tempt them in other worlds, England asserts its public stance that marriage means one man, one wife." In short, "polygamy is un-English." (Nussbaum, 1994: 141, 149, 153; also Nussbaum, 1995.) Thus, the multiplicity of the female "other" defined the European woman as she who is singular; plurality was an attribute of the "them" that served to construct, by the act of contrasting, the "us."

Nussbaum's argument points to what might be termed an "inner-directed" aspect of the trope, in the sense that it was used in a process of self-definition. In her discussion of Diderot's *Bijoux indiscrets*, Suz-anne Rodin Pucci has also suggested an "outer-directed" aspect of the trope, wherein the plurality of the women, each of whose sexual confession constitutes a manifestation of difference and alterity relative to the master/voyeur, represents a model for the multiplicity of differences in the real world:

> Each representation of female desire and passion reinforces the plurality necessary for construing Western male mastery at the same time that it exhibits the multiple differences of a supposed sexual, political and cultural unknown. [. . . E]mphasis on multiple female differences is constitutive of the male dominant perspective and of the metaphysics involved in the concept and notion of Western 'Man.'

Hence, the construction of European Man, with all the unicity and hegemony capitalization implies, was contingent in part upon the plurality and subservience of "oriental" women, from whom he differs and over whom he is dominant. Furthermore, Pucci writes:

> to cast the exotic Orient in the fictional 'parts,' in the synecdoche, of the multiple harem women is to represent the objects of the Other as commodit[ies] that Western men could and indeed did appropriate in the name of those delightful exchangeable and seemingly inexhaustible minimal differences. . . . Even as she represents cultural difference, woman is stripped of individual sexual characteristics that (un)cover her nature as an aggregation

of the multiple and interchangeable objects of male desire. (Pucci, 1990: 150, 154, 160, 167–8.)[7]

The image of the Orient as a space to be appropriated by the West is thus metonymically constructed through the generic plurality of its women, different yet nameless, alluring yet interchangeable, other yet ripe for the picking.

Foreign Bodies

Speaking of "cast[ing] the exotic Orient in the fictional 'parts,' in the synecdoche, of the multiple harem women," another subject that greatly preoccupied Western writers was the personal grooming habits of oriental women: they lavished particular attention on exactly what they did with their "parts," that is, on such topics as bathing, the application of henna to the hands and feet, the dyeing of eyelids with kohl, and the removal of body (particularly pubic) hair.

In her essay "The Fiction of Fiction," Susan Koppelman Cornillon describes the centrality of the grooming rituals of depilating "legs, armpits, chests, chins, cheeks, upper lips, and eyebrows" to the lives of American women, noting "and yet, with all this that attaches itself to female leg-shaving slavery, I have never seen any fictional female character either shave or pluck a hair." (Cornillon, 1973: 116–17.) She is in part making the point that the "real" lives of women are not always factored into their fictional depiction, and that is no doubt correct; in the representation of "other" women in xenological literature, by contrast, grooming practices were part and parcel of what makes them different, they are determinants of their alterity. Hence, they recur with great regularity.

For instance, Sonnini described in painful detail how women "are unmercifully stripped of the veil of nature" since they are "anxious to

---

[7] Interesting parallels are drawn by Patricia Parker between the "discourse of the blazon," the rhetorical appropriation of a woman's body through its division into parts and their inventory, and the narratives of exploration and mercantilist colonization of the New World. However, she is concerned with the multiple parts of a particular woman, rather than a particular part of multiple women as in Diderot. (Parker, 1987: chapter 7.)

preserve over their whole bodies an exact and uniform polish." (Sonnini, 1800: 179.) Likewise, Stern writes that "on the day before her marriage, the Fellah bride in Syria takes the greatest care of her body. Accompanied by friends and relatives she goes to the bath. There she is washed, scrubbed, rouged, and decorated. It is an important duty of the friends with the aid of a plaster made of honey and other ingredients to rip all the hair from the body of the bride—she becomes smooth and shiny, like a small immature girl." Similarly, in Egypt, "several days before the wedding the bride takes a bath. On a fixed evening she comes together with her friends and they remove the hair from every part of her body except her head; for this they need a sticky Colophonium heart in a turgid state, which they pour on the hair which is to be removed, and after it cools, they tear it off violently with the hair. . . . Twenty-four hours after this procedure there follows the *lelet el henne*, the night of henna." (Stern, 1934: 172–3.)[8] And Vierath (1927) devotes an entire chapter to the subject of corporal care among oriental women.

Next to such dry and clinical accounts, the theme also crops up in erotic works—as for instance in the following rather poetic passage from the anonymously published *La Fleur lascive orientale* [The oriental lascivious flower] (1882), another collection of tales that has been attributed to Decourdemanche:

> Softly she then parts her *féradje* [coat] and offers herself whole as prey to my gaze. I saw her angelic body as white as camphor or virgin wax; then, continuing downwards, I admired her secret recess with gracefully rounded hare's lips, and, for greater pleasure still, absolutely free of down. For starkness one could have hardly better compared her than to crystal or to the eye of the phoenix; in the middle, a slit, due to the steady and infallible penknife of the Creator, divided it into two parts. (Anon./*Fleur lascive*, 1955: 121, translation mine.)[9]

---

[8] The "night of henna" is called "*lailatu'l-khannah*" in Arabic.

[9] The garment to which the anonymous author refers is called "*ferâce*" in Turkish. The attribution of this translation to Decourdemanche is due to Gershon Legman, who also mentions "a rare English translation being later privately issued (by Smithers in Sheffield) as by the 'Erotika Biblion Society.'" (Legman, 1964: 463.) However, Pascal Pia argues that Decourdemanche may have merely collaborated on its preparation. (Pia, 1978: cols. 473–6.)

And in Mardaan's *Kama Houri*, the subject is conflated with sado-masochism, as the English heroine is tied spreadeagled and forcibly depilated by her native lover's child bride: "Ann watched with horror, as the little girl, flicking her fingers, approached the sensitive forest of her mound. She groaned and writhed for it seemed as if a thousand little needles were being driven into her body. The little girl looked up and laughed." (Mardaan, 1967: 80.)

Whether clinical or pornographic, such discussions were always strongly eroticized; thus, John Richards wrote in 1699 that "upon solemn occasions, when a virgin does prepare herself for her husband's bed, they make a feast in the baths to which they invite their friends, at which time she takes off the hair of her body, which she never does before, and is always practised afterwards in these hot countries. *With how much modesty this is done I cannot tell.*" (Cited in Cleugh, 1955: 92, italics mine.) Substituting innuendo for fact, Richards thus made sure at least to plant a doubt in the reader's mind as to the sexual nature of the custom. Indeed, if Theille is to be believed, the beauty products used by oriental women are themselves sexual stimulants: "The science of cosmetics holds no secrets for them; all of Arabia is drawn upon to derive from those balsamic pastes that fineness, that brightness, that sweetness that renders the skin as beautiful as it is attractive by virtue of the suave and *aphrodisiac* scent it exhales." (Theille, 1839: 1: 235, translation mine.)[10]

Like travelers' descriptions of exotic costumes or tattoos and other body modification, or the European fascination with Hottentot women's steatopygia and distended labia, the emphasis placed by Western commentators on women's depilation or adornment with henna or kohl clearly served the function of constructing difference. Luigi Bassano, who was in İstanbul during the late 1530s, wrote that Turks:

> like the hair black, and she whom nature has not so endowed resorts to
> trickery, so that when it is blond, or white from old age, they dye it red with

[10] The word I have rendered as "aphrodisiac" is "*cantharidée*" in the original, indicating that it is not their natural scent that makes these women sexually alluring, but the cosmetics they use.

Archenda, which they call Chnà, with which they dye their pony tails; with the same medicine they dye their nails, many dye their entire hands, some their feet, but in the form of the shoe; there are some who also dye their pubic hair and four fingers above it; and they make the hair fall out because they consider it a sin to have hair in the secret parts." (Bassano, 1963: 20, translation mine.)[11]

It is impossible not to see in Bassano's repeated use of the third person a statement of difference, and this is even more clear in James Dallaway's comment, in his *Constantinople Ancient and Modern* (1797), that "they have a custom too of drawing a black line with a mixture of powder of antimony and oil, called Surmèh, above and under the eyelashes, in order to give the eye more fire. . . . The nails both of the fingers and feet are always stained of a rose colour. *Such is the taste of Asiatics.*" (Dallaway, 1797: 30, italics mine.)[12] The modes of personal hygiene and grooming practiced by or ascribed to the women of the Orient thus worked to set them apart in the Western imagination, to underscore their difference: they were technologies of alterity.

This is made quite evident in a relatively recent work based on early travelers' accounts, James Cleugh's *Ladies of the Harem* (1955), where the author writes that when the Sultan selected a concubine to spend the night with him, "the lucky girl—for this great occasion may mean a lot of privileges later—is bathed, perfumed, depilated, massaged, dressed and otherwise adorned for hours and hours, amid comings and goings which could not be rivalled, for alternate frenzy and solemnity, in any European bride's preparation for monogamy." (Cleugh, 1955: 57.)[13] An even starker example, one that clearly illustrates the conflation of race and class in xenological discourse, is the following passage by Roland Burton, which concerns not the Middle East but the South Sea Islands: "The pubic hair in some tribes is

---

[11] Babinger notes in his index that the word "archenda" is of uncertain origin, but signifies a dye; evidently it must refer to henna, which is called "*kına*" in Turkish.

[12] The eye makeup to which Dallaway refers is called "*sürme*" in Turkish.

[13] Peter Tompkins elaborates on this passage, stating that "the lucky damsel was being bathed, depilated, shampooed, perfumed, mascaraed, hennaed, anointed, finely dressed, and, according to some authorities, plied with strong liquor (to dispel shyness) and with strong aphrodisiacs (to help in the performance of her delicate duties)." (Tompkins, 1962: 96.)

plucked out with the fingers, resulting, judging from external behavior of the individual, only in some pleasurable sensation. In all cases *the pain born so indifferently by the savage would kill or drive insane a European of the more educated classes.*" (Burton, 1935: 30, italics mine.) The comparisons made in these passages between what are viewed as the practices of Europe's "others" and their Western counterparts underscore particularly well the role of this trope in constructing difference. Such preoccupation with the absence of body hair, incidentally, gains particular significance when one considers that eighteenth- and nineteenth-century mainstream pornography in Europe generally tended to emphasize a thick growth of pubic hair.

Such "alterization" also took place, as I suggested earlier, in the countless descriptions of Turkish baths. Cleugh's assertion that "bathing was one of the main preoccupations of Turkish harem inmates, whether inside the establishment or, preferably, out of it. For the public baths afforded opportunities for meetings with friends in less restricted conditions" (Cleugh, 1955: 82) is only one of many such statements. Nicolas de Nicolay, who traveled in the Ottoman Empire in 1551–52, and whose *Les Quatre premiers livres des navigations et pérégrinations orientales* (1567) [translated as *The Navigations, Peregrinations and Voyages, Made into Turkie*], reprinted many times and translated into several languages, was immensely influential, wrote of:

the Turky women being shut up without permission to go abroad, nor to appear in the streets openly, except it be going to the bathes, wherto they neverthelesse goe with their faces covered too bring their Ielous husbands out of suspition, which continually so keepe them under subiection and closed in, & oftentimes under colour of goyng to bathes, they resort to other places where they think good to accomplish their pleasures, & come home againe in good time without the knowledge or perceiving of their husbands, wherein they feare nothing at al, for that to those bathes no men do frequent, so long as the women are there. (Nicolay, 1585: 60r.)

And Bassano, whose descriptions of women's baths Nicolay appropriated verbatim, complained that even when women do end up in the bath, their behavior is far from innocent:

[T]hey intimately wash one another, & one neighbor the other, or one sister the other: for which reason there is great love between women, due to the familiarity that develops from washing and rubbing each other. Because of this one frequently sees women very much in love with one another, not unlike a man with a woman, & I have already met Greek and Turkish women who, seeing a beautiful young woman, seek the occasion to wash together, to see her nude, and to handle her. . . . This and much more dishonesty is born from the bathing of women. (Bassano, 1963: 17–18, translation mine.)[14]

Nicolay concluded that "considering the reasons aforesaid, to wit, the cleansing of their bodies, health, superstition, liberty to go abroad, & lascivious voluptuousness, it is not to be marvelled at that these baths are so accustomably frequented of the Turks." (Nicolay, 1585: 60r.) Although eyewitnesses like Lady Montagu and Julia Pardoe later took great pains to stress that nothing unseemly went on in the baths, many travelers (primarily men who had, of course, never seen them first-hand) were only too willing to indulge in such erotic fantasies; they described stark naked women reclining languorously as their slaves braided their hair or massaged their limbs, consuming large quantities of sweets, talking about sex, carressing each other, and making love, far from the despotic control of the eunuchs. Compared to the spartan bathrooms of England, such luxury inevitably portrayed Turkish baths as the nuclei of an empire of the senses, depicting oriental women as preoccupied, indeed obsessed, with their own bodies and hence with sex.

The effect of frequent bathing on women's flesh, incidentally, was the site of another interesting discursive inconsistency: while some travelers claimed it caused women to age prematurely, others wrote that it made their skin firm and beautiful. (Schiffer, 1987.) For example, Lady Craven wrote that "the frequent use of hot-baths destroys the solids, and these women at nineteen look older than I am at this moment" (Craven, 1789: 226), a view echoed by Dallaway who stated that "warm baths used without moderation, and unrelieved idleness, spoil in most instances, by a complete relaxation of the solids, forms that nature intended should rival the elegance of their

---

[14] There is an identical passage in Nicolay, 1585: 60r.

countenances." (Dallaway, 1797: 30.) By contrast, John Auldjo, who visited İstanbul in 1833, gave the following effusive description of a "handsome Turkish lady," which he qualified as "a perfect specimen of oriental beauty": "Her skin was very white and beautiful; the constant use of dry vapour bath having reduced it to a fineness which I can only compare to highly polished marble; and it looked as glossy and as cold." (Auldjo, 1835: 160–61.) This change, of course, heralds the great upsurge of interest in the curative powers of Turkish baths that took hold of Europe in the second half of the nineteenth century: dozens of books and pamphlets were published on this subject from the 1850s on, and numerous baths were constructed in Britain and elsewhere. Be that as it may, the medium was once again the message here: the point was not whether frequent steam baths make women firm or flabby, but rather that "they" have customs that make them a particular way, and different from "us."

Unquenchable Desires

In a book rather pretentiously entitled *The Real Turk* (1914), Stanwood Cobb states that "*Ennui* is the fatal disease of the Oriental woman. She does not, as a rule, know how to read; her head is empty of ideas, and her language is vile. The talk of the harem, in which wives, servants, and little children join, is pornographic to a degree." (Cobb, 1914: 68.) The idleness and indolence of harem women is a recurring theme in orientalist discourse, and is closely linked to the process of sexualization: as Foucault points out, "it is worth remembering that the first figure to be invested by the deployment of sexuality [in Western discourse], one of the first to be 'sexualized,' was the 'idle' woman." (Foucault, 1978–85: 1: 121.)

Thus, the anonymous author of *L'Odalisque* wrote that "women, in Turkey, have no distraction of any sort or description: they may think, are permitted to think and permitted to be occupied only with love." (Anon./*Odalisque*, 1928: 9–10.)[15] Lieutenant Murray wrote in *The*

---

[15] On sexualized depictions of "idle" Turkish women, see also Schiffer, 1987.

Turkish Slave or the Dumb Dwarf of Constantinople that "in a land where personal beauty alone makes the market value for a woman, and where the main occupation is bathing, eating and administering to the amusement of their Turkish masters ... it is not to be supposed that there is any great degree of intelligence to be found among the gentle sex." (Murray, 1863: 9.) And in Akbar Del Piombo's *Skirts* (1956) (subsequently republished as *Into the Harem*), a piece of erotic burlesque detailing the sexual adventures of a young American endowed with a prodigious and indefatigable erection, the hero is kidnapped and taken to Turkey, where he ends up helping the sultan satisfy the many sex-starved women in his harem and thereby restore social peace.

Idle or not, Turks in general (like other "orientals") were stereotyped early on as people of unbridled sexuality. Thus, for example, Henry Maundrell lamented in 1697 that a beautiful orange grove which, "were [it] under the Cultivation of an English Gardner, it is impossible any thing could be made more delightful," was being used as "a fold for sheep and goats," and declared: "so little sense have the Turks, of such refin'd delights as these; being a people generally of the grossest apprehension, and *knowing few other pleasures, but such sensualitys, as are equally common both to Men and Beasts.*" (Maundrell, 1703: 39–40, italics mine.) And Fromaget similarly declared that "the Mussulmans, who know of no other pleasures in this life than those of the senses, devote themselves to the devices of love with a comprehensive sensuality that seems inborn in the Oriental." (Fromaget, 1932: 103.) But why was sensuality "inborn" to Turks?

Climatic factors, of course, were believed to play an important role: after all, Hippocrates had declared of Asia Minor that "courage, endurance, industry and high spirit could not arise in such conditions ... but pleasure must be supreme." (Hippocrates, 1923–28: 1: 109.) And in his *Esprit des lois* [Spirit of the laws] (1748), an instant classic that went through at least 22 editions within his own lifetime, Montesquieu claimed to have demonstrated that heat made sensory organs more sensitive. He went on to say:

From this delicacy of organs peculiar to warm climates it follows that the soul is most sensibly moved by whatever relates to the union of the two sexes:

here everything leads to this end. In northern climates scarcely does the physical aspect of love have the power to make itself felt. In temperate climates, love, attended by a thousand accessories, renders itself agreeable by things that have at first the appearance, though not the reality, of this passion. In warm climates it is liked for its own sake, it is the only cause of happiness, it is life itself. In southern countries a machine delicate, weak, but sensitive engages either in *a love that ceaselessly swells and ebbs in a seraglio,* or to a passion which leaves women in a greater independence, and is consequently exposed to a thousand anxieties. (Montesquieu, 1949: 223–4, italics mine.)[16]

In the nineteenth and twentieth centuries, such environmental explanations mingled freely with racialist ones, leading to sweeping statements such as the following: "The Turkic temperament is not unlike the temperament of other Oriental races. It is one of extreme sensuality and unrestrained sexual desire. It is therefore natural that modesty among them should not be very strict, for modesty is always in inverse ratio to the sensuality of any race. Their hot climate and their scant loose clothing are also factors against the development or prevalence of sexual modesty." (Pinhas, 1933: 19.)

The subject of "modesty," incidentally, came up frequently in sexualized xenological discourse. I mentioned earlier that Casanova quoted the Comte de Bonneval in his memoirs as asserting that the Muslim woman "wears her modesty only on her face"; this claim is repeated with noteworthy regularity in the literature, and a very typical example is afforded by Carsten Niebuhr, who wrote in 1772:

The veil seems to be the most important piece of their dress: their chief care is always to hide their face. There have been many instances of women, who, upon being surprised naked, eagerly covered their faces, without shewing any concern about their other charms. The Egyptian peasants never give their daughters shirts till they are eight years of age. We often saw little girls running about quite naked, and gazing at us as we passed: None, however, had her face uncovered; but all wore veils. (Niebuhr, 1799: 1: 90.)

---

[16] I have modified Nugent's translation considerably—see the French edition of 1951: 2: 477.

If this claim was (at least in some cases) based on empirical obser-vation, I would speculate that what was at work here was a fairly straightforward cultural difference: while exposing oneself naked cer-tainly *would* be frowned upon in Islamic societies (Bousquet, 1990: 104–6), the naked body itself was not viewed as shameful or impure; thus, a woman surprised in the nude might simply try to conceal her identity, that is, make sure that no connection could be established between the exposed body and the primary referent of identity, which is the face. In Christian Europe, on the other hand, the body itself was regarded as the source of evil and sin, and hence one's primary concern would be to conceal the body, not just its identity. But I am only guessing.

Western writers' preoccupation with women's modesty stemmed in part from the consolidation of bourgeois mores, which increasingly called for the de-sexualization of women. "Proper" women were expected to be modest, that is, not only to be sexless but also to conceal any physical reminder of their sexuality. Not surprisingly, therefore, the sexuality of "oriental" women was the object of special attention. Burton wrote in *Sindh, and the Races that Inhabit the Valley of the Indus* (1851) that "in warm and damp countries, lying close to mountains, the amativeness of the female here appears to be stronger than that of the male," and in *Zanzibar, City, Island, Coast* (1872) that "as usual in damp-hot climates, for instance, Sind, Egypt, and lowlands of Syria, Mazenderan, Malabar, and California, the sexual requirements of the passive exceed those of the active sex; and the usual result is a dissolute social state." (Burton, 1966: 12, 93.) A good many years before Burton, moreover, Ottaviano Bon had written of harem women that:

> it is not lawfull for any one to bring ought in unto them, with which they may commit the deeds of beastly, and unnaturall uncleanesse; so that if they have a will to eat, radishes, cucumbers, gourds, or such like meats; they are sent in unto them sliced, to deprive them of the means of playing the wantons: for they being all young, lusty, and lascivious wenches, and wanting the society of men (which would better instruct them, and questionlesse far better employ them) are doubtless of themselves inclined to that which is naught, and will often be possest with unchast thoughts. (Bon, 1650: 59.)

And this view was echoed by Alexander Pope, who, in a 1716 letter to Lady Montagu, wrote of Turkey as "the Land of Jealousy, where the unhappy Women converse with none but Eunuchs, and where the very Cucumbers are brought to them Cutt." (Pope, 1956: 1: 368.) In short, women in Turkey were slaves of passion, victims of uncontrollable urges that led them to immoral behavior on a scale unseen in Europe—at least in the upper classes.

From the most innocent virgin to the wife hungry for her absent husband's attention, women in Fromaget's *Le Cousin de Mahomet* are unconditionally willing to engage in sexual escapades with the young French protagonist, as much when he charms them with his flute or his verbal gallantry as when he feigns madness in order to escape execution, or appears before them all bloody and dirty after his latest misadventure. Perhaps finding climate not poetic enough, and not yet acquainted with racial theories, Fromaget offered an interesting explanation for their behavior:

> Mahomet must be held responsible for the ease with which the favors of a Turkish lady may be won. In depriving them of Paradise and of immortality the legislator has opened the door to incontinence. "When I die," thinks a Turkish woman, "all is at an end. I have no rewards to gain or punishments to fear in the life to come; let us enjoy in this one everything that can make it more agreeable." They act accordingly, and this way of thinking combined with the extreme constraint in which they are kept by their husbands is the main reason for their being sometimes willing to risk everything to satisfy their desires. (Fromaget, 1932: 106.)[17]

The oft repeated (but apocryphal) claim that Islam does not recognize that women have souls, and therefore does not provide for them in the afterlife, was thus presented as the reason for their dissolute behavior, for their lacking in the temperance that Christian women would necessarily exercise since they harbor the hope of going to heaven.

Of course insatiable women are a staple of pornography, which has always been primarily male-oriented and promises its consumers sex objects that are simultaneously submissive to their every whim *and*

---

[17] See also Pinhas, 1933: 27–8.

sexually ravenous. Oriental women—that is, naturally amative chat-
tels—provided a perfect fit.

Submissive Slaves

Aaron Hill, who saw fit to include stories of Westerners' escapades with
Turkish women in *A Full and Just Account of the Present State of the
Ottoman Empire in All its Branches*, offers the following manifestly eroti-
cized description of an "oriental" slave market:

> There is in *Constantinople*, a *Slave-Market twice* or *thrice* a Week, thither the
> People go, and see the miserable *Christian Captive-Virgins*, dress'd in all the
> tempting Ornaments, that can allure the Looks of *amorous Passengers*; they
> speak to those they are inclin'd to like, and having ask'd them any Questions
> they think fit to start, they feel their *Breasts, Hands, Cheeks*, and *Foreheads*; nay
> proceed, if curious in the nicety of Search, to have the young, and wretched
> Creatures taken privately to some convenient Place, where, *undisturb'd*, and
> *free* to use the utmost of their Will, they find out certain subtle Means of
> boasted Efficacy, to discover instantly by *Proofs*, and *Demonstration*, whether
> the *pretended Virgin* has *as yet* been rob'd of that so celebrated *Jewel*, she
> affirms her self Possessor of. (Hill, 1709: 103.)[18]

From Hill's encyclopedic account of the Ottoman Empire to light-
weight erotic novels, this theme creeps up again and again: in real life
slavery may well have been both *serious* business and serious *business*,
but in the xenological literature, it was primarily an opportunity for
staging sadistic fantasies in which women were stripped naked, chained,
fondled, and otherwise humiliated. In *La Rose d'Amour; or the Adventures
of a Gentleman in Search of Pleasure*, the French narrator goes to Turkey
to procure beautiful female slaves with whom to populate his "harem."
(Anon./*Rose d'Amour*, 1967: 3: 10–15, 42–6.) And the evil Bey of Tunis
declares in *The Lustful Turk* that "if there is anything that tends to the
subjection of a haughty woman, it is the attacking her modesty at once
in the most sensible part. To have this effect nothing tends to humble

[18] For roughly contemporary comparable accounts of slave markets, see also Chew,
1937: 189–90.

coy chastity so much as our system of the slave market, where they are exposed naked, and left unreservedly to the sight and feel of whoever chooses to bid for them. The most stubborn beauty will in time inevitably fall under its subduing influence." (Anon./ *Lustful Turk*, 1984: 140.) Reflecting more the prevalent sexual discourse in Western Europe than the customs of the Orient, this passage is quite paradigmatic.

The anonymous *Marché aux esclaves et harem*, for instance, is for all practical purposes just one long meditation on being publicly undressed and displayed in a slave market. As soon as they are captured by pirates, the young Sidonie and her aunt are divested of most of their clothes and taken to shore where they are paraded before the towns-folk, ever conscious of being "offered to their gaze, half-naked and chained as we were." Viewed by "men whose lascivious and indiscreet gaze, fixed upon the nakedness of our persons, made us lower our eyes and blush from shame," they finally arrive at the slave market where, Sidonie observes, she and her aunt are the only white women for sale. The latter then expresses her fear that "very soon those rascals will strip off the clothing they left us and expose us totally naked before everybody, as is, in any case, the rule for slaves sold in their markets." Upon hearing this, Sidonie exclaims: "Oh my God! we shall then be as naked as the negroes." Eventually, their worst fears come true and potential buyers demand that they be undressed; after a frantic struggle, recounted with great relish, Sidonie is "forced to yield in spite of myself to the violence" and compelled, "overcome by despair, to let myself be unclothed completely and be exposed, there and then, naked as a monkey." The slave merchant then touches her all over, "drawing attention to each of my natural perfections," treating her "no better than an animal." Finally, the would-be buyer inspects her personally:

> He subjected me entirely to precisely what I had feared the most, namely, a most detailed examination which, from my teeth and eyes, extended down to the most secret and delicate parts of my body; he did so with touches that not only outraged my modesty and my young girl's innocence . . . but also betrayed this hideous eunuch's habit of handling naked women even in the most hidden recesses of their bodies. And mine was in his hands, shielded by nothing, all natural and with no embellishments, and, feeling at the moment somewhat neglected by virtue of the voyage, it was, one might say,

nature captured in the act. (Anon./*Marché*, 1875: 12, 16, 18, 29, 39–41, 44–5, translation mine.)

All of this is described in a manner that not only irresistibly sexualizes xenotopia, but also marks it insistently as different, as foreign and inferior. Thus, when Sidonie and her aunt are first taken ashore, she reflects that "it was into a country totally foreign and unknown to us that we were setting foot, with other mores that we would be dealing, and towards a crude and barbaric civilization that we were now walking." Later too she notes how "terrible it is to be ignorant of the fate that awaits one among a people so foreign and unknown." Referring repeatedly to her new surroundings as "this barbaric land," Sidonie laments how different its customs are "from those we had known until this day in our happy France." (Anon./*Marché*, 1875: 8–9, 24–5, 28, translation mine.) Just like the Bey's reference to "our system of the slave market," these passages situate the fantasy in a particular setting and give it "reality." So while their sexual details titillated the reader, such stories also worked to produce the Orient as France's "other," a place whose alterity was established as much by its customs and religion as by its sexual practices. In this manner, too, the French, British, or Italian victims in these tales of slavery in effect served as a metonym for native women, by taking the position of participant observers—ethnographers, as it were, reporting on the way women are treated "there."

As mentioned earlier, the harem provided a perfect setting for the topos of the slave-nymph, portraying women as unselfish and submissive on the one hand, and lustful and sexually voracious on the other. Sidonie relates, for example, how "with smiles and glittering eyes," her fellow-concubines "praised the joys of lying with a man and letting oneself be deflowered by him." (Anon./*Marché*, 1875: 63, translation mine.) Indeed, this was elevated to a doctrine in *L'Odalisque*, where the new concubine is educated by the harem superintendent. Their dialogue begins thus:

Q – Why have women been put into the world by the great Allah?
A – To give pleasure to Mussulmans and provide for them some notion of Paradise. (Anon./*Odalisque*, 1928: 30.)

From there, the lessons go into great detail, and the teacher imparts to the student all the subtleties of (selfless) lovemaking: "You must part your legs and have no object other than to weld your stomach to the belly of the Friend of God; that is, to push your fundament with all your strength against the member of His Highness." (Anon./*Odalisque*, 1928: 35.)

The sultan's sexual doings is a subject that Aaron Hill could have hardly passed up, and while his account is less explicit, it is no less notable for its eroticization of power: after discussing the "Lascivious Customs of the Ladies of the *Seraglio*" and "How the Sultan chuses a Mistress," he offers the following account of the introduction of a virgin to the Sultan's chamber:

> She enters, only cover'd with a *Wrapping Night-gown*, and advancing to the Feet of the *Grand Signior*'s *Bed*, falls down upon her Knees, and in an humble manner asks this Question. *A Slave to your Commands*, Great Monarch, *waits your beckon, may, or may she not be now admitted?* You may be sure the *Sultan* answers *Yes*, and if impatient to possess her Beauties, takes her in as soon and kindly as your self *young Reader* wou'd your Mistress: But alas poor Women! common Custom *generally* forces them to a more humble Entrance, for, in token of Submission, *dropping their Night-gown*, they must gently raise the *Bed Cloaths* at the Feet, and so creep gradually up to those Embraces, which an *Englishman* wou'd be so civil to believe deserving of a kinder Welcome; and an *Englishwoman*, if I know them rightly, think too worthy to bestow in such a *mortifying* and submissive manner. (Hill, 1709: 166.)

The contrast with English ways in Hill's narrative is at least as important as the account itself.

The claim that Islam held women to be nothing more than instruments of male pleasure occurs repeatedly, and, like so many aspects of sexuality in the "East," functions as a technology of alterity. In *Memoires turcs, avec l'histoire galante de leur séjour en France* (1743), pseudonymously published by Claude Godard d'Aucour immediately after the visit of an Ottoman ambassador to France and at the height of public interest in *turqueries*, a Muslim heretic named Jatab is mentioned, whose heresy consisted in the fact that "women, according to him, are not pure machines made simply for our pleasure; he does not deprive these admirable automata of all feeling after death: he promises them Paradise just as he does us, where they will ceaselessly enjoy, he says, a pleasure as vivid as that procured them by the most loving man to whom they surrendered themselves during their lifetime." Although brought up in Turkey, Godard d'Aucour's hero is half-Turkish and half-French, and in an apparent fit of relativism, his father (the Turkish half of his parentage) speaks to him as follows: "My son, he said to me with kindness, each Country has its own customs; the women whom you see here, our slaves who submit entirely to our will, are in France as free as we are, if not more so." The young man, however, has no stomach for the subjection of women; later, he resists temptation: "I know not who held me back & tempered the violent transports that agitated my spirit; born of a French mother, my heart is often French, & belies the habit which I wear: it is thence that I draw the respect that I feel for the fair sex, & that is the origin of the kind of sadness that I have always felt upon seeing in Turkey women destined to be our Slaves, I who have all my life felt compelled to adore them." (Godard d'Aucour, 1743: 1: 14, 26–8, translation mine.)

Little wonder, under the circumstances, that Pinhas ben Nahum bluntly declared that "the nobler concept of love, such as is found in Europe and America, does not exist among the Turks, or at least very rarely." (Pinhas, 1933: 131.) And that in Murray's *The Turkish Slave or the Dumb Dwarf of Constantinople*, it is a Greek slave who taught the Turkish woman "the true dignity of her sex, and how woman was esteemed and cherished in other countries." (Murray, 1863: 12.) Paying heed neither to the subordinate position of women in Europe, nor to the socio-historical circumstances under which romance and chivalry arose in Europe and the role they played in the consolidation of patriarchy, such representations of sex in Turkey served only to construct difference.

Wily Women

A story in the anonymous collection *From a Turkish Harim* declared poetically (if no less mysogynistically) that "the virtue of women is as water; when it is held confined it stays there, but should it find an outlet, however small, it all runs away." (Anon./*Harim*, 1930: 188.) Indeed, a common rationalization for the harem system in Western literature was that, being so sexually desirous, oriental women must be restrained; in turn, a corollary of that notion was that they are always engaged in trying to outwit their captors, often with success. Thus, the theme of faithless and promiscuous women was quite central to xenological discourse, and was particularly well-represented in the corpus of translations and pseudo-translations from Arabic, Persian, and Turkish.

For example, two of the translations published by Decourdemanche, *Le Livre des femmes* and *Les Ruses des femmes*, stress that women are faithless, cunning, and mischievous. Nafzāwī's *The Perfumed Garden*, made so famous by Sir Richard Burton's translation, also contained a chapter entitled "On the Deceits and Treacheries of Women." (Nafzāwī, 1963: chapter 11.) Likewise, the frame stories of many translations of "oriental" tales touched upon this theme. It is well enough known, for instance, that the *Thousand and One Nights* stories were occasioned by King Shahryar's conviction that women are faithless and his decision to marry a different one each day and have her executed the following morning; the tales resulted from Shahrazad's creative efforts to stay alive by keeping him in suspense. A less-known version of this plot is found in Nakhshabī's *Ṭūṭīnāmah* [translated as *The Tooti Nameh, or Tales of a Parrot*] (1972), where an eloquent parrot prevents his master's wife from being unfaithful to him by distracting her each night with a different story. Similarly, Şeyhzâde's *The History of the Forty Vezirs* is written in the form of a dialogue between forty vezirs intent on proving women evil, and forty ladies defending their gender. *La Fleur lascive orientale* also features variations on the same theme. So, for that matter, do 'Alī al-Baghdādī's recently translated *Les Fleurs éclatantes dans les baisers et l'accolement* (Brilliant flowers in kisses and copulation), and a contemporary book claiming to be a translation, *Memoirs of a Harem Girl* (1968)—whose original title, judging from the translator/author's comments, was to be *The Tricks of Women*. (Phillips, 1968: 147.) In the late 1960s, one must assume, the vaguely suggestive first title was judged a better marketing tool than the second one.

To be sure, this theme is not foreign to the Muslim world, and one could perhaps argue that in societies where women are deprived of direct power, the strategies to which they necessarily turn are likely to be viewed by men (who do not lack direct power) as devious.[19] Nevertheless, the fact is that the image of woman as liar or trickster was quite widespread in the West independently of these translations of Islamic sources, and a good deal of humor and folklore was in fact based on the themes of cuckoldry and the wiles of women from medieval times onward.[20] Thus, the publication of Decourdemanche's *Les Ruses des femmes* and other comparable works amounted to little more than "oriental" confirmation of pre-existing Western sexist stereotypes.

Billie Melman has recently highlighted another version of this trope, in which the imagined promiscuity of the "oriental" woman was used as a metaphor for freedom. Interestingly, such representations are not very unusual in xenological literature, and Pratt has coined the term "feminotopia" to denote "idealized worlds of female autonomy, empowerment, and pleasure." (Pratt, 1992: 166–7.)[21] Melman points to a well-known passage in which Lady Montagu wrote of Ottoman women that:

'Tis very easy to see, they have in reality more liberty than we have. No woman, of what rank soever, is permitted to go into the streets without two *Mu[s]lins*, one that covers her face, all but her eyes; and another, that hides the whole dress of her head, and hangs half way down her back. Their shapes are also wholly concealed, by a thing they call a *Ferigee*, which no woman of any sort appears without ... You may guess then, how effectually this

---

[19] On harem women's intrigues as reflected in the Western travel literature, see Davis, 1986: chapter 10. On the theme of the trickery of women in Islamic culture, see Malti-Douglas, 1991: chapters 2 and 3; also Aït Sabbah, 1986: 70–72. (The English translation is of the earlier edition, where this subject is treated more briefly.) On misogyny and sexuality in Islamic texts, see Bouhdiba, 1975: chapter 10. For an interesting and cross-cultural study of some aspects of misogynistic discourse, see Penzer, 1952: 3–71; this is a revised version of an appendix originally published in Penzer's *The Ocean of Story* (1924).

[20] See for instance Wiesner, 1993: chapter 1. Among printed books dealing with the subject, Reade mentions *Alphabet de l'imperfection et malice des femmes* (Alphabet of the imperfection and malice of women, Lyon, 1648) and *The Art of Cuckoldom, or, the Intrigues of the City Wifes* (London, 1697). (Reade, 1936: nos. 85 and 301.) See also Wagner, 1988: 143–61; and Gallop, 1980: 274. (The amusing pun in Gallop's title, "Snatches of Conversation," refers to Diderot's *Les Bijoux indiscrets*.)

[21] See also Nussbaum, 1995: chapter 6.

disguises them, so that there is no distinguishing the great lady from her slave. 'Tis impossible for the most jealous husband to know his wife, when he meets her, and no man dare either touch or follow a woman in the street. This perpetual masquerade gives them entire liberty of following their inclinations without danger of discovery." (Montagu, 1763: 2: 33–4.)

Another eighteenth-century woman traveler, Lady Elizabeth Craven, similarly wrote: "Judge, Sir, if all these coverings do not confound all shape or air so much, that men or women, princesses and slaves, may be concealed under them. I think I never saw a country where women may enjoy so much liberty, and free from all reproach, as in Turkey." (Craven, 1789: 205.)

The notion that the veil provided Muslim women with ample opportunity to engage in mischief undetected was repeated by numerous subsequent authors, and while this passage is, in itself, not unlike those innumerable other references to the wiles of Oriental women—and the impunity with which they habitually cheat on their husbands—there is an important distinction, namely the fact that both Lady Montagu and Lady Craven associated sexual freedom in the Ottoman Empire with economic independence. (Melman, 1992: 88.) This was not out of character for Enlightenment England, where sexuality was seen "less as a sin or vice, and more as part of the economy of Nature," hence as a central constituent of the pursuit of happiness. In the latter half of the century, furthermore, travelers' reports increasingly captured the British imagination with accounts of the sexually free societies of the South Seas, providing images of a society not governed by sexual possessiveness, guilt, or jealousy as a desirable alternative form of social organization. (Porter, 1982: 6–8.)[22] Thus, "*sexuality bec[ame] a metaphor for geographical and cultural diversity*," as tolerance of sexual alterity emerged as "the ultimate test of the openness of the *philosophes* or the enlightened traveler." (Melman, 1992: 70, italics mine.) The challenge presented by natural law to the stranglehold of religion, and the emergence of the pursuit of individual freedom and fulfillment as a legitimate political cause, could thus hardly fail to catapult sexuality

---

[22] By contrast, it is noteworthy that one of the leitmotivs of orientalist discourse is the jealousy of oriental men and the rivalries of harem women.

into discursive prominence. In this climate, Lady Montagu and Lady Craven articulated critiques of their own economic precariousness and lack of liberty (both women eventually separated from their husbands and, without independent means, were left at the mercy of the latters' good will) in terms of sexual freedom in the Orient.

A century later, interestingly enough, the trope of oriental sexuality was utilized to the exact opposite effect: " 'Liberty' for the Augustans is licence, the liberty to indulge the natural sexual drives. To the Victorians it is freedom *from* sex, within marriage. Woman's *privacy* within her own sphere and her control of her own body." (Melman, 1992: 111, 87–8.) This time around, it was the motif of slippers, which, according to Lady Craven, would customarily be placed before the entrance to the harem to indicate a wife's desire for privacy, that gained center stage: to the nineteenth-century English woman, her Oriental counterpart seemed to have greater freedom not because she could hide behind her veil and seek sex, but because she could hide behind her slippers and avoid it. The diversity of discursive uses to which sexuality has been put is truly remarkable.

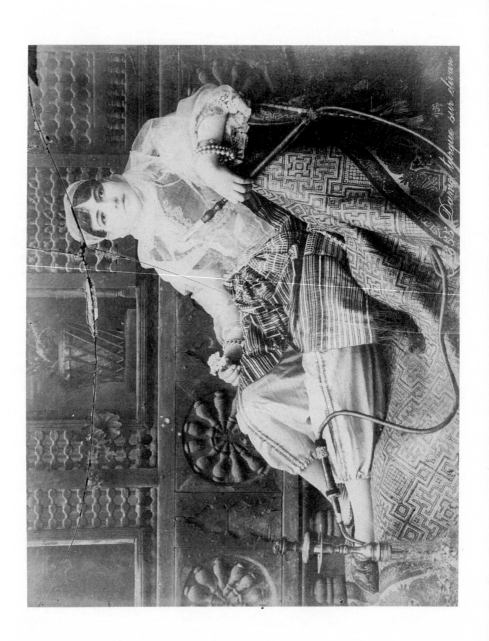

Dame turque sur divan

Conclusion:
The Mutability of Place

There are cases in which a person's own body, even portions of his own mental life—his perceptions, thoughts and feelings—appear alien to him and as not belonging to his ego; there are other cases in which he ascribes to the external world things that clearly originate in his own ego and that ought to be acknowledged by it. Thus even the feeling of our own ego is subject to disturbances and the boundaries of the ego are not constant. (Freud, 1961: 13.)[1]

The particular mix of social relations which are ... part of what defines the uniqueness of any place is by no means all included within that place itself. Importantly, it includes relations which stretch beyond—the global as part of what constitutes the local, the outside as part of the inside. Such a view of place challenges any possibility of claims to internal histories or to timeless identities. The identities of place are always unfixed, contested, and multiple. (Massey, 1994: 5.)

In this study I have argued that sexuality played an important role in the construction of Europe's spaces of otherness, by establishing the

---

[1] To be fair, I should point out that I am quoting Freud out of context: this passage is preceded by the sentence "Pathology has made us acquainted with a great number of states in which the boundary lines between the ego and the external world become uncertain or in which they are actually drawn incorrectly." I am of course not referring to pathologies here, but rather to what I take to be the usual way in which members of collectivities define themselves and their group boundaries.

alterity of the non-European. In turn, these spaces of otherness were instrumental in helping Europe signify itself, that is, define its own identity and place in the world. They also constituted the spatial imaginary within which colonialism became comprehensible and metropolitan subjects were conscripted in its service.

From the anti-Islamic polemics of the Middle Ages, through fiction-alized descriptions of the Ottoman seraglio in the seventeenth century, the South Seas in the eighteenth, and the "dark continent" in the nineteenth, to contemporary science fiction tales depicting sexual relations between humans and extra-terrestrial aliens (Heldreth, 1986), sexuality and alterity have historically been intertwined in the European imagination. But this pattern is not limited to Europe: while I am not prepared to suggest that it constitutes a universal invariant, examples of the sexualization of the "other" can be found in different societies as well. Take the Muslim world, for instance. Usāmah ibn Munqidh, a twelfth-century Syrian whose memoirs provide a fascinating glimpse into the Levant during the times of the Crusades, claimed that Chris-tian men lacked jealousy in sexual matters; and to illustrate his point, he related a story about a Frankish knight who, having had his pubic hair removed, was so satisfied with the result that he called for his wife and asked the (male) bath-keeper to give her the same treatment. (Usāmah, 1987: 165–6.) Many Muslim travelers to Europe told of the loose morals of Western women, as evidenced by the way men and women freely mingled in society, conversing, drinking, and even engag-ing in dances that brought them into close physical proximity.[2] The eighteenth-century Ottoman poet Enderunlu Fâzıl Bey wrote at length of the supposed sexual temperaments of the men and women of various nations, declaring the Frankish women of Constantinople to be partial to beardless youths, Bosnian women to be sexually cold, and Damas-cene women to be entirely devoid of virtue. (Mathers, 1930: 1: 167, 182–3.) Sexuality has provided a lexicon for mutual accusations and insults traded between Sunnis and Shi'ites, with Turkish Sunnis, for

---

[2] Numerous examples are given in Lewis, 1982: chapter 11. On the portrayal of Christian women as both sex objects and sexual predators in the early Ottoman novel, see Parla, 1990.

example, accusing the Alevî minority of engaging in orgies and incest.[3] On a more contemporary note, the novel *Mawsimu'l-hijrah ilā ash-shimāl* [Season of migration to the north] (1969) by Tayeb Salih tells of a Sudanese man who set out to redress the wrongs visited on his country by British colonialism by committing violence against British women— his sexual exploits, stated in explicitly politico-military language, eventually leading him to murder and self-destruction.[4] And one regularly encounters, in present-day Turkish newspapers, the image of the West as a combined paradise-cum-inferno of sexual promiscuity, often manifested in verbiage that, by decrying foreign women's low morals, conveniently serves to justify the publication of endless photo spreads of topless Western tourists.

While the theme does, therefore, exist in other contexts as well, my focus here has been on European discourses of alterity. "Places and spaces," Shields writes, "are hypostatized from the world of real space relations to the symbolic realm of cultural significations. Traces of these cultural place-images are also left behind in the litter of historical popular cultures: postcards, advertising images, song lyrics and in the settings of novels. These images connected with a place may even come to be held as signifiers of its essential character." (Shields, 1991: 47.) It is precisely some of these cultural artifacts that I have reviewed, stressing many different forms taken by sexuality in xenological discourse—from available femininity to violent masculinity, from threatening woman to effeminate man. It could be pointed out that this variability is easy to explain, for each form was linked to a particular conjuncture in Europe's relations with the rest of the world. That would of course be true; but it would also be besides the point. My aim has been not so much to associate with each trope its "material" conditions of existence, but rather to underscore the ways in which sexuality was instrumentalized for the purpose of drawing boundaries between self and other, and between "here" and "there." The function of sexuality in xenological (or alteritist) discourse was not *merely* to set

---

[3] The orgies allegedly practiced by the Alevî are referred to as "*mum söndü*," literally "the candle has gone out"; incest is known as "*kızılbaşlık*," literally "redheadness," after the red headgear worn by some Alevîs.

[4] For an insightful reading of this novel, see Makdisi, 1994.

up the image of a male/active colonizer penetrating a female/passive territory, as is often claimed, nor *merely* to create a climate of emergency in which repression could be naturalized as the protection of white womanhood. It was each of these, and it was more. The sexuality of the "other" was a technology of place; its function was the spatialization of difference, the differentiation of space. This is, I believe, the substratum of what has been a tremendously varied, and yet in certain ways highly united body of knowledge and representations.

But the construction of identity, alterity, and place is a means, not an end in itself. Today, as in the past, sexualized images of the "other" are used in support of hegemonic practices. In the popular film *Rising Sun* (1993), for example, sexual signifiers—such as straps tied to the four corners of an unmade bed—are enlisted in the service of Japan-bashing, casting the Japanese not only as an economic "yellow peril" poised to take over American business, but as a nation of sexual "others" as well. It is true that both the sexual "perversity," and the murder that occasions the film's storyline, are ultimately revealed to be the work of white Americans, but by that point, the damage is done. Much worse, at the height of the recent genocide carried out by Serb nationalists against Bosnia and Herzegovina, a Serbian academic named Nada Todorov attempted to blame the victims, portraying them as naturally disposed towards violence by virtue of their sexual development:

> According to her analysis, carried by the military press, the traditional *Thousand and One Nights* tales, which Muslims are supposed to have read in their childhood, deserve special blame, since these stories have provided "subliminal direction" to the Muslims to torture and kill Christians. As Todorov explains: "Since these stories are full of eroticism, it is certain that they [the Muslims] read them carefully during puberty, so that their effect on the personality of the latter is clearly evident. In committing atrocities in Bosnia-Herzegovina, [their] conscious, sub-conscious, and unconscious levels of personality have been at work." (Cited in Cigar, 1995: 70.)[5]

---

[5] Not that this ridiculous statement should be dignified with a serious rebuttal, but *The Thousand and One Nights* was translated into Serbo-Croat-Bosnian only very recently. It is worth placing Todorov's preposterous claim in the context of the systematic rape

This brazen perversion of reality, in which the aggressors project onto their victims their own evil deeds, shows the power of instrumentalized sexuality. And in Israel, the right-wing discourse of the settlers and their political allies makes much capital out of a supposed Arab male threat to Jewish women. (Shipler, 1986: 292–5.)[6] Indeed, in that case the function of sexuality as a technology of place is doubly insidious, since Israel's "space of otherness" is not physically distinct from itself, but must be *constructed as such*. Creating a space of otherness characterized by a sexual threat, in that instance, logically calls for the creation of a space that is safe from any such threat—something that can only be achieved, since the "other" is seen as congenitally threatening, through his *physical* displacement.

The communications explosion of our century seems to have had relatively little effect on the persistence of sexualized racial and geographical stereotypes, not only in novels but also in cinema and other mass media.[7] Getting to know the "others" better, in other words, has not brought about fundamental changes in the tropes, sexual or otherwise, used to represent them. Whatever the "reality" of any given point on the globe may once have been, however, this much is certain: the ravages of colonialism, the growth of multinational capitalism, the progressive incorporation of every spot on the map into the world economic system, the invention of electronic media and their relentless penetration everywhere, wars and migration, all have altered it irrevocably. Still, place-images live on. They do so for the simple reason that "changes necessitate not just an adjustment of the myth, 'cleaning out' the inappropriate images and installing new ones, but a restructuring of the entire mythology and the development of new metaphors by which ideology is presented." (Shields, 1991: 256.) The change must be epistemological, not empirical.

As the "cement" that binds society together, to follow Gramsci,

---

campaign waged by Serb nationalists, whose Bosnian and Croatian victims number in the tens of thousands.
[6] For some (very preliminary) remarks on this motif in Israeli literature, see also Shammas, 1994: 167–73, as well as, more generally, the large literature on images of the Arab in Israeli literature.
[7] See, for example, Feret, 1984; Shohat, 1990.

ideology functions to contain differences or antagonisms that threaten to tear it apart; and it can do that most effectively by setting up differences of its own, in other words, by appropriating difference and reconstructing it on the hegemonic powers' own terms. (Williamson, 1986: 100.)[8] Take racism, for instance: it is most useful not as the starting point of, but as posterior justification for, politically and socially directed attitudes—most notably, ways of thinking that legitimate existing societal inequities.Thus, for instance, it is when slavery is revealed to be the barbaric, inhuman practice that it is that the "inferiority" of its victims, who happen to have black skin, becomes a useful idea. To put it another way, it is when the transparency of race can no longer be presumed, when transracial relations of domination and subordination that hitherto appeared natural no longer do so, that the deployment of race becomes expedient. (Ridley, 1983: 78; Sharpe, 1993: 5.)

In short, differences are discursively produced in order to cover up or legitimate existing socio-economic imbalances. As Bhabha writes, "the construction of the colonial subject in discourse, and the exercise of colonial power through discourse, demand an articulation of forms of difference—racial and sexual. Such an articulation becomes crucial if it is held that the body is always simultaneously (if conflictually) inscribed in both the economy of pleasure and desire, and the economy of discourse, domination and power." (Bhabha, 1994: 67.) Socially constructed space plays a central role in this process.

Human differences and spatial differences mutually support and reinforce each other; ideology can therefore be assisted by representations of space. Place is not merely the domain of thought, it is an integral part of political praxis, since people act less upon realities than upon their perceptions of those realities. The socially constructed cognitive/significational structures that mediate geographical facts thus shape human actions. (Shields, 1991: 30; Lefebvre, 1991: 26.) Such is the power of representation: like art, it does not just mean, it also *does*.

---

[8] As Levy writes of anthropology, for instance, "universality is a convenient fiction, even an illusion, behind which lurks a new supremacist logic for subordinating the racial other within a new hierarchy." (Levy, 1991: 52.) See also Laclau, 1977: 161.

Beyond merely reflecting relations of power, the social production of space and its functioning to construct difference also produce and reproduce them. Spatial differentiation is not just an outcome of social processes, in other words, it is a fundamental part of the reproduction of society and its dominant social relations. (Massey, 1984: 300.)[9] But if socially constructed space is so intimately tied to the practice of power and domination, it must also be both the site and the means of contest and resistance: as Soja puts it, "concrete spatiality—actual human geography—is thus a competitive area for struggles over social production and reproduction, for social practices aimed either at the maintenance and reinforcement of existing spatiality or at significant restructuring and/or radical transformation." (Soja, 1989: 130.) Understanding social spatiality—that is, the ways in which socially produced systems of signification are articulated with physical space so as to fulfill certain socially useful functions—can help demystify the manner in which spatiality partakes in the establishment and naturalization of relations of domination and subordination, thereby opening avenues for radical social change. (Keith and Pile, 1993: 225.)

I entertain the hope, therefore, that studies such as this one amount to a bit more than mere "representations of representation," that they also have some emancipatory potential. Foucault has written that he set out "to learn to what extent the effort to think one's own history can free thought from what it silently thinks, and so enable it to think differently." (Foucault, 1978–85, 2: 9.) To write history is to chronicle change; and to chronicle change is to show that reality has not always been, and therefore need not always be, as it is today: "only the difference of the past can demonstrate that the inscriptions of the 'other' are variable, encouraging the recognition that the images our culture so obsessively projects in advertising, movies, fiction, and so forth, need not exhaust the possible. All inscriptions and legitimations are human products, and the future need not be like the present."

---

[9] This is a common theme in Marxist geography. It is worth noting that the same point has been made about gender; see Kelly, 1984: 61; Barrett, 1985. On the points of intersection of Marxist and feminist geography and their conceptions of the role of space in the reproduction of social relations, see Rose, 1993: 117–22. On the role of space in the reproduction of gender, see Massey, 1994.

(Boheemen, 1987: 43.) It is only by showing that stereotypes are not fixed, that diametrically opposed views were held at different times by different people equally convinced of the truth of their beliefs, that one can demonstrate this simple fact: stereotypes only make sense within specific discursive networks, and invariably owe their existence to specific social conditions. They are, therefore, subject to change.

And so it is for place. As Huggan writes, "the map's systematic inscription on a supposedly 'uninscribed' earth reveals it ... as a palimpsest covering over alternative spatial configurations which, once brought to light, indicate both the plurality of possible perspectives on, and the inadequacy of any single model of, the world." (Huggan, 1990: 128.) All our maps, our trove of spatially organized knowledge, thus only represent a link in a long chain of writings and overwritings. But recognizing the mutability of our most cherished spatial truths is the surest way to undermine the hegemonic practices which they support. My undertaking of this study has been inspired precisely by this conviction.

Bibliography

Adorno, Rolena. "El Sujeto colonial y la construccion cultural de la alteridad" (The colonial subject and the cultural construction of alterity), *Revista de crítica literaria latinoamericana*, 14, 28 (1988), pp. 55–68.

Ahmed, Leila. "Western Ethnocentrism and Perceptions of the Harem," *Feminist Studies*, 8 (1982), pp. 521–34.

Aijaz Ahmad. *In Theory: Classes, Nations, Literatures*, London and New York, Verso, 1992.

Aït Sabbah, Fatna (pseud. of Fatima Mernissi). *La Femme dans l'inconscient musulman* (Woman in the Muslim Unconscious), Paris, Éditions Albin Michel, 1986. English translation of earlier edition: *Woman in the Muslim Unconscious*, translated by Mary Jo Lakeland, New York, Pergamon Press, 1984.

Ali, Muhsin Jassim. *Scheherazade in England: A Study of Nineteenth-Century English Criticism of the "Arabian Nights,"* Washington, Three Continents Press, 1981.

Allgrove, George. *Love in the East*, London, Anthony Gibbs & Phillips, 1962.

Alloula, Malek. *The Colonial Harem*, translated by Myrna Godzich and Wlad Godzich, introduction by Barbara Harlow, Minneapolis, University of Minnesota Press, 1986.

Allport, Gordon W. *The Nature of Prejudice*, Cambridge, MA, Addison-Wesley Publishing Company, Inc., 1954.

Anderson, Benedict. *Imagined Communities: Reflections on the Origin and Spread of Nationalism*, London, Verso, 1983.

Anderson, Kay and Fay Gale, eds. *Inventing Places: Studies in Cultural Geography*, Melbourne, Longman Cheshire; n.p.: Halstead Press, John Wiley & Sons, Inc., 1992.

Anon. [Lord George Herbert?]. *A Night in a Moorish Harem*, Paris, Isidore Liseux, 1909.

Anon. *Arabian Love Tales: Being Romances Drawn from the Book of the Thousand Nights and One Night*, translated (from the French) by [Edward] Powys Mathers, London, The Folio Society, 1949.

Anon. *Der persische Dekameron* [The Persian *Decameron*], with an Introduction by Franz Blei, Vienna and Leipzig, Verlag für Kulturforschung, 1927.

Anon. [Mouchet de Troyes]. *Dictionnaire contenant les anecdotes historiques de l'amour, depuis le commencement du monde jusqu'à ce jour* [Dictionary containing historical anecdotes of love, from the beginning of the world to this day], 5 vols. Troyes, Gobelet, 1811.

Anon. *Die Liebesgeschichten des Orients: Aus den tausend Nächten und der einen Nacht* [The love stories of the Orient: from the *Thousand Nights and a Night*], translated by Carl Theodor Ritter von Riba, Berlin and Leipzig, Wilhelm Borngräber Verlag, n.d. [ca. 1920].

Anon. *Eastern Love Stories: Classic Tales of Oriental Love*, New York, Shakespeare House, 1951.

Anon. *From a Turkish Harim*, translated by John C. Kraemer, New York, [The Lotus Society], 1930.

Anon. *Geschichten der Liebe aus den tausendundein Nächten* [Love stories from the *Thousand and One Nights*], Wiesbaden, Insel-Verlag, 1953.

Anon. *La Rose d'Amour; or the Adventures of a Gentleman in Search of Pleasure*, serialized in *The Pearl: a Journal of Facetiae and Voluptuous Reading* 8–16 (1880), reprint edition, 3 vols. in 1, with an Introduction by Jack Hirschman, North Hollywood, Brandon House, 1967.

Anon. *L'Art d'aimer à travers les âges et les littératures* [The art of love through the ages and the literatures], Vol. I, *En Orient: Anthologie des maîtres de la littérature orientale* [In the Orient: anthology of the masters of oriental litterature], Paris, Les Éditions Georges-Anquetil, n.d. [ca. 1920].

Anon. *La Fleur lascive orientale* [The oriental lascivious flower], translation attributed to Jean-Adolphe Decourdemanche, n.p., L'Astrée, 1955.

Anon. [Tifāshī?]. *Le Livre de volupté (Bah Nameh)* [The book of voluptuousness *(Bahnâme)*], translated by Abdul-Haqq Efendi, Erzeroum, Qizmich-Aga, Libraire-Éditeur, n.d. [Brussels, Jules Gay, ca. 1878–79].

Anon. *Les Ruses des femmes (Mikri-zenan), et extraits du Plaisir après la peine (Feredj bad chiddeh)* [The wiles of women *(Mekr-i Zenân)*, and selections from Pleasure after pain *(Ferec ba'de Şiddet)*], translated by J.-A. [Jean-Adolphe] Decourdemanche, Paris, Ernest Leroux, Éditeur, 1896. English translation: *The wiles of women*, translated (from the French) by J. [John] Mills Whitham and S. F. Mills Whitham, New York, Lincoln Mac Veagh, Dial Press, 1929.

Anon. *Liebesgeschichten des Orients* [Love stories of the Orient], with an Introduction by Franz Blei, Hannover, Paul Steegemann Verlag, 1922.

Anon. [Pigeon de Saint-Paterne?]. *L'Odalisque: Ouvrage traduit du Turc* [The odalisque: a work translated from the Turkish], Constantinople, Ibrahim Bectas, 1779. English translation: *The Odalisque by Voltaire*, translated by M. Clyboret, n.p., privately printed for The Voltaire Society, 1928.

Anon. *Marché aux esclaves et harem: épisode inédit de la piraterie barbaresque au XVIIIe siècle* [Slave market and harem: a hitherto unpublished episode of Barbary Coast piratry in the eighteenth century], Paris, Ernest Leroux, Éditeur, 1875.

Anon. *Memoirs of a Harem Girl: the Story of Aisha, a Woman of Tangier, an Erotic Masterpiece Long Suppressed*, edited and translated by Ary Caldwell Phillips, New York, Tower Books, 1968.

Anon. ["Walter"]. *My Secret Life*, 11 vols., [Amsterdam], s.n., ca. 1890. Reprint edition: New York, Grove Press, 1966.

Anon. *Nights of the Rajah; or the Indian Loves of Captain Charles de Vane*, with an Introduction by Richard Manton, New York, Grove Press, 1983.

Anon. *The Amatory Adventures of the Lustful Turk, or Lascivious Scenes in a Harem*, New York, Warner Books, 1984.

Anon. *The Amorous Memoirs of Captain Charles de Vane: Being the Military and Amorous Reminiscences of Captain Charles de Vane, Royal Sussex*

Regiment, with an Introduction by Richard Manton, New York, Grove Press, 1982.

Anon. *The Arabian Droll Stories*, translated by Carlo De Fornaro. New York, [The Lotus Society], 1929.

Anon. *The Pleasures of Cruelty, being a Sequel to the Reading of Justine et Juliette by The Marquis de Sade*, New York, Grove Press, Inc., n.d.

Anon. *Traffic in Women, including Detailed Descriptions of the Customs and Manners of the White Women Slaves and Wives of Asia, Turkey, Egypt, etc.*, no publication information.

Anon. [William Rufus Chetwood?]. *The Voyages and Adventures of Captain Robert Boyle in Several Parts of the World, intermix'd with the Story of Mrs. Villars, an English Lady with whom he made his Surprizing Escape from Barbary*, London, John Watts, 1726.

Apollinaire, Guillaume, Fernand Fleuret, and Louis Perceau. *L'Enfer de la Bibliothèque Nationale: Icono-bio-bibliographie descriptive, critique et raisonnée, complète a ce jour de tous les ouvrages composant cette célèbre collection, avec un index alphabétique des titres et noms d'auteurs* (The "Hell" of the Bibliothéque Nationale: descriptive, critical, and comprehensive icono-bio-bibliography of all the works comprising this famous collection, complete as of today, with an alphabetical index of titles and authors' names), Paris, Mercure de France, 1913.

Apter, Emily. "Female Trouble in the Colonial Harem," *Differences: a Journal of Feminist Cultural Studies*, 4, 1 (1992), pp. 205–24.

Armstrong, Hamilton Fish. *Where the East Begins*, New York and London, Harper & Brothers Publishers, 1929.

Armstrong, Meg. "'A Jumble of Foreignness': The Sublime Musayums of Nineteenth-Century Fairs and Expositions," *Cultural Critique*, 23, (1992–93), pp. 199–250.

Armstrong, Nancy. *Desire and Domestic Fiction: a Political History of the Novel*, New York and Oxford, Oxford University Press, 1987.

Arnold, David. *Colonizing the Body: State Medicine and Epidemic Disease in Nineteenth-Century India*, Berkeley, Los Angeles, and London, University of California Press, 1993.

[Ashbee, Henry Spencer] Pisanus Fraxi [pseud.]. *Index Librorum Prohibitorum: Being Notes Bio- Biblio- Icono-graphical and Critical on Curious and Uncommon Books*, London, Privately Printed, 1877.

[Ashbee, Henry Spencer] Pisanus Fraxi [pseud.]. *Centuria Librorum Absconditorum: Being Notes Bio- Biblio- Icono-graphical and Critical on Curious and Uncommon Books*, London, Privately Printed, 1879.

[Ashbee, Henry Spencer] Pisanus Fraxi [pseud.]. *Catena Librorum Tacendorum: Being Notes Bio- Biblio- Icono- graphical and Critical on Curious and Uncommon Books*, London, Privately Printed, 1885.

Ashcroft, Bill, Gareth Griffiths, and Helen Tiffin. *The Empire Writes Back: Theory and Practice in Post-Colonial Literatures*, London and New York, Routledge, 1995.

Auldjo, John. *Journal of a Visit to Constantinople, and Some of the Greek Islands, in the Spring and Summer of 1833*, London, Longman, Rees, Orme, Brown, Green, and Longman, 1835.

Azim, Firdous. *The Colonial Rise of the Novel*, London and New York, Routledge, 1993.

Bachelard, Gaston. *The Poetics of Space*, translated by Maria Jolas, foreword by Etienne Gilson, New York, The Orion Press, 1964.

Baecque, Antoine de. "The 'Livres remplis d'horreur': Pornographic Literature and Politics at the Beginning of the French Revolution," in *Erotica and the Enlightenment*, edited by Peter Wagner, Frankfurt am Main, Bern, New York, and Paris, Peter Lang, 1991, pp. 123–65.

[al-Baghdādī, Abū ʿAbdu'r-raḥman ʿAlī] al-Baghdâdî. *Les Fleurs éclatantes dans les baisers et l'accolement* [Brilliant flowers in kisses and copulation], translated and with an Introduction by René R. Khawam, Paris, Éditions Albin Michel, 1973.

Baker, Kathryn Hinojosa. "Delinquent Desire: Race, Sex, and Ritual in Reform Schools for Girls," *Discourse*, 15, 1 (1992), pp. 46–68.

Bakhtin, M.M. [Mikhail Mikhailovich]. "Forms of Time and of the Chronotope in the Novel: Notes toward a Historical Poetics," *The Dialogic Imagination: Four Essays*, edited by Michael Holquist, translated by Caryl Emerson and Michael Holquist, Austin and London, University of Texas Press, 1981, pp. 84–258.

Balibar, Etienne. "The Nation Form: History and Ideology," in *Race, Nation, Class: Ambiguous Identities*, by Etienne Balibar and Immanuel Wallerstein, translated by Chris Turner, London and New York, Verso, 1991, pp. 86–106.

Ballhatchet, Kenneth. *Race, Sex, and Class under the Raj: Imperial Attitudes and Policies and their Critics, 1793–1905*, New York, St. Martin's Press, 1980.

Bammer, Angelika (ed.). *Displacements: Cultural Identities in Question*, Bloomington and Indianapolis, Indiana University Press, 1994.

Barbier, A.-A. [Antoine-Alexandre]. *Dictionnaire des ouvrages anonymes* [Dictionary of anonymous works], 4 vols., Paris, P. Daffis, 1872–79. Reprint edition: Paris, G.P. Maisonneuve & Larose, 1964.

Bardakçı, Murat. *Osmanlı'da Seks* [Sex in the Ottoman Empire], İstanbul, Gür Yayınları, 1992.

Barrett, Michèle. "Ideology and the Cultural Production of Gender," in *Feminist Criticism and Social Change: Sex, Class and Race in Literature and Culture*, edited by Judith Newton and Deborah Rosenfelt, New York and London, Methuen, 1985, pp. 65–85.

Barthes, Roland. *Mythologies*, translated by Annette Lavers, New York, Hill and Wang, 1994.

Başcı, K. Pelin. "Shadows in the Missionary Garden of Roses: Women of Turkey in American Missionary Texts," in *Deconstructing Images of 'The Turkish Woman,'* edited by Zehra Arat, New York, St. Martin's Press, 1998, pp. 101–23.

Bassano (da Zara), Luigi. *I Costumi et i Modi Particolari de la Vita de Turchi* [The special customs and manners of the life of the Turks], [Rome, Antonio Blando Asolano, 1545]. Reprint edition, with an Introduction by Franz Babinger, Monaco di Baviera [Munich], Max Hueber, 1963.

Basset, René (ed.). *Mille et un contes, récits, & légendes arabes* [Thousand and one arabic tales, stories, and legends], 3 vols., Paris, Librairie Orientale et Américaine Maisonneuve Frères, 1924–27.

Baudet, Henri. *Paradise on Earth: Some Thoughts on European Images of Non-European Man*, translated by Elizabeth Wentholt, New Haven and London, Yale University Press, 1965.

Baudier (de Languedoc), Michel. *Histoire géneralle du serrail, et de la Cour du Grand Seigneur Empereur des Turcs* [General history of the seraglio and the court of the sultan, emperor of the Turks, translated as *The history of the imperiall estate of the grand seigneurs*], Paris, Claude Cramoisy, 1624.

Baughman, Laurence Alan. *Southern Rape Complex: Hundred Year Psychosis*, Atlanta, Pendulum Books, 1966.

Beauchamps, [Pierre-François Godart] de. *Histoire du Prince Apprius, extraite des Fastes du monde, depuis sa création. Manuscrit Persan trouvé dans la bibliothèque de Schah-Hussain, Roi de Perse, détrôné par Mamouth en 1722. Traduit en français par Monsieur Esprit* [Story of Prince Apprius, excerpted from the Festivities of the world, since its creation. Persian manuscript found in the library of Shah Hussain, King of Persia, dethroned by Mamouth in 1722. Translated into French by Mr. Esprit], La Haye [The Hague], s.n., 1745.

Beckford, William. *Vathek*, in *Three Gothic Novels*, edited by Peter Fairclough, with an Introduction by Mario Praz, Harmondsworth, Middlesex, Penguin Books, 1987, pp. 149–255.

Behdad, Ali. "The Eroticized Orient: Images of the Harem in Montesquieu and his Precursors," *Stanford French Review*, 13, 2–3 (1989), pp. 109–26.

Behdad, Ali. *Belated Travelers: Orientalism in the Age of Colonial Dissolution*, Durham and London, Duke University Press, 1994.

Bell, David and Gill Valentine. "The Sexed Self: Strategies of Performance, Sites of Resistance," in *Mapping the Subject: Geographies of Cultural Transformation*, edited by Steve Pile and Nigel Thrift, London and New York, Routledge, 1995a, pp. 143–57.

Bell, David and Gill Valentine (eds.). *Mapping Desire: Geographies of Sexualities*, London and New York, Routledge, 1995b.

[Benjamin ben Jonah]. *The Itinerary of Benjamin of Tudela*, critical text, translation and commentary by Marcus Nathan Adler, London, Henry Frowde; Oxford University Press, 1907.

Berger, Peter L. and Thomas Luckmann. *The Social Construction of Reality: a Treatise in the Sociology of Knowledge*, Garden City, Doubleday & Company, Inc., 1966.

Berry, Chris. *A Bit on the Side: East-West Topographies of Desire*, Sydney, Empress Publishing, 1994.

Betsky, Aaron. *Building Sex: Men, Women, Architecture, and the Construction of Sexuality*, New York, William Morrow and Company, Inc., 1995.

Bhabha, Homi K. "The Other Question: Stereotype, Discrimination and the Discourse of Colonialism," *The Location of Culture*, London and New York, Routledge, 1994, pp. 66–84.

Bhabha, Homi K. (ed.). *Nation and Narration*, London and New York, Routledge, 1990.

Biddiss, Michael D. *Father of Racist Ideology: The Social and Political Thought of Count Gobineau*, London, Weidenfeld and Nicolson, 1970.

Blanch, Lesley. *The Wilder Shores of Love*, New York, Simon and Schuster, 1954.

Bloch, Iwan. *Anthropological Studies in the Strange Sexual Practises in All Races of the World*, translated by Keene Wallis, New York, Falstaff Press, Inc., 1933.

Bloch, Iwan. *Anthropological and Ethnological Studies in the Strangest Sex Acts in Modes of Love of All Races Illustrated: Oriental, Occidental, Savage, Civilized*, translated by Ernst Vogel, New York, Falstaff Press, Inc., 1935.

Blunt, Alison. *Travel, Gender, and Imperialism: Mary Kingsley and West Africa*, New York and London, The Guilford Press, 1994.

Blunt, Alison and Gillian Rose. "Introduction: Women's Colonial and Postcolonial Geographies," in *Writing Women and Space: Colonial and Postcolonial Geographies*, edited by Alison Blunt and Gillian Rose, New York and London, The Guilford Press, 1994, pp. 1–25.

[Blunt, John Elijah, Mrs]. *The People of Turkey: Twenty Years' Residence among Bulgarians, Greeks, Albanians, Turks, and Armenians, by a Consul's Daughter and Wife*, 2 vols., edited by Stanley Lane Poole, London, John Murray, 1878.

[Bobovi, Albert]. "Topkapı Sarayı in the Mid-Seventeenth Century: Bobovi's Description," translated and with an Introduction by C. [Carol] G. Fisher and A. [Alan] Fisher, *Archivum Ottomanicum*, 10 (1985 [1987]), pp. 5–81.

Boheemen, Christine van. *The Novel as Family Romance: Language, Gender, and Authority from Fielding to Joyce*, Ithaca and London, Cornell University Press, 1987.

Bolen, Carl van. *Erotik des Orients: Eine Darstellung der orientalischen Hochkulturen* [Erotic of the Orient: a description of oriental high cultures], Teufen, Bücher des Lebens, 1955.

[Bon, Ottaviano] Robert Withers [trans.]. *A Description of the Grand Signor's Seraglio, or Turkish Emperours Court*, edited by John Greaves, London, Jo. Martin and Jo. Ridley, 1650.

Bonaparte, Marie. "Notes on Excision," translated by John Rodker, *Female Sexuality*, New York, International University Press, Inc., 1953.

Bongie, Chris. *Exotic Memories: Literature, Colonialism, and the Fin de Siècle*, Stanford, Stanford University Press, 1991.

Boone, Joseph A. "Mapping of Male Desire in Durrell's *Alexandria Quartet*," *The South Atlantic Quarterly*, 88, 1 (1989), pp. 73–106.

Borges, Jorge Luis. "Los traductores de las *1001 Noches*" [The translators of the *1001 Nights*], *Historia de la Eternidad*, Buenos Aires, Emecé Editores, 1953, pp. 99–134.

[Bougainville, Louis-Antoine de]. *Voyage autour du monde par la frégate du Roi la Boudeuse, et la flûte l'Etoile; en 1766, 1767, 1768 & 1769* [A voyage round the world by the king's frigate La Boudeuse and the store ship l'Etoile], Paris, Saillant & Nyon, 1771. English translation: *A Voyage Round the World. Performed by Order of His Most Christian Majesty, in the Years 1766, 1767, 1768, and 1769 by Lewis de Bougainville, Colonel of Foot, and Commodore of the Expedition, in the Frigate La Boudeuse, and the Store-ship L'Etoile*, 2 vols., translated by John Reinhold Forster, London, J. Nourse and T. Davies, 1772.

Bouhdiba, Abdelwahab. *La Sexualité en Islam* [Sexuality in Islam], Paris, Presses Universitaires de France, 1975. English translation: *Sexuality in Islam*, London and Boston, Routledge & Kegan Paul, 1985.

Bourdieu, Pierre. *Outline of a Theory of Practice*, translated by Richard Nice, Cambridge, U.K., Cambridge University Press, 1977.

Bousquet, G.-H. [Georges-Henri]. *L'Éthique sexuelle de l'Islam* [The sexual ethics of Islam], Paris, Desclée de Brouwer, 1990.

Brantlinger, Patrick. *Rule of Darkness: British Literature and Imperialism, 1830–1914*, Ithaca and London, Cornell University Press, 1988.

Bristow, Joseph. *Empire Boys: Adventures in a Man's World*, London, Harper Collins Academic, 1991.

Brodie, Fawn M. *The Devil Drives: a Life of Sir Richard Burton*, New York, W.W. Norton & Company, Inc., 1967.

Bronson, Bill. *Sexual Paradises of Earth: A Single Man's Guide to International Travel*, Southfield, BB Press, 1993.

Brontë, Charlotte. *Jane Eyre*, New York and London, W.W. Norton & Co., 1971.

Brooks, Peter. *Body Work: Objects of Desire in Modern Narrative*, Cambridge, MA and London, Harvard University Press, 1993.

Brown, Laura. *Ends of Empire: Women and Ideology in Early Eighteenth-Century English Literature*, Ithaca and London, Cornell University Press, 1993.

Brown, Paul. "'This thing of darkness I acknowledge mine': *The Tempest* and the Discourse of Colonialism," in *Political Shakespeare: New Essays in Cultural Materialism*, edited by Jonathan Dollimore and Alan Sinfield, Ithaca and London, Cornell University Press, 1985, pp. 48–71.

Brownmiller, Susan. *Against Our Will: Men, Women and Rape*, New York, Simon & Schuster, 1975.

Brunet, Gustave. *Imprimeurs imaginaires et libraires supposés: Étude bibliographique* [Imaginary printers and spurious booksellers: bibliographic study], Paris, Librairie Tross, 1866.

Brunet, Gustave. *Dictionnaire des ouvrages anonymes, suivi des Supercheries littéraires dévoilées: Supplément à la Dernière édition de ces deux ouvrages* [Dictionary of anonymous works, followed by Literary fakes exposed: supplement to the last edition of these two works], Paris, F.-J. Féchoz, Éditeur, 1889.

Bryk, Felix. *Voodoo-Eros: Ethnological Studies in the Sex-Life of the African Aborigines*, translated by Mayne R. Sexton, New York, Privately Printed, 1933.

Buber, Martin. "Afterword: the History of the Dialogical Principle," translated by Maurice Friedman, *Between Man and Man*, translated by Ronald Gregor Smith, with an Introduction by Maurice Friedman, New York, The Macmillan Company, 1965, pp. 209–24.

Buonaventura, Wendy. *Serpent of the Nile: Women and Dance in the Arab World*, London, Saqi Books, 1989.

Burkitt, Ian. "The Shifting Concept of Self," *History of the Human Sciences* 7, 2 (1994), pp. 7–28.

Burnaby, Fred. *On Horseback through Asia Minor*, 2 vols., London, Sampson Low, Marston, Searle, and Rivington, 1877.

Burroughs, Edgar Rice. *Tarzan of the Apes*, New York, Grosset & Dunlap, 1914.

Burton, Richard [F.], Sir. *Love, War and Fancy: the Customs and Manners of the East, from writings on "The Arabian Nights,"* edited by Kenneth Walker, New York, Ballantine Books, 1964.

Burton, Richard [F.], Sir. *The Erotic Traveller*, edited by Edward Leigh, London, The Ortolan Press, 1966.

Burton, Richard F., Sir. *A Plain and Literal Translation of the Arabian Nights' Entertainments, now entituled The Book of the Thousand Nights and a Night [. . .]* 10+7 vols., n.p., printed by the Burton Club, n.d. ("The Mecca Edition").

Burton, Richard [F.], Sir. *The Sotadic Zone*, New York, The Panurge Press, n.d.

Burton, R. [Roland] (ed.). *Venus Oceanica: Anthropological Studies in the Sex Life of the South Sea Natives*, New York, The Oceanica Research Press, 1935.

Busia, Abena P. A. "Miscegenation as Metonymy: Sexuality and Power in the Colonial Novel," *Ethnic and Racial Studies*, 9, 3 (1986), pp. 360–72.

Busia, Abena P. A. "Silencing Sycorax: On African Colonial Discourse and the Unvoiced Female," *Cultural Critique*, 14 (1989–90), pp. 81–104.

Buzard, James. *The Beaten Track: European Tourism, Literature, and the Ways to Culture, 1800–1918*, Oxford, The Clarendon Press of Oxford University Press, 1993.

Byron, Lord [George Gordon Byron, Baron]. *Byron's Letters and Journals*, 12 vols., edited by Leslie A. Marchand, Cambridge, MA, The Belknap Press of Harvard University Press, 1973–82.

Callan, Hilary and Shirley Ardener (eds.). *The Incorporated Wife*, London, Croom Helm; Oxford, Centre for Cross Cultural Research on Women, 1984.

Callaway, Helen. *Gender, Culture and Empire: European Women in Colonial Nigeria*, Urbana and Chicago, University of Illinois Press, 1987.

Camille, Michael. *Image on the Edge: the Margins of Medieval Art*, London, Reaktion Books, 1992.

Campbell, Mary B. *The Witness and the Other World: Exotic European Travel Writing, 400–1600*, Ithaca and London, Cornell University Press, 1988.

Camus, Albert. "The Adulterous Woman," in *Exile and the Kingdom*, translated by Justin O'Brien, New York, Alfred A. Knopf, 1963, pp. 3–33.

Carby, Hazel V. "'On the Threshold of Woman's Era': Lynching, Empire, and Sexuality in Black Feminist Theory," in *'Race,' Writing, and Difference*, edited by Henry Louis Gates, Jr., Chicago and London, The University of Chicago Press, 1986, pp. 301–16.

Carlyle, Thomas. "Chartism," in *Past and Present, Chartism, and Sartor Resartus*, New York, Harper & Brothers, Publishers, 1848, pp. 299–386.

Carr, David, *Time, Narrative, and History*, Bloomington and Indianapolis, Indiana University Press, 1991.

Carr, Helen. "Woman/Indian: 'The American' and His Others," in *Europe and its Others: Proceedings of the Essex Conference on the Sociology of Literature, July 1984*, edited by Francis Barker, Peter Hulme, Margaret Iversen, and Diana Loxley, 2 vols., Colchester, University of Essex, 1985, vol. 2, pp. 46–60.

Carter, Angela. *The Sadeian Woman and the Ideology of Pornography*, New York, Pantheon Books, 1988.

Carter, Erica, James Donald, and Judith Squires (eds.). *Space and Place: Theories of Identity and Location*, London, Lawrence & Wishart, 1993.

Carter, Paul. *The Road to Botany Bay: An Essay in Spatial History*, London and Boston, Faber and Faber, 1987.

Casanova, Giacomo, Chevalier de Seingalt [Giacomo Girolamo Casanova de Seingalt]. *History of My Life*, translated and with an Introduction by Willard R. Trask, 6 vols. in 3, New York, Harcourt, Brace & World, Inc., 1966–68.

Çelik, Zeynep. *Displaying the Orient: Architecture of Islam at Nineteenth-Century World's Fairs*, Berkeley, Los Angeles, and Oxford, University of California Press, 1992.

Çelik, Zeynep and Leila Kinney. "Ethnography and Exhibitionism at the Expositions Universelles," *Assemblage: A Critical Journal of Architecture and Design Culture*, 13 (1990), pp. 34–59.

Certeau, Michel de. *The Practice of Everyday Life*, translated by Steven F. Rendall, Berkeley, Los Angeles, and London, University of California Press, 1984.

Certeau, Michel de. "Montaigne's 'Of Cannibals': the Savage 'I.'" in *Heterologies: Discourse on the Other*, translated by Brian Massumi, with a Foreword by Wlad Godzich, Minneapolis and London, University of Minnesota Press, 1986, pp. 67–79.

Chakravarti, Uma. "Whatever Happened to the Vedic *Dasi*? Orientalism, Nationalism and a Script from the Past," in *Recasting Women: Essays in Colonial History*, edited by Kumkum Sangari and Sudesh Vaid, New Delhi, Kali for Women, 1989, pp. 27–87.

[Chardin, Jean]. *Voyages de Monsieur le Chevalier Chardin, en Perse, et autres lieux de l'Orient* [Voyages of the Chevalier Chardin, in Persia and other places of the Orient, translated as *Sir John Chardin's Travels in Persia*], 3 vols., Amsterdam, Jean Louis de Lorme, 1711.

Chaudhuri, Nupur and Margaret Strobel (eds.). *Western Women and Imperialism: Complicity and Resistance*, Bloomington, Indiana University Press, 1992.

Chebel, Malek. *Encyclopédie de l'amour en Islam: Érotisme, beauté et sexualité dans le monde arabe, en Perse et en Turquie* [Encyclopaedia of love in Islam: eroticism, beauty, and sexuality in the Arab world, in Persia, and in Turkey], Paris, Éditions Payot & Rivages, 1995.

Chester, Suzanne. "Writing the Subject: Exoticism/Eroticism in Marguerite Duras's *The Lover* and *The Sea Wall*," in *De/Colonizing the Subject: The Politics of Gender in Women's Autobiography*, edited by Sidonie Smith and Julia Watson, Minneapolis, University of Minnesota Press, 1992, pp. 436–57.

Chew, Samuel C. *The Crescent and the Rose: Islam and England during the Renaissance*, New York, Oxford University Press, 1937.

Cheyfitz, Eric. *The Poetics of Imperialism: Translation and Colonization from "The Tempest" to "Tarzan,"* New York and Oxford, Oxford University Press, 1991.

Cigar, Norman. *Genocide in Bosnia: The Policy of "Ethnic Cleansing,"* College Station, Texas A&M University Press, 1995.

Cixous, Hélène. "Sorties: Out and Out: Attacks/Ways Out/Forays," in *The Newly Born Woman*, by Hélène Cixous and Catherine Clément, translated by Betsy Wing, with an Introduction by Sandra M. Gilbert, Minneapolis, University of Minnesota Press, 1986, pp. 63–132.

Cleland, John. *Memoirs of a Woman of Pleasure* [*Fanny Hill*], 2 vols., London, G. Fenton, 1749.

Cleugh, James. *Ladies of the Harem*, London, Frederick Muller, Ltd., 1955. Revised and expanded edition: *A History of Oriental Orgies: an Account of Erotic Practices Among the Peoples of the East and the Near East*, New York, Crown Publishers, Inc., 1968.

Clifford, James. "Introduction: Partial Truths," in *Writing Culture: The Poetics and Politics of Ethnography*, edited by James Clifford and George E. Marcus, Berkeley, Los Angeles and London, University of California Press, 1986, pp. 1–26.

Clissold, Stephen. *The Barbary slaves*, New York, Barnes & Noble, 1977.

Cobb, Stanwood. *The Real Turk*, Boston, New York, and Chicago, The Pilgrim Press, 1914.

Colomina, Beatriz (ed.). *Sexuality & Space*, New York, Princeton Architectural Press, 1992.

Conant, Martha Pike. *The Oriental Tale in England in the Eighteenth Century*, New York, The Columbia University Press, 1908.

Conrad, Joseph. *Heart of Darkness*, edited by Robert Kimbrough, New York and London, W.W. Norton & Co., 1988.

Corbey, Raymond. *Wildheid en Beschaving: De Europese Verbeelding van Afrika* [Savagery and civilization: the European imagining of Africa], Baarn, Ambo, 1989.

Cornillon, Susan Koppelman. "The Fiction of Fiction," in *Images of Women in Fiction: Feminist Perspectives*, edited by Susan Koppelman Cornillon, Bowling Green, Bowling Green University Popular Press, 1973, pp. 113–30.

Cosgrove, Denis E. *Social Formation and Symbolic Landscape*, Totowa, Barnes & Noble Books, 1985.

Cosgrove, Denis and Stephen Daniels (eds.). *The Iconography of Landscape: Essays on the Symbolic Representation, Design and Use of Past Environments*, Cambridge, UK, Cambridge University Press, 1988.

[Courthop, George, Sir]. *The Memoirs of Sir George Courthop, 1616–1685*, edited by S.C. [Sophia Crawford] Lomas, *The Camden Miscellany*, Vol. 11, London, Offices of the Royal Historical Society, 1907, pp. 91–157.

Crapanzano, Vincent. *Hermes' Dilemma and Hamlet's Desire: On the Epistemology of Interpretation*, Cambridge, MA and London, Harvard University Press, 1992.

[Craven, Elizabeth, Lady]. *A Journey through the Crimea to Constantinople in a Series of Letters from the Right Honourable Elizabeth Lady Craven, to his*

Serene Highness the Margrave of Brandebourg, Anspach, and Bareith, Written in the Year 1786, London, G.G.J. and J. Robinson, 1789.

Crawley, [Alfred] Ernest. *The Mystic Rose: A Study of Primitive Marriage*, London, Macmillan and Co., 1902.

Crawley, [Alfred] Ernest. *Studies of Savages and Sex*, edited by Theodore Besterman, London, Methuen & Co., Ltd., 1929.

Crawley, [Alfred] Ernest. *Dress, Drinks, and Drums: Further Studies of Savages and Sex*, edited by Theodore Besterman, London, Methuen & Co., Ltd., 1931.

[Crébillon, Claude-Prosper Jolyot de, le fils]. *Le Sopha, conte moral* [The sofa: moral tale], 2 vols., Gaznah, de l'imprimerie du Très-Pieux, Très-Clément & Très-Auguste Sultan des Indes, l'an de l'Hégire MCXX [Paris, ca. 1745]. English translation: *The Sofa: a Moral Tale*, translated and with an Introduction by Bonamy Dobrée, London, George Routledge & Sons, Ltd., 1927.

Croutier, Alev Lytle. *Harem: The World Behind the Veil*, New York, Abbeville Press, 1989.

[Crowley, Aleister (Edward Alexander)] Alain Lutiy [pseud.]. *The Scented Garden of Abdullah the Satirist of Shiraz*, London, Privately Printed, 1910. Reprint edition, with an Introduction by Martin P. Starr, Chicago, The Teitan Press, 1991.

Curtis, John. *Shipwreck of the Stirling Castle, Containing a Faithful Narrative of the Dreadful Sufferings of the Crew, and the Cruel Murder of Captain Fraser by the Savages; also, the Horrible Barbarity of the Cannibals Inflicted upon the Captain's Widow, whose Unparalleled Sufferings are Stated by Herself, and Corroborated by other Survivors*, London, George Virtue, 1838.

Dallaway, James. *Constantinople Ancient and Modern, with Excursions to the Shores and Islands of the Archipelago and to the Troad*, London, Printed by T. Bensley for T. Cadell Junior & W. Davies, 1797.

Daniel, Norman [A.] *Islam and the West: The Making of an Image*, Edinburgh, The University Press, 1960.

Daniel, Stephen H. "Reading Places: The Rhetorical Basis of Place," in *Commonplaces: Essays on the Nature of Place*, edited by David W. Black, Donald Kunze, and John Pickles, Lanham, New York, and London, University Press of America, 1989, pp. 17–23.

Das, Veena. "Gender Studies, Cross-Cultural Comparison, and the Colonial Organization of Knowledge," *Berkshire Review*, 21 (1986), pp. 58–76.

D'Astorg, Bertrand. *Les Noces orientales: Essai sur quelques formes féminines dans l'imaginaire occidental* [The oriental wedding: an essay on some feminine forms in the Western imagination], Paris, Éditions du Seuil, 1980.

David, Deirdre. "Children of Empire: Victorian Imperialism and Sexual Politics in Dickens and Kipling," in *Gender and Discourse in Victorian Literature and Art*, edited by Antony H. Harrison and Beverly Taylor, DeKalb, Northern Illinois University Press, 1992, pp. 124–42.

Davis, Fanny. *The Ottoman Lady: A Social History from 1718 to 1918*, New York, Westport, and London, Greenwood Press, 1986.

Deakin, Terence J. *Catalogi Librorum Eroticorum: A Critical Bibliography of Erotic Bibliographies and Book-Catalogues*, London, Cecil and Amelia Woolf, 1964.

Deane, Seamus. Introduction to *Nationalism, Colonialism, and Literature*, by Terry Eagleton, Fredric Jameson, and Edward W. Said, Minneapolis, University of Minnesota Press, 1990.

Decker, Jeffrey Louis. "Terrorism (Un)Veiled: Frantz Fanon and the Women of Algiers," *Cultural Critique*, 17, (1990–91), pp. 177–95.

De Groot, Joanna. " 'Sex' and 'Race': the Construction of Language and Image in the Nineteenth Century," in *Sexuality and Subordination: Interdisciplinary Studies of Gender in the Nineteenth Century*, edited by Susan Mendus and Jane Rendall, London and New York, Routledge, 1989, pp. 89–128.

Dehoï, Enver F. *L'Érotisme des "Mille et une nuits"* [The eroticism of the Thousand and One Nights], Paris, Jean-Jacques Pauvert, Éditeur, 1963.

De Lauretis, Teresa. "The Technology of Gender," *Technologies of Gender: Essays on Theory, Film, and Fiction*, Bloomington and Indianapolis, Indiana University Press, 1987, pp. 1–30.

De Leeuw, Hendrik. *Cities of Sin*, London, Neville Spearman, Ltd., 1953.

Del Piombo, Akbar [pseud. of Norman Rubington]. *Into the harem*, [New York], The Traveller's Companion, Inc. [The Olympia Press, Inc.], 1970.

De Martino, Ferdinando and Abdel-Khalek Bey Saroit (eds.). *Anthologie de l'amour arabe* [Anthology of Arabic love], with an Introduction by Pierre Louÿs, Paris, Société du Mercure de France, 1902.

Denis, Armand. *Taboo: Sex and Morality Around the World*, London, Four Square Books, 1967.

De Rachewiltz, Boris. *Black Eros: Sexual Customs of Africa from Prehistory to the Present Day*, translated by Peter Whigham, New York, Lyle Stuart, Inc., 1964.

Derounian-Stodola, Kathryn Zabelle and James Arthur Levernier. *The Indian Captivity Narrative, 1550–1900*, New York, Twayne Publishers, Toronto, Maxwell Macmillan Canada, Inc., 1993.

Derrida, Jacques. "Differance." *Speech and Phenomena, and Other Essays on Husserl's Theory of Signs*, translated and with an Introduction by David B. Allison, with a Preface by Newton Garver, Evanston, Northwestern University Press, 1973, pp. 129–60.

Derrida, Jacques. "Racism's Last Word," translated by Peggy Kamuf, in *'Race,' Writing, and Difference*, edited by Henry Louis Gates, Jr., Chicago and London, The University of Chicago Press, 1986, pp. 329–38.

Desmet-Grégoire, Hélène. "De la perception d'une femme ottomane à celle des femmes ottomanes: le récit de voyage d'une européenne du XIXe siècle, la princesse de Belgiojoso" [From the perception of an Ottoman woman to that of Ottoman women: the travelogue of a nineteenth-century European, the Princess of Belgiojoso], in *Contributions à l'histoire économique et sociale de l'Empire ottoman*, edited by Jean-Louis Bacqué-Grammont and Paul Dumont, Leuven, Éditions Peeters, 1983, pp. 429–49.

Devereaux, Charles, Captain [pseud. of Dan Harding?]. *Venus in India*, with an Introduction by Milton van Sickle, Los Angeles, Holloway House Publishing Co., 1967.

Diderot, Denis. "Supplément au Voyage de Bougainville" [Supplement to the *Voyage* of Bougainville], in *Opuscules philosophiques et littéraires, la plupart posthumes ou inédites*, edited by S.J. [Simon-Jacques] Bourlet de Vauxcelles and J.B.A. [Jean Baptiste Antoine] Suard, Paris, De l'Imprimerie de Chevet, 1796.

Diderot, Denis. "Les Bijoux indiscrets" [The indiscreet jewels], in *Œuvres romanesques*, edited by Henri Bénac and reviewed by Lucette Perol, Paris, Éditions Garnier Frères, 1981, pp. 1–233.

Dijkstra, Bram. *Idols of Perversity: Fantasies of Feminine Evil in Fin-de-Siècle Culture*, New York and Oxford, Oxford University Press, 1986.

Diprose, Rosalyn and Robyn Ferrell (eds.). *Cartographies: Poststructuralism and the Mapping of Bodies and Spaces*, Sydney, Allen & Unwin, 1991.

Doane, Mary Ann. *Femmes Fatales: Feminism, Film Theory, Psychoanalysis*, New York and London, Routledge, 1991.

Donaldson, Laura E. *Decolonizing Feminisms: Race, Gender, and Empire-Building*, Chapel Hill and London, The University of North Carolina Press, 1992.

[Donne, John]. *The Complete English Poems of John Donne*, edited by C.A. Patrides, London and Melbourne, J.M. Dent & Sons, Ltd., 1985.

Douthwaite, Julia V. *Exotic Women: Literary Heroines and Cultural Strategies in Ancien Régime France*, Philadelphia, University of Pennsylvania Press, 1992.

Doyle, Arthur Conan, [Sir]. *The Lost World*, New York, Hodder & Stoughton; George H. Doran Company, 1912.

Duben, Alan and Cem Behar. *Istanbul Households: Marriage, Family and Fertility, 1880–1940*, Cambridge, UK, Cambridge University Press, 1991.

Duchet, Michèle. *Anthropologie et histoire au siècle des lumières: Buffon, Voltaire, Rousseau, Helvétius, Diderot* [Anthropology and history in the Age of Enlightenment: Buffon, Voltaire, Rousseau, Helvétius, Diderot], Paris, François Maspero, 1971.

Dufrenoy, Marie-Louise. *L'Orient romanesque en France, 1704–1789: Étude d'histoire et de critique littéraires* [The romantic orient in France, 1704–89: a study in literary history and criticism], 2 vols., Montreal, Beauchemin, 1946–47.

Durel, Pétrus. *La Femme dans les colonies françaises: Étude sur les mœurs au point de vue myologique et social* [Women in the French colonies: a study of mores from a myological and social viewpoint], Paris, J. Dulon, 1898.

Edwardes, Allen. *The Jewel in the Lotus: A Historical Survey of the Sexual Culture of the East*, with an Introduction by Albert Ellis, New York, The Julian Press, Inc., 1959.

Edwardes, Allen. "A Historical Survey of Sex Savages and Sexual Savagery in the East," in *Sex Crimes in History: Evolving Concepts of Sadism, Lust-*

Murder, and Necrophilia—from Ancient to Modern Times, by R. [Robert] E.L. Masters and Eduard Lea, New York, The Julian Press, Inc., 1963, pp. 185–216.

Edwardes, Allen. *The Rape of India: a Biography of Robert Clive and a Sexual History of the Conquest of Hindustan,* New York, The Julian Press, Inc., 1966.

Edwardes, Allen and Robert E.L. Masters. *The Cradle of Erotica: A Study of Afro-Asian Sexual Expression and an Analysis of Erotic Freedom in Social Relationships,* New York, The Julian Press, Inc., 1963.

Edwards, Elizabeth (ed.). *Anthropology and Photography, 1860–1920,* New Haven and London, Yale University Press, London, The Royal Anthropological Institute, 1992.

Elisséeff, Nikita. *Thèmes et motifs des Mille et une nuits: Essai de classification* [Themes and motifs of the *Thousand and One Nights*: a taxonomic essay], Beirut, Institut Français de Damas, 1949.

Ellison, Grace. *An Englishwoman in a Turkish Harem,* with an Introduction by Edward G. Browne, London, Methuen & Co., Ltd., 1915.

Englisch, Paul. *Sittengeschichte des Orients* [Moral history of the Orient], Berlin, Kiepenheuer Verlag; Vienna, Phaidon Verlag, 1932.

Entrikin, J. Nicholas. *The Betweenness of Place: Towards a Geography of Modernity,* Baltimore, The Johns Hopkins University Press, 1991.

Erdem, Yahya. "18. Yüzyıl'da Avrupa'da Basılan Constantinople Rumuzlu Kitaplar" [Books bearing the Constantinople imprint published in Europe during the eighteenth century], *Müteferrika,* 5 (1995), pp. 17–41.

Everard, John. *Oriental Model,* with an Introduction and Commentary by Jane Everard, London, Robert Hale, Limited, 1955.

Fabian, Johannes. *Time and the Other: How Anthropology Makes Its Object,* New York, Columbia University Press, 1983.

Fanon, Frantz. *Studies in a Dying Colonialism,* translated by Haakon Chevalier, with an Introduction by Adolfo Gilly, New York, Monthly Review Press, [1965].

Fanon, Frantz. *Black Skin, White Masks,* translated by Charles Lam Markmann, New York, Grove Press, Inc., 1967.

Fanon, Frantz. *The Wretched of the Earth,* translated by Constance Farrington, with a Preface by Jean-Paul Sartre, New York, Grove Press, 1968.

[Fâzıl Hüseyin Bey, Enderunlu] Fazil-Bey. *Le Livre des femmes (Zenan-nameh)* [The book of women (*Zenânnâme*)], translated by J.-A. [Jean-Adolphe] Decourdemanche, Paris, Ernest Leroux, Éditeur, 1879. English translation in *Eastern Love*, edited and translated (from the French) by E. Powys Mathers, 3 vols., New York, Horace Liveright, London, J. Rodker, 1930, Vol. 1, pp. 145–95.

[Fâzıl Hüseyin Bey, Enderunlu] Fazil-Bey. *Le Livre des beaux* [The book of handsome men], translated and with an Introduction by "un pacha à trois queues" [Edmond Fazy?], Paris, Bibliothèque Internationale d'Édition, 1909.

Fazy, Edmond and Abdul-Halim Memdouh (eds.). *Anthologie de l'amour turc* [Anthology of Turkish love], Paris, Société du Mercure de France, 1905.

Fehlinger, H. [Hans]. *Sexual Life of Primitive People*, translated by S. [Solomon] Herbert and Mrs. S. [Fanny Segaller] Herbert, London, A. & C. Black, 1921.

Feret, Bill. *Lure of the Tropix: A Pictorial History of the Jungle Heroine, Jungle Queens, White Goddesses, Harem Girls and Huntresses*, London and New York, Proteus Books, 1984.

Ferguson, Adam. *An Essay on the History of Civil Society*, edited and with an Introduction by Duncan Forbes, Edinburgh, Edinburgh University Press, 1966.

Ferguson, Moira. *Colonialism and Gender Relations from Mary Wollstonecraft to Jamaica Kincaid: East Caribbean Connections*, New York, Columbia University Press, 1993.

Finck, Henry T. *Primitive Love and Love-Stories*, New York, Charles Scribner's Sons, 1899.

Fitzpatrick, William. *Istanbul After Dark*, New York, MacFadden-Bartell, 1970.

Flaherty, Gloria. "Sex and Shamanism in the Eighteenth Century," in *Sexual Underworlds of the Enlightenment*, edited by G.S. [George Sebastian] Rousseau and Roy Porter, Manchester and New York, Manchester University Press, 1990, pp. 261–80.

Flaubert, Gustave. *Sentimental Education; or, the History of a Young Man*, 2 vols., Akron, St Dunstan Society, 1904.

[Flaubert, Gustave]. *Flaubert in Egypt: A Sensibility on Tour. A Narrative*

Drawn from Gustave Flaubert's Travel Notes & Letters, translated and edited by Francis Steegmuller, London, Sydney, and Toronto, The Bodley Head Ltd., 1972.

Flaubert, Gustave. *Œuvres complètes illustrées de Gustave Flaubert: Correspondance* [The complete works of Gustave Flaubert, illustrated: correspondence], 4 vols., edited by René Descharmes, Paris, Librairie de France, 1922–25. English translation: *The Letters of Gustave Flaubert*, 2 vols., translated and edited by Francis Steegmuller, Cambridge, MA and London, The Belknap Press of Harvard University Press, 1980.

Forster, E.M. [Edward Morgan]. *A Passage to India*, New York, Harcourt, Brace & World, Inc., 1952.

Foucault, Michel. *Madness and Civilization: A History of Insanity in the Age of Reason*, translated by Richard Howard, New York, Pantheon Books, 1965.

Foucault, Michel. *The Archeology of Knowledge and the Discourse on Language*, translated by A.M. Sheridan Smith, New York, Pantheon Books, 1972.

Foucault, Michel. *The Order of Things: An Archaeology of the Human Sciences*, New York, Vintage Books, 1973.

Foucault, Michel. *The History of Sexuality*. Vol. I, *An Introduction*, translated by Robert Hurley, New York, Pantheon Books, 1978. Vol. II, *The Use of Pleasure*, translated by Robert Hurley, New York, Pantheon Books, 1985.

Foucault, Michel. "Questions on Geography," an interview by the editors of the journal *Hérodote*, translated by Colin Gordon, in *Power/Knowledge: Selected Interviews and Other Writings, 1972–1977*, edited by Colin Gordon, translated by Colin Gordon, Leo Marshall, John Mepham, and Kate Soper, New York, Pantheon Books, 1980a, pp. 63–77.

Foucault, Michel. "The Eye of Power," a conversation with Jean-Pierre Barou and Michelle Perrot, translated by Colin Gordon, in *Power/Knowledge: Selected Interviews and Other Writings, 1972–1977*, edited by Colin Gordon, translated by Colin Gordon, Leo Marshall, John Mepham, and Kate Soper, New York, Pantheon Books, 1980b, pp. 146–65.

Foucault, Michel. "Of Other Spaces," translated by Jay Miskowiec, in *Diacritics: A Review of Contemporary Criticism*, 16, 1 (1986), pp. 22–7.

Foucault, Michel. "Technologies of the Self," in *Technologies of the Self: A Seminar with Michel Foucault*, edited by Luther H. Martin, Huck Gutman, and Patrick H. Hutton, Amherst, The University of Massachusetts Press, 1988, pp. 16–49.

France, Hector. *Musk, Hashish and Blood*, London and Paris, Printed for Subscribers Only, 1900.

France, Hector. *The Amatory Adventures of Sheik Mansour, a Master of the Art of Love*, [translated by A.R. (Alfred Richard) Allinson?], New York, Jul-Mar Press, 1932.

Fredrickson, George M. *The Black Image in the White Mind: The Debate on Afro-American Character and Destiny, 1817–1914*, New York, Hagerstown, San Francisco, and London, Harper & Row, Publishers, 1972.

Freud, Sigmund. "The Question of Lay Analysis," in *The Standard Edition of the Complete Psychological Works of Sigmund Freud*, translated under the general editorship of James Strachey in collaboration with Anna Freud, assisted by Alix Strachey and Alan Tyson, 24 vols., London, The Hogarth Press and the Institute of Psycho-Analysis, 1953–74, Vol. 20, pp. 183–250.

Freud, Sigmund. *Civilization and Its Discontents*, translated and edited by James Strachey, New York, W.W. Norton & Company, Inc., 1961.

Friedenthal, Albert. *Das Weib im Leben der Völker* [Woman in the life of nations], 2 vols., Berlin, Verlagsanstalt für Litteratur und Kunst, ca. 1910.

Friedman, John Block. *The Monstrous Races in Medieval Art and Thought*, Cambridge, MA and London, Harvard University Press, 1981.

Fromaget, Nicolas. *Eunuchs, Odalisques and Love: a Frenchman's Amatory Adventures in Turkey*, with an Introduction by Winifred Moroney, New York, The Panurge Press, 1932.

Fuss, Diana. "Interior Colonies: Frantz Fanon and the Politics of Identification," *Diacritics*, 24, 2–3 (1994), pp. 20–42.

Gallop, Jane. "Snatches of Conversation," in *Women and Language in Literature and Society*, edited by Sally McConnell-Ginet, Ruth Borker, and Nelly Furman, New York, Praeger Publishers, 1980, pp. 274–83.

Garber, Marjorie. *Vested Interests: Cross-Dressing and Cultural Anxiety*, New York and London, Routledge, 1992.

[Gauthier-Villars, Henry] Willy and Pol Prille. *Les Bazars de la volupté* [The bazaars of voluptuousness], Paris, Éditions Montaigne, 1926.

[Gay, Jules] C. D'I***. *Bibliographie des ouvrages relatifs à l'amour, aux femmes, au mariage, et des livres facétieux pantagruéliques, scatologiques, satyriques, etc.* [Bibliography of works concerning love, women, marriage, and of facetious, Pantagruelian, scatological, satyrical, etc. books], 4 vols., expanded and edited by J. Lemonnyer, Paris, J. Lemonnyer, Éditeur, and Ch. Gilliet, Libraire, 1894; Lille, Stéphane Becour, Libraire, 1897–1900.

Gay, Peter. *The Bourgeois Experience: Victoria to Freud*, 3 vols., New York and Oxford, Oxford University Press, 1984–86; W.W. Norton, 1993.

Gaya, [Louis de]. *Marriage Ceremonies, as Now Used in All Parts of the World*, London, John Nutt, 1704.

Gerhardt, Mia I. *The Art of Story-Telling: A Literary Study of the Thousand and One Nights*, Leiden, E.J. Brill, 1963.

Gilman, Sander L. *Difference and Pathology: Stereotypes of Sexuality, Race, and Madness*, Ithaca and London, Cornell University Press, 1985.

Gilman, Sander L. *Sexuality: An Illustrated History, Representing the Sexual in Medicine and Culture from the Middle Ages to the Age of AIDS*, New York, John Wiley & Sons, 1989.

Gilman, Sander L. "Plague in Germany, 1939/1989: Cultural Images of Race, Space, and Disease," in *Nationalisms and Sexualities*, edited by Andrew Parker, Mary Russo, Doris Sommer, and Patricia Yaeger, New York and London, Routledge, 1992, pp. 175–200.

Girodias, Maurice (ed.). *The Olympia Reader: Selections from the Traveller's Companion Series*, New York, Ballantine Books, 1967.

Glover, David. "'Dark Enough fur Any Man': Bram Stoker's Sexual Ethnology and the Question of Irish Nationalism," in *Late Imperial Culture*, edited by Román De la Campa, E. Ann Kaplan, and Michael Sprinker, London and New York, Verso, 1995, pp. 53–71.

Gobineau, A. [Joseph Arthur] de. *Trois ans en Asie (de 1855 à 1858)* [Three years in Asia, from 1855 to 1858], Paris, Librairie de L. Hachette et Cie., 1859.

[Godard d'Aucour, Claude] Achmet Dely-Azet. *Mémoires turcs, avec l'histoire galante de leur séjour en France, par un auteur Turc de toutes les Académies Mahométanes, licencié en droit Turc, & Maître-ès-Arts de l'Université de Constantinople* [Turkish memoirs, with the gallant story of their stay in France, by a Turkish author of all the Mohammedan academies, certified in Turkish law, Master of Arts from the University of Constantinople], 3 vols. in 1, La Haye, Chez Isaac Beauregard, 1743.

Godlewska, Anne and Neil Smith (eds.). *Geography and Empire*, Oxford and Cambridge, MA, Blackwell Publishers, 1994.

Goffman, Erving. *The Presentation of Self in Everyday Life*, New York, Doubleday Anchor Books, 1959.

Goldberg, David Theo. *Racist Culture: Philosophy and the Politics of Meaning*, Oxford and Cambridge, MA, Blackwell Publishers, 1993.

Goldsmith, Oliver. *The Citizen of the World*, 2 vols., edited by Austin Dobson, London, J.M. Dent and Co., 1891.

Goodland, Roger. *A Bibliography of Sex Rites and Customs: An Annotated Record of Books, Articles, and Illustrations in All Languages*, London, George Routledge & Sons, Ltd., 1931.

Gouda, Frances. "*Nyonyas* on the Colonial Divide: White Women in the Dutch East Indies, 1900–1942," *Gender & History*, 5, 3 (1993), pp. 318–42.

Goulemot, Jean Marie. *Ces livres qu'on ne lit que d'une main: Lecture et lecteurs de livres pornographiques au XVIIIe siècle* [Those books that are read with one hand only: reading and readers of pornographic books in the eighteenth century], Aix-en-Provence, Éditions Alinea, 1991.

Gourdault, Jules. *La Femme dans tous les pays* [Woman in all countries], Paris, Jouvet et Cie, Libraires, Éditeurs, 1882.

Gove, Philip Babcock. *The Imaginary Voyage in Prose Fiction: a History of its Criticism and a Guide for its Study, with an Annotated Check List of 215 Imaginary Voyages from 1700 to 1800*, London, The Holland Press, 1961.

Granamour, A. de [pseud. of Paul Little]. *Turkish Delights*, n.p., Venus Editions, 1973.

Grandjean, Georges. *L'Amour en Islam* [Love in Islam], Paris, Société française d'éditions littéraires et techniques, Edgar Malfère, Directeur, 1931.

Green, Martin. *Dreams of Adventure, Deeds of Empire*, New York, Basic Books, Inc., 1979.

Greenberg, Mitchell. "Racine's *Bérénice*: Orientalism and the Allegory of Absolutism," *L'Esprit créateur*, 32, 3 (1992), pp. 75–86.

Gregory, Derek. *Geographical Imaginations*, Cambridge, MA and Oxford, Blackwell, 1994.

Grewal, Inderpal and Caren Kaplan (eds.). *Scattered Hegemonies: Postmodernity and Transnational Feminist Practices*, Minneapolis and London, University of Minnesota Press, 1994.

Grosrichard, Alain. *Structure du sérail: La fiction du despotisme asiatique dans l'Occident classique* [Structure of the seraglio: the fiction of asiatic despotism in the classical West], Paris, Éditions du Seuil, 1979.

Grosz, Elizabeth. "Inscriptions and Body-Maps: Representations and the Corporeal," in *Feminine/Masculine and Representation*, edited by Terry Threadgold and Anne Cranny-Francis, Sydney, London, Boston, and Wellington, Allen & Unwin, 1990, pp. 62–74.

Guiraud, Pierre. *Dictionnaire historique, stylistique, rhétorique, étymologique, de la littérature érotique; précédé d'une introduction sur les structures étymologiques du vocabulaire érotique* [Historical, stylistic, rhetorical, etymological dictionary of the erotic literature; preceded by an introduction on the etymological structures of the erotic vocabulary], Paris, Payot, 1978.

Habesci, Elias. *The Present State of the Ottoman Empire, Containing a More Accurate and Interesting Account of the Religion, Government, Military Establishment, Manners, Customs, and Amusements of the Turks than Any Yet Extant: Including a Particular Description of the Court and Seraglio of the Grand Signor*, London, R. Baldwin, 1784.

Haggard, H. [Henry] Rider. *The Favorite Novels of H. Rider Haggard*, New York, Blue Ribbon Books, Inc., 1928.

Hakluyt, Richard. *The Principal Navigations, Voiages, Traffiques and Discoveries of the English Nation, made by Sea or Over-Land, to the Remote and Farthest Distant Quarters of the Earth at any Time within the Compasse of these 1600 yeeres [. . .]*, 3 vols., London, George Bishop, Ralph Newberie and Robert Barker, 1598.

Hall, C. Michael. "Sex Tourism in South-East Asia," in *Tourism and the Less Developed Countries*, edited by David Harrison, London, Belhaven Press, New York and Toronto, Halstead Press, 1992, pp. 64–74.

Hall, Kim F. "'I Rather Would Wish to be a Black-Moor': Beauty, Race, and Rank in Lady Mary Wroth's *Urania*," in *Women, 'Race,' and Writing in the Early Modern Period*, edited by Margo Hendricks and Patricia Parker, London and New York, Routledge, 1994, pp. 178–94, 335–39.

Hampton, Timothy. "'Turkish Dogs': Rabelais, Erasmus, and the Rhetoric of Alterity," *Representations*, 41 (1993), pp. 58–82.

Hansen, Christian, Catherine Needham, and Bill Nichols. "Skin Flicks: Pornography, Ethnography, and the Discourses of Power," *Discourse*, 11, 2 (1989), pp. 65–79.

Harbison, Robert. *Eccentric Spaces*, New York, Alfred A. Knopf, 1977.

Harbsmeier, Michael. "On Travel Accounts and Cosmological Strategies: Some Models in Comparative Xenology," *Ethnos*, 50, 3–4 (1985), pp. 273–312.

Hardy, E.J. [Edward John]. *The Unvarying East: Modern Scenes and Ancient Scriptures*, New York, Charles Scribner's Sons, London, T. Fisher Unwin, 1912.

Harley, J.B. [John Brian]. "Maps, Knowledge, and Power," in *The Iconography of Landscape: Essays on the Symbolic Representation, Design and Use of Past Environments*, edited by Denis Cosgrove and Stephen Daniels, Cambridge, UK, Cambridge University Press, 1988, pp. 277–312.

Harris, Walter B. *The Land of an African Sultan: Travels in Morocco, 1887, 1888 and 1889*, London, Sampson Low, Marston, Searle & Rivington, 1889.

Harrison, Brian. *Separate Spheres: the Opposition to Women's Suffrage in Britain*, London, Croom Helm, 1978.

Hart, Lynda. *Fatal Women: Lesbian Sexuality and the Mark of Aggression*, Princeton, Princeton University Press, 1994.

Hartley, L.P. [Leslie Poles]. *The Go-Between*, New York, Alfred A. Knopf, 1954.

Hartog, François. *The Mirror of Herodotus: The Representation of the Other in the Writing of History*, translated by Janet Lloyd, Berkeley, Los Angeles, and London, University of California Press, 1988.

Harvey, David. "Class Relations, Social Justice and the Politics of Difference," in *Place and the Politics of Identity*, edited by Michael Keith and Steve Pile, London and New York, Routledge, 1993, pp. 41–66.

Hawley, John Stratton (ed.). *Sati: The Blessing and the Curse. The Burning of Wives in India*, New York and Oxford, Oxford University Press, 1994.

Heldreth, Leonard G. "Close Encounters of the Carnal Kind: Sex with Aliens in Science Fiction," in *Erotic Universe: Sexuality and Fantastic Literature*, edited by Donald Palumbo, New York, Westport, and London, Greenwood Press, 1986, pp. 131–44.

Hendricks, Margo and Patricia Parker (eds.). *Women, 'Race,' and Writing in the Early Modern Period*, London and New York, Routledge, 1994.

Hennessy, Rosemary and Rajeswari Mohan. "The Construction of Woman in Three Popular Texts of Empire: Towards a Critique of Materialist Feminism," *Textual Practice*, 3, 3 (1989), pp. 323–59.

Henriques, Fernando. *Children of Caliban: Miscegenation*, London, Secker & Warburg, 1974.

Hernton, Calvin C. *Sex and Racism in America*, Garden City, Doubleday & Company, Inc., 1965.

Herzog, Kristin. *Women, Ethnics, and Exotics: Images of Power in Mid-Nineteenth-Century American Fiction*, Knoxville, University of Tennessee Press, 1983.

Hesse, Barnor. "Black to Front and Black Again: Racialization through Contested Times and Spaces," in *Place and the Politics of Identity*, edited by Michael Keith and Steve Pile, London and New York, Routledge, 1993, pp. 162–82.

Higginbotham, Evelyn Brooks. "African-American Women's History and the Meta-language of Race," in *Revising the Word and the World: Essays in Feminist Literary Criticism*, edited by VèVè A. Clark, Ruth-Ellen B. Joeres, and Madelon Sprengnether, Chicago and London, The University of Chicago Press, 1993, pp. 91–114.

Hill, Aaron. *A Full and Just Account of the Present State of the Ottoman Empire in All its Branches: with the Government, and Policy, Religion, Customs, and Way of Living of the Turks, in General, Faithfully Related from a Serious Observation, taken in Many Years Travels thro' those Countries*, London, John Mayo, 1709.

Hill, Gillian. *Cartographical Curiosities*, London, Published for The British Library by British Museum Publications Ltd., 1978.

Hippocrates. *Airs Waters Places*, translated by W.H.S. Jones, in [Collected Works], 4 vols., Cambridge, MA, Harvard University Press; London, William Heinemann Ltd., 1923–28, Vol. 1, pp. 65–137.

Hirschfeld, Magnus. *Men and Women: The World Journey of a Sexologist*, New York, G.P. Putnam's Sons, 1935.

Hodes, Martha. "The Sexualization of Reconstruction Politics: White Women and Black Men in the South after the Civil War," *Journal of the History of Sexuality*, 3, 3 (1993), pp. 402–17.

Hodgen, Margaret T. *Early Anthropology in the Sixteenth and Seventeenth Centuries*, Philadelphia, University of Pennsylvania Press, 1964.

hooks, bell [pseud. of Gloria Watkins]. "Choosing the Margin as a Space of Radical Openness," *Yearning: Race, Gender, and Cultural Politics*, Boston, South End Press, 1990, pp. 145–53.

Houghton, Walter E. *The Victorian Frame of Mind, 1830–70*, New Haven, published for Wellesley College by Yale University Press; London, Oxford University Press, 1957.

Howard, Jean E. "An English Lass Amid the Moors: Gender, Race, Sexuality, and National Identity in Heywood's *The Fair Maid of the West*," in *Women, 'Race,' and Writing in the Early Modern Period*, edited by Margo Hendricks and Patricia Parker, London and New York, Routledge, 1994, pp. 101–17, 321–3.

Huart, Annabelle d' and Nadia Tazi. *Harems*, with a Preface by Lawrence Durrell, Paris, Éditions du Chêne/Hachette, 1980.

Huggan, Graham. "Decolonizing the Map: Post-Colonialism, Post-Structuralism and the Cartographic Connection," in *Past the Last Post: Theorizing Post-Colonialism and Post-Modernism*, edited by Ian Adam and Helen Tiffin, Calgary, University of Calgary Press, 1990, pp. 125–38.

Hughes-Hallett, Lucy. *Cleopatra: Histories, Dreams and Distortions*, New York, Harper & Row, Publishers, 1990.

Hull, E.M. [Edith Maude]. *The Sheik: A Novel*, Boston, Small, Maynard & Company, Publishers, 1921.

Hulme, Peter. "Polytropic Man: Tropes of Sexuality and Mobility in Early Colonial Discourse," in *Europe and its Others: Proceedings of the Essex Conference on the Sociology of Literature, July 1984*, edited by Francis Barker, Peter Hulme, Margaret Iversen, and Diana Loxley, 2 vols., Colchester, University of Essex, 1985, Vol. 2, pp. 17–32.

Hulme, Peter. *Colonial Encounters: Europe and the Native Caribbean, 1492–1797*, London and New York, Routledge, 1992.

Hunt, Lynn (ed.). *Eroticism and the Body Politic*, Baltimore and London, The Johns Hopkins University Press, 1991.

Hurley, Kelly. " 'The Inner Chambers of All Nameless Sin': *The Beetle*, Gothic Female Sexuality, and Oriental Barbarism," in *Virginal Sexuality and Textuality in Victorian Literature*, edited by Lloyd Davis, Albany, State University of New York Press, 1993, pp. 193–213.

Husserl, Edmund. *The Crisis of European Sciences and Transcendental Phenomenology: An Introduction to Phenomenological Philosophy*, translated by David Carr, Evanston, Northwestern University Press, 1970.

Hyam, Ronald. *Empire and Sexuality: The British Experience*, Manchester and New York, Manchester University Press, 1990.

Ilex, E. [pseud. of Emile Duhousset?]. *Mœurs orientales: Les Huis-clos de l'ethnographie* [Oriental mores: the closed doors of ethnography], London, Imprimerie particulière de la Société d'Anthropologie et d'Ethnologie Comparées, 1878.

Ingilis, Amirah. *The White Women's Protection Ordinance: Sexual Anxiety and Politics in Papua*, New York, St. Martin's Press, 1975.

Jackson, Peter. *Maps of Meaning: An Introduction to Cultural Geography*, London, Unwin Hyman, 1989.

Jacob, Margaret C. "The Materialist World of Pornography," in *The Invention of Pornography: Obscenity and the Origins of Modernity, 1500–1800*, edited by Lynn Hunt, New York, Zone Books, 1993, pp. 157–202.

Jacobus X [pseud.]. *Untrodden Fields of Anthropology: Observations on the Esoteric Manners and Customs of Semi-Civilized Peoples; Being a Record of Thirty Years' Experience in Asia, Africa, America and Oceania by a French Army Surgeon*, 2 vols., Paris, Charles Carrington, 1898.

Jameson, Fredric. *The Political Unconscious: Narrative as a Socially Symbolic Act*, Ithaca, Cornell University Press, 1981.

Jameson, Fredric. *Postmodernism, or, the Cultural Logic of High Capitalism*, Durham, Duke University Press, 1991.

JanMohamed, Abdul R. "The Economy of Manichean Allegory: The Function of Racial Difference in Colonialist Literature," in *'Race,' Writing, and Difference*, edited by Henry Louis Gates, Jr., Chicago and London, The University of Chicago Press, 1986, pp. 78–106.

JanMohamed, Abdul R. "Sexuality on/of the Racial Border: Foucault,

Wright, and the Articulation of 'Racialized Sexuality'," in *Discourses of Sexuality: From Aristotle to AIDS*, edited by Domna C. Stanton, Ann Arbor, The University of Michigan Press, 1992, pp. 94–116.

Jay, Nancy. "Gender and Dichotomy," *Feminist Studies*, 7, 1 (1981), pp. 38–56.

Jones, Ann Rosalind and Peter Stallybrass. "Dismantling Irena: The Sexualizing of Ireland in Early Modern England," in *Nationalisms and Sexualities*, edited by Andrew Parker, Mary Russo, Doris Sommer, and Patricia Yaeger, New York and London, Routledge, 1992, pp. 157–71.

Jordan, Winthrop. *White Over Black: American Attitudes Towards the Negro*, Chapel Hill, University of North Carolina Press, 1968.

Joyce, T. Athol and N.W. [Northcote Whitridge] Thomas. *Women of All Nations: A Record of their Characteristics, Habits, Manners, Customs, and Influence*, London and New York, Cassell and Company, Ltd., 1908.

Kabbani, Rana. *Europe's Myths of Orient*, Bloomington, Indiana University Press, 1986.

[Kalyāna Mall]. *Ananga-Ranga; (Stage of the Bodiless One) or, the Hindu Art of Love (Ars Amoris Indica)*, translated and annotated by A.F.F. [Forster Fitzgerald Arbuthnot] and B.F.R. [Richard F. Burton], Cosmopoli, for the Kama Shastra Society of London and Benares, 1885.

Kanneh, Kadiatu. "The Difficult Politics of Wigs and Veils: Feminism and the Colonial Body," paper presented at the Conference on Gender and Colonialism, University College, Galway, May 1992. Published in part in *The Post-Colonial Studies Reader*, edited by Bill Ashcroft, Gareth Griffiths, and Helen Tiffin, London and New York, Routledge, 1995, pp. 346–8.

Kaplan, Caren. "'Getting to Know You': Travel, Gender, and the Politics of Representation in *Anna and the King of Siam* and *The King and I*," in *Late Imperial Culture*, edited by Román De la Campa, E. Ann Kaplan, and Michael Sprinker, London and New York, Verso, 1995, pp. 33–52.

Kaplan, Cora. "Pandora's Box: Subjectivity, Class and Sexuality in Socialist Feminist Criticism," in *Making a Difference: Feminist Literary Criticism*, edited by Gayle Greene and Coppélia Kahn, London and New York, Methuen, 1985, pp. 146–76.

Kappler, Claude. *Monstres, démons et merveilles à la fin du Moyen Age*

[Monsters, demons, and marvels at the end of the Middle Ages], Paris, Payot, 1980.

Kearney, Patrick J. *The Private Case: An Annotated Bibliography of the Private Case Erotica Collection in the British (Museum) Library*, with an Introduction by G. [Gershon] Legman, London, Jay Landesman, Limited, 1981.

Keith, Michael and Steve Pile (eds.). *Place and the Politics of Identity*, London and New York, Routledge, 1993.

Keith, W.J. [William John]. *Regions of the Imagination: The Development of British Rural Fiction*, Toronto, Buffalo, and London, University of Toronto Press, 1988.

Kelly, Joan. "The Doubled Vision of Feminist Theory: A Postscript to the 'Women and Power' Conference," *Women, History, & Theory: the Essays of Joan Kelly*, Chicago and London, The University of Chicago Press, 1984, pp. 51–64.

[Kemâl Paşa Zâde Şemseddin Ahmed bin Süleyman (a.k.a. İbn-i Kemâl Paşa), possibly translated from Tīfāshī]. *The Old Man Young Again, or Age-Rejuvenescence in the Power of Concupiscence (Kitab Ruju'a as-Shaykh ila Sabah Fi-l-Kuwwat 'ala-l-Bah)* [*Kitāb Rudjū' ash-Shaykh ilā Sabāh fī'l-Quwwah 'alā'l-Bāh*], translated, annotated, and with a Foreword by an English "Bohemian," Paris, Charles Carrington, 1898.

Kerr, Robert. *A General History and Collection of Voyages and Travels, Arranged in Systematic Order; Forming a Complete History of the Origin and Progress of Navigation, Discovery and Commerce, by Sea and Land, from the Earliest Ages to the Present Time*, 18 vols., Edinburgh and London, W. Blackwood and T. Cadell, 1811–24.

Kiernan, V.G. [Victor Gordon]. *The Lords of Human Kind: Black Man, Yellow Man, and White Man in an Age of Empire*, Boston and Toronto, Little, Brown and Company, 1969.

Kincaid, James R. *Child-Loving: The Victorian Child and Victorian Culture*, New York and London, Routledge, 1992.

Kipling, Rudyard. *Plain Tales from the Hills*, New York, Charles Scribner's Sons, 1899.

Kipling, Rudyard. *Kim*, London, Macmillan and Co., Ltd., 1901.

Kleinlogel, Cornelia. *Exotik-Erotik: Zur Geschichte des Türkenbildes in der deutschen Literatur der frühen Neuzeit (1453–1800)* [Exotic-Erotic: on the history of the image of the Turk in German literature during the early modern period, 1453–1800], Frankfurt am Main, Bern, New York, and Paris, Verlag Peter Lang, 1989.

Knibiehler, Yvonne and Régine Goutalier. *La Femme au temps des colonies* [Woman in the times of the colonies], Paris, Éditions Stock, 1985.

Kolodny, Annette. *The Lay of the Land: Metaphor as Experience and History in American Life and Letters*, Chapell Hill, The University of North Carolina Press, 1975.

Kunze, Donald. *Thought and Place: The Architecture of Eternal Place in the Philosophy of Giambattista Vico*, New York, Bern, Frankfurt am Main, and Paris, Peter Lang, 1987.

Kuoh-Moukoury, Thérèse. *Les Couples dominos* [Domino couples], Paris, Julliard, 1973.

Laclau, Ernesto. *Politics and Ideology in Marxist Theory: Capitalism–Fascism–Populism*, London, NLB [New Left Books]; Atlantic Highlands, Humanities Press, 1977.

Laclau, Ernesto. *New Reflections on the Revolution of Our Time*, London and New York, Verso, 1990.

Lafitau, [Joseph-François]. *Mœurs des sauvages ameriquains, comparées aux mœurs des premiers temps* [Mores of the American savages, compared to the mores of the earliest times], 2 vols., Paris, Saugrain l'Aîné & Charles Estienne Hochereau, 1724.

[La Mesnardière, Hippolyte Jules Pilet de]. *La Poëtique de Jules de la Mesnardière* [The Poetics of Jules de la Mesnardière], Paris, Antoine de Sommaville, 1640.

[La Roche-Guilhem, Mlle. de] Mademoiselle D***. *Histoire des favorites, contenant ce qui c'est passé de plus remarquable sous plusieurs régnes* [History of the favorites, containing the most remarkable events that occurred under several reigns], Amsterdam, Paul Marret, 1697.

Laubscher, B.J.F. [Barend Jacob Frederick]. *Sex, Custom and Psychopathology: A Study of South African Pagan Natives*, London, George Routledge & Sons Ltd., 1937.

Lavrin, Asunción (ed.). *Sexuality and Marriage in Colonial Latin America*, Lincoln and London, University of Nebraska Press, 1989.

Lawrence, T.E. [Thomas Edward]. *Seven Pillars of Wisdom: A Triumph*, Garden City, Doubleday & Company, Inc., 1938.

Lawrence, T.E. [Thomas Edward]. *The Mint: Notes Made in the R.A.F. Depot between August and December, 1922, and at Cadet College in 1925*, New York, W.W. Norton & Company, Inc., 1963.

[Le Camus, Antoine]. *Abdeker, or The Art of Preserving Beauty*, London, Printed for A. Millar, 1754.

Le Corbeiller, Clare. "Miss America and Her Sisters: Personifications of the Four Parts of the World," *The Metropolitan Museum of Art Bulletin*, 19, 8 (1961), pp. 208–23.

Leed, Eric J. *The Mind of the Traveler: From Gilgamesh to Global Tourism*, n.p., Basic Books, 1991.

Lefebvre, Henri. *The Production of Space*, translated by Donald Nicholson-Smith, Oxford and Cambridge, MA, Blackwell, 1991.

Legh-Jones, Alison. *English Woman Arab Man*, London, Paul Elek, 1975.

Legman, G. [Gershon]. *The Horn Book: Studies in Erotic Folklore and Bibliography*, New Hyde Park, University Books Inc., 1964.

Le Rouge, Gustave [pseud. of Georges Grassal]. *Encyclopédie de l'amour: Turquie. Mariage, adultère, prostitution, psychologie de l'eunuchisme. Anthologie* [Encyclopedia of Love: Turkey. Marriage, adultery, prostitution, psychology of eunuchism. Anthology], Paris, H. Daragon Libraire-Éditeur, 1912.

Levine, Philippa. "Venereal Disease, Prostitution, and the Politics of Empire: The Case of British India," *Journal of the History of Sexuality*, 4, 4 (1994), 579–602.

Levy, Anita. *Other Women: The Writing of Class, Race, and Gender, 1832–1898*, Princeton, Princeton University Press, 1991.

Lew, Joseph W. "Lady Mary's Portable Seraglio," *Eighteenth-Century Studies*, 24, 4 (1991), pp. 432–50.

Lewis, Bernard. *The Muslim Discovery of Europe*, New York and London, W.W. Norton & Company, 1982.

[Linné, Carl von]. *The Elements of Botany: Containing the History of the Science; with Accurate Definitions of all the Terms of Art, [. . .] the Theory of Vegetables; the Scientific Arrangement of Plants, and Names used in Botany; Rules Concerning the General History, Virtues, and Uses of Plants. Being a Translation of the "Philosophia Botanica," and other Treatises of the celebrated Linnæus. To which is added an Appendix, wherein are Described some Plants lately found in Norfolk and Suffolk [. . .]*, translated by Hugh Rose, London, T. Cadell, 1775.

Livingstone, Daniel N. "Climate's Moral Economy: Science, Race and Place in Post-Darwinian British and American Geography," in *Geography and Empire*, edited by Anne Godlewska and Neil Smith, Oxford and Cambridge, MA, Blackwell Publishers, 1994, pp. 132–54.

Löbel, D. Theophil. *Hochzeitsbräuche in der Türkei* [Marriage customs in Turkey], with an Introduction by H. [Hermann, or Arminius] Vambéry, Amsterdam, J.H. de Bussy, 1897.

Lockwood, Vere. *Son of the Turk*, condensed by Barbara Cartland, New York, Toronto, and London, Bantam Books, 1980.

Lo Duca, [Giuseppe]. *Die Erotik im fernen Osten* [The erotic in the Far East], Basel, Verlag Kurt Desch, 1969.

Lorimer, Douglas A. *Colour, Class and the Victorians: English Attitudes to the Negro in the Mid-Nineteenth Century*, [Leicester], Leicester University Press; New York, Holmes & Meier Publishers, Inc., 1978.

Loti, Pierre [pseud. of Julien Viaud]. *Disenchanted (Désenchantées)*, translated by Clara Bell, New York and London, The Macmillan Company, 1912.

Loti, Pierre [pseud. of Julien Viaud]. *The Romance of a Spahi*, translated by G.F. Monkshood, New York, Brentano's, 1930.

Low, Gail Ching-Liang. "His Stories?: Narratives and Images of Imperialism," in *Space and Place: Theories of Identity and Location*, edited by Erica Carter, James Donald, and Judith Squires, London, Lawrence & Wishart, 1993a, pp. 187–219.

Low, Gail Ching-Liang. "White Skins/Black Masks: The Pleasures and Politics of Imperialism," in *Space and Place: Theories of Identity and Location*, edited by Erica Carter, James Donald, and Judith Squires, London, Lawrence & Wishart, 1993b, pp. 241–66.

Lowe, Lisa. *Critical Terrains: French and British Orientalisms*, Ithaca and London, Cornell University Press, 1991.

Lowenthal, David. *The Past is a Foreign Country*, Cambridge, UK, Cambridge University Press, 1985.

Luebbers, Leslie. "Documenting the Invisible: European Images of Ottoman Women, 1567–1867," *The Print Collector's Newsletter*, 24, 1 (1993), pp. 1–7.

Lutwack, Leonard. *The Role of Place in Literature*, Syracuse, Syracuse University Press, 1984.

Lutz, Catherine A. and Jane L. Collins. *Reading "National Geographic"*, Chicago and London, The University of Chicago Press, 1993.

Mabro, Judy (ed.). *Veiled Half-Truths: Western Travellers' Perceptions of Middle Eastern Women*, London and New York, I.B. Tauris & Co. Ltd., Publishers, 1991.

Maccagnani, Roberta. "Esotismo-Erotismo. Pierre Loti: dalla Maschera Esotica alla Sovranità Coloniale" [Exoticism-Eroticism. Pierre Loti: from exotic mask to colonial rule], in *Letterature, Esotismo, Colonialismo*, by Anita Licari, Roberta Maccagnani, and Lina Zecchi, with an Introduction by Gianni Celati, Bologna, Capelli Editore, 1978, pp. 63–99.

MacKenzie, John M. *Orientalism: History, Theory and the Arts*, Manchester and New York, Manchester University Press, 1995.

MacKenzie, John M. (ed.). *Imperialism and Popular Culture*, Manchester, UK and Dover, NH, Manchester University Press, 1986.

Makdisi, Saree S. "The Empire Renarrated: *Season of Migration to the North* and the Reinvention of the Present," in *Colonial Discourse and Post-Colonial Theory: A Reader*, edited by Patrick Williams and Laura Chrisman, New York, Columbia University Press, 1994, pp. 535–50.

Malinowski, Bronislaw. *The Sexual Life of Savages in North-Western Melanesia: An Ethnographic Account of Courtship, Marriage and Family Life Among the Natives of the Trobriand Islands, British New Guinea*, with a Preface by Havelock Ellis, New York, Halcyon Press, [1929?].

Malleret, Louis. *L'Exotisme indochinois dans la littérature française depuis 1860* [Indochinese exoticism in French literature since 1860], Paris, Larose Éditeurs, 1934.

Malti-Douglas, Fedwa. *Woman's Body, Woman's Word: Gender and Discourse in Arabo-Islamic Writing*, Princeton, Princeton University Press, 1991.

Mandel, Gabriele. *Oriental Erotica*, translated by Evelyn Rossiter, Ware, Omega Books, 1983.

Manganyi, N. Chabani. "Making Strange: Race, Science and Ethnopsychiatric Discourse," in *Europe and its Others: Proceedings of the Essex Conference on the Sociology of Literature, July 1984*, edited by Francis Barker, Peter Hulme, Margaret Iversen, and Diana Loxley, 2 vols., Colchester, University of Essex, 1985, Vol. 1, pp. 152–69.

Mani, Lata. "The Production of an Official Discourse on *Sati* in Early Nineteenth-Century Bengal," in *Europe and its Others: Proceedings of the Essex Conference on the Sociology of Literature, July 1984*, edited by Francis Barker, Peter Hulme, Margaret Iversen, and Diana Loxley, 2 vols., Colchester, University of Essex, 1985, Vol. 1, pp. 107–27.

Mani, Lata. "Contentious Traditions: The Debate on *Sati* in Colonial India," in *Recasting Women: Essays in Colonial History*, edited by Kumkum Sangari and Sudesh Vaid, New Delhi, Kali for Women, 1989, pp. 88–126.

Mani, Lata and Ruth Frankenberg. "The Challenge of *Orientalism*," *Economy and Society*, 14, 2 (1985), pp. 174–92.

Mannoni, O. [Octave]. *Prospero and Caliban: The Psychology of Colonization*, translated by Pamela Powesland, with a Foreword by Maurice Bloch, [Ann Arbor], The University of Michigan Press, 1990.

Mannsåker, Frances. "Elegancy and Wildness: Reflections of the East in the Eighteenth-Century Imagination," in *Exoticism in the Enlightenment*, edited by G.S. [George Sebastian] Rousseau and Roy Porter, Manchester and New York, Manchester University Press, 1990, pp. 175–95.

Mantegazza, Paolo. *Anthropological Studies of Sexual Relations of Mankind*, translated by James Bruce, New York, Anthropological Press, 1932.

[Marana, Giovanni Paolo]. *The First Volume of Letters Writ by a Turkish Spy, who Lived Five and Forty Years, Undiscover'd at Paris*, London, Henry Rhodes, 1691.

Marchitello, Howard. "Political Maps: The Production of Cartography and Chorography in Early Modern England," in *Cultural Artifacts and the Production of Meaning: The Page, the Image, and the Body*, edited by Margaret J.M. Ezell and Katherine O'Brien O'Keeffe, Ann Arbor, The University of Michigan Press, 1994, pp. 13–40.

Marcus, Steven. *The Other Victorians: A Study of Sexuality and Pornography in Mid-Nineteenth Century England*, London, Corgi Books, 1966.

Mardaan, Ataullah [pseud.] [on the title page: Robert Desmond]. *Kama Houri*, Covina, Collectors Publications, 1967.

Marshall, P.J. [Peter James] and Glyndwr Williams. *The Great Map of Mankind: Perceptions of New Worlds in the Age of Enlightenment*, Cambridge, MA, Harvard University Press, 1982.

Martinkus-Zemp, Ada. "Européocentrisme et exotisme: L'Homme blanc et la femme noire (dans la littérature française de l'entre-deux-guerres)" [Eurocentricism and exoticism: the white man and the black woman (in interwar French literature)], *Cahiers d'études africaines*, 49 (1973), pp. 60–81.

Martino, Pierre. *L'Orient dans la littérature française au XVIIe et au XVIIIe siècle* [The Orient in French literature during the seventeenth and eighteenth centuries], Paris, Hachette, 1906.

[Marx, Karl]. *Karl Marx on Colonialism and Modernization: His Despatches and Other Writings on China, India, Mexico, the Middle East and North Africa*, edited and with an Introduction by Shlomo Avineri, Garden City, Doubleday & Company, Inc., 1968.

Marx, Karl. *Capital: A Critique of Political Economy*, 3 vols., translated by Samuel Moore and Edward Aveling, edited by Frederick Engels, London, Lawrence & Wishart, 1970.

Marx, Karl and Friedrich Engels. *The German Ideology, Parts I & III*, [translated by W. Lough and C.P. Magill], edited by R. [Roy] Pascal, New York, International Publishers, 1963.

Marx, K. [Karl], F. [Friedrich] Engels, and V. [Vladimir Ilich] Lenin. *On Historical Materialism: A Collection*, edited by T. Borodulina, Moscow, Progress Publishers, 1972.

Massey, Doreen. *Spatial Divisions of Labour: Social Structures and the Geography of Production*, London and Basingstoke, Macmillan, 1984.

Massey, Doreen. *Space, Place, and Gender*, Minneapolis, University of Minnesota Press, 1994.

Mathers, E. Powys (ed. and trans.). *Eastern Love*, 3 vols., New York, Horace Liveright; London, J. Rodker, 1930.

Maundrell, Hen[ry]. *A Journey from Aleppo to Jerusalem at Easter AD 1697*, Oxford, Printed at the Theater, 1703.

Maupassant, Guy de. *À la Feuille de Rose, Maison turque; Suivi de la correspondance de l'auteur avec Gisèle d'Estoc et Marie Bashkirtseff et de quelques poèmes libres* [At the Rose Petal, Turkish house; followed by the author's correspondence with Gisèle d'Estoc and Marie Bashkirtseff, and by a few free poems], edited by Alexandre Grenier, Paris, Encre, 1984.

McBratney, John. "Images of Indian Women in Rudyard Kipling: A Case of Doubling Discourse," *Inscriptions*, 3/4 (1988), pp. 47–57.

McClintock, Anne. "Maidens, Maps, and Mines: The Reinvention of Patriarchy in Colonial South Africa," *The South Atlantic Quarterly*, 87, 1 (1988), pp. 147–92.

McClintock, Anne. *Imperial Leather: Race, Gender and Sexuality in the Colonial Contest*, New York and London, Routledge, 1995.

McDowell, Linda. "Space, Place and Gender Relations: Part I, Feminist Empiricism and the Geography of Social Relations," *Progress in Human Geography*, 17, 2 (1993), pp. 157–79; "Space, Place and Gender Relations: Part II, Identity, Difference, Feminist Geometries and Geographies," *Progress in Human Geography*, 17, 3 (1993), pp. 305–18.

McNelly, Cleo. "Nature, Women and Claude Lévi-Strauss," *Massachusetts Review*, 16 (1975), pp. 7–29.

Mead, Margaret. *Coming of Age in Samoa: A Psychological Study of Primitive Youth for Western Civilisation*, New York, William Morrow & Company, 1928.

Mead, Margaret. *Growing up in New Guinea: A Comparative Study of Primitive Education*, New York, William Morrow & Company, 1930.

Mead, Margaret. *Sex and Temperament in Three Primitive Societies*, New York, William Morrow & Company, 1935.

Meadows, Robert. *A Private Anthropological Cabinet of 500 Authentic Racial-Esoteric Photographs and Illustrations*, New York, Falstaff Press, 1934.

Méhémet-Saïd-Effendi [Mehmed Sa'id Efendi]. *La Morale musulmane; ou, L'Akhlaqi-Hamidé* [The Muslim morality; or, the *Ahlâk-ı Hamîde* (The praiseworthy morality)], translated by J.-A. [Jean-Adolphe] Decourdemanche, Paris, Ernest Leroux, Éditeur, 1888.

Melman, Billie. *Women's Orients: English Women and the Middle East, 1718–1918; Sexuality, Religion, and Work*, Ann Arbor, University of Michigan Press, 1992.

Memmi, Albert. *The Colonizer and the Colonized*, translated by Howard Greenfeld, New York, The Orion Press, 1965.

Metlitzki, Dorothee. *The Matter of Araby in Medieval England*, New Haven and London, Yale University Press, 1977.

Mignolo, Walter D. *The Darker Side of the Renaissance: Literacy, Territoriality, and Colonization*, Ann Arbor, The University of Michigan Press, 1995.

Miller, Christopher L. *Blank Darkness: Africanist Discourse in French*, Chicago and London, The University of Chicago Press, 1985.

Miller, Jane. *Seductions: Studies in Reading and Culture*, London, Virago Press, 1990.

Millingen, Frederick, Major. *Wild Life among the Koords*, London, Hurst and Blackett, Publishers, 1870.

Mills, Sara. *Discourses of Difference: An Analysis of Women's Travel Writing and Colonialism*, London and New York, Routledge, 1993.

Mills, Sara. "Knowledge, Gender, and Empire," in *Writing Women and Space: Colonial and Postcolonial Geographies*, edited by Alison Blunt and Gillian Rose, New York and London, The Guilford Press, 1994, pp. 29–50.

Mitchell, Timothy. *Colonizing Egypt*, Cambridge, Cambridge University Press, 1988.

Moi, Toril. *Sexual/Textual Politics: Feminist Literary Theory*, London and New York, Methuen, 1985.

[Moll, Herman]. *A Complete System of Geography, being a Description of All the Countries, Islands, Cities, Chief Towns, Harbours, Lakes, and Rivers, Mountains, Mines, &c. of the Known World [. . .]*, 2 vols., London, Printed for William Innys, 1744–47.

Monmonier, Mark. *How to Lie with Maps*, Chicago and London, The University of Chicago Press, 1991.

[Montagu, Mary Wortley, Lady]. *Letters of the Right Honourable Lady M—y W—y M—e: Written during her Travels in Europe, Asia and Africa, to Persons of Distinction, Men of Letters, &c. in different Parts of Europe. Which Contains, among other curious Relations, Accounts of the Policy and Manners of the Turks; Drawn from Sources that have been inaccessible to other Travelers*, 3 vols., London, T. Becket and P.A. De Hondt, 1763.

Montesquieu [Charles-Louis de Secondat, Baron de la Brède et de Montesquieu]. *Esprit des lois* [Spirit of the laws], in *Œuvres complètes*, 2 vols., edited by Roger Caillois, [Paris], Librairie Gallimard, 1951, Vol. 2, pp. 225–995. English translation: *The Spirit of the Laws*, 2 vols. in 1, translated by Thomas Nugent, with an Introduction by Franz Neumann, New York, Hafner Publishing Company, 1949.

Montesquieu [Charles-Louis de Secondat, Baron de la Brède et de Montesquieu]. *The Persian Letters*, translated and with an Introduction by George R. Healy, Indianapolis and New York, The Bobbs-Merrill Company, Inc., 1964.

Montrose, Louis. "The Work of Gender and Sexuality in the Elizabethan Discourse of Discovery," in *Discourses of Sexuality: From Aristotle to AIDS*, edited by Domna C. Stanton, Ann Arbor, The University of Michigan Press, 1992, pp. 138–84.

Moon, Michael and Cathy N. Davidson (eds.). *Subjects and Citizens: Nation, Race, and Gender from "Oroonoko" to Anita Hill*, Durham and London, Duke University Press, 1995.

Moore, Thomas. *Lalla Rookh: An Oriental Romance*, London, Longman, Brown, Green, and Longmans, 1849.

Morton, Benjamin A. *The Veiled Empress: An Unacademic Biography*, New York and London, G.P. Putnam's Sons, 1923.

Morton, Thomas. *New English Canaan or New Canaan. Containing an Abstract of New England, Composed in Three Bookes*, Amsterdam, Jacob Frederick Stam, 1637.

Moruzzi, Norma Claire. "Veiled Agents: Feminine Agency and Masquerade in *The Battle of Algiers*," in *Negotiating at the Margins: The Gendered Discourses of Power and Resistance*, edited by Sue Fisher and Kathy Davis, New Brunswick, Rutgers University Press, 1993, pp. 255–77.

Mosse, George L. *Nationalism and Sexuality: Respectability and Abnormal Sexuality in Modern Europe*, New York, Howard Fertig, 1985.

Mouffe, Chantal. "For a Politics of Nomadic Identity," in *Travellers' Tales: Narratives of Home and Displacement*, edited by George Robertson, Melinda Mash, Lisa Tickner, Jon Bird, Barry Curtis, and Tim Putnam, London and New York, Routledge, 1994, pp. 105–13.

Murphy, Alexander B. "Regions as Social Constructs: The Gap between Theory and Practice," *Progress in Human Geography*, 15, 1 (1991), pp. 23–35.

[Murray Ballou, Maturin] Lieutenant Murray. *The Turkish Slave or the Dumb Dwarf of Constantinople: A Story of the Eastern World*, Boston, Elliott, Thomes & Talbot, [ca. 1863].

Nabokov, Vladimir. "On a Book Entitled *Lolita*," in *The Annotated Lolita*, edited and annotated by Alfred Appel, Jr, New York and Toronto, McGraw-Hill Book Company, 1970, pp. 313–19.

Naddaff, Sandra. *Arabesque: Narrative Structure and the Aesthetics of Repetition in the "1001 Nights,"* Evanston, Northwestern University Press, 1991.

[an-Nafzāwī, ʿUmar ibn Muḥammad] Cheikh Nefzaoui. *The Perfumed Garden*, translated by Sir Richard [F.] Burton, London, Luxor Press, 1963.

[an-Nafzāwī, ʿUmar ibn Muḥammad]. *The Glory of the Perfumed Garden: the Missing Flowers. An English Translation from the Arabic of the Second and Hitherto Unpublished Part of Shaykh Nafzawi's Perfumed Garden*, [translated by H.E.J.], London, Neville Spearman, 1975.

[Nakhshabī, Ziyāu'd-Dīn]. *The Tooti Nameh, or Tales of a Parrot* [*Tūtīnāmah*], Calcutta; printed in London, J. Debrett, 1801.

Namias, June. *White Captives: Gender and Ethnicity on the American Frontier*, Chapel Hill and London, The University of North Carolina Press, 1993.

Nandy, Ashis. *The Intimate Enemy: Loss and Recovery of Self under Colonialism*, Delhi, Oxford University Press, 1983.

Nay, H. [pseud. of Hugo Hayn]. *Bibliotheca Germanorum erotica: Verzeichniss der gesammten deutschen erotischen Literatur min Einschluss der Uebersetzungen* [The German erotic library: bibliography of the entire German erotic literature, including translations], Leipzig, s.n., 1875.

Nederveen Pieterse, Jan. *White on Black: Images of Africa and Blacks in Western Popular Culture*, New Haven and London, Yale University Press, 1992.

Newman, Karen. *Fashioning Femininity and English Renaissance Drama*, Chicago and London, The University of Chicago Press, 1991.

Nicolaidès [or Nicolaïdes], Jean (ed.). *Contes licencieux de Constantinople et de l'Asie Mineure* [Ribald tales of Constantinople and Asia Minor], with introductory essays by C. de W. and G. Froidure d'Aubigné, Paris, Gustave Ficker; Kleinbronn, Jacob Martin, 1906.

[Nicolay Dauphinois, Nicolas de, Seigneur d'Arfeuile] Nicholas Nicholay Daulphinois, Lord of Arfeuile. *The Navigations, Peregrinations and Voyages, made into Turkie [. . .]*, London, Thomas Dawson, 1585.

Niebuhr, [Carsten]. *Travels through Arabia and Other Countries in the East*, 2 vols., translated by Robert Heron, Perth, R. Morison Junior, 1799.

Nussbaum, Felicity. "The Other Woman: Polygamy, *Pamela*, and the Prerogative of Empire," in *Women, 'Race,' and Writing in the Early Modern Period*, edited by Margo Hendricks and Patricia Parker, London and New York, Routledge, 1994, pp. 138–59, 326–30.

Nussbaum, Felicity A. *Torrid Zones: Maternity, Sexuality, and Empire in Eighteenth-Century English Narratives*, Baltimore and London, The Johns Hopkins University Press, 1995.

O'Gorman, Edmundo. *The Invention of America: an Inquiry into the Historical Nature of the New World and the Meaning of its History*, Bloomington, Indiana University Press, 1961.

[Omer Haleby, Abou Othman, Khôdja]. *El Ktab des lois secrètes de l'amour d'après le Khôdja Omer Haleby, Abou Othman* [*al-Kitāb* (the book) of the secret laws of love according to Khôdja Omer Haleby, Abou Othman], translated by Paul de Régla [Paul André Desjardin], Paris, Georges Carré, Éditeur, 1893. Second edition: Paris, Albin Michel, Éditeur, 1906. English translation: *El Ktab: The Book of the Secret Laws of Love according to the Khôdja Omer Haleby Abou Othmân*, translated (from the French) by Adolph F. Niemoeller, New York, Panurge Press, 1935 [unpublished].

Orme, Robert. *Historical Fragments of the Mogul Empire, of the Morattoes, and of the English Concerns in Indoostan, from the year M.DC.LIX*, London, F. Wingrave, 1805.

Orr, Bridget. " 'The Only Free People in the Empire': Gender Difference in Colonial Discourse," in *De-Scribing Empire: Post-Colonialism and Textuality*, edited by Chris Tiffin and Alan Lawson, London and New York, Routledge, 1994, pp. 152–68.

Özege, M. Seyfettin. *Eski Harflerle Basılmış Türkçe Eserler Kataloğu* [Catalogue of works in Turkish printed in the old alphabet], 5 vols., İstanbul, Fatih Yayınevi Matbaası, 1971–79.

Parker, Andrew, Mary Russo, Doris Sommer, and Patricia Yaeger (eds.). *Nationalisms and Sexualities*, New York and London, Routledge, 1992.

Parker, Patricia. *Literary Fat Ladies: Rhetoric, Gender, Property*, London and New York, Methuen & Co., 1987.

Parker, Patricia. "Fantasies of 'Race' and 'Gender': Africa, *Othello* and Bringing to Light," in *Women, 'Race,' and Writing in the Early Modern Period*, edited by Margo Hendricks and Patricia Parker, London and New York, Routledge, 1994, pp. 84–100, 315–21.

Parla, Jale. *Babalar ve Oğullar: Tanzimat Romanının Epistemolojik Temelleri* [Fathers and sons: epistemological foundations of the *Tanzimat* (Reformation Era) novel], İstanbul, İletişim Yayınları, 1990.

Pastner, Carroll McC. "Englishmen in Arabia: Encounters with Middle Eastern Women," *Signs: Journal of Women in Culture and Society*, 4, 2 (1978), pp. 309–23.

Paxton, Nancy L. "Mobilizing Chivalry: Rape in British Novels about the Indian Uprising of 1857," *Victorian Studies*, 36, 1 (1992), pp. 5–30.

Peirce, Leslie P. *The Imperial Harem: Women and Sovereignty in the Ottoman Empire*, New York and Oxford, Oxford University Press, 1993.

Penzer, Norman M. *An Annotated Bibliography of Sir Richard Francis Burton K.C.M.G.*, with a Preface by F. Grenfell Baker, London, A.M. Philpot, 1923. Reprint edition: Mansfield, Maurizio Martino Publisher, n.d.

Penzer, N. [Norman] M. *Poison-Damsels and Other Essays in Folklore and Anthropology*, London, Chas. J. Sawyer, Ltd., 1952.

Perbal, Albert. "La Race nègre et la malédiction de Cham" [The black race and the curse of Ham], *Revue de l'Université d'Ottawa*, 10, 2 (1940), pp. 157–77.

Perceau, Louis. *Bibliographie du roman érotique au XIXe siècle* [Bibliography of the erotic novel in the nineteenth century], Paris, Georges Fourdrinier, Éditeur, 1930.

Perera, Suvendrini. *Reaches of Empire: The English Novel from Edgeworth to Dickens*, New York, Columbia University Press, 1991.

Pétis de la Croix, François. *Les Mille et un jours: contes persans* [The thousand and one days: Persian tales], edited and annotated by Paul Sebag, Paris, Christian Bourgeois, Éditeur, 1980. English translation:*The Persian and the Turkish Tales, Compleat*, translated by [William] King, 2 vols., London, W. Mears and J. Browne, 1714. Reprint edition: New York and London, Garland Publishers, Inc., 1972.

Pia, Pascal. *Les Livres de l'Enfer du XVIe siècle à nos jours* [The books of "Hell" from the sixteenth century to our time], 2 vols., Paris, C. Coulet and A. Faure, 1978.

Pickles, John. *Phenomenology, Science and Geography: Spatiality and the Human Sciences*, Cambridge, UK, Cambridge University Press, 1985.

Pile, Steve and Nigel Thrift (eds.). *Mapping the Subject: Geographies of Cultural Transformation*, London and New York, Routledge, 1995.

Pinhas ben Nahum [pseud.]. *The Turkish Art of Love*, New York, Panurge Press, 1933.

Ploss, H. [Hermann Heinrich]. *Das Weib, in der Natur- und Völkerkunde:*

Anthropologische Studien [Woman, in natural science and ethnology: anthropological studies], 2 vols., edited by Max [Maximilian Carl August] Bartels, Leipzig, Th. Grieben's Verlag, 1897. English translation: *Woman: An Historical, Gynaecological and Anthropological Compendium*, 3 vols., translated by Eric John Dingwall. London, W. Heinemann, Ltd., 1935. Selections: *Femina Libido Sexualis: Compendium of the Psychology, Anthropology and Anatomy of the Sexual Characteristics of the Woman*, edited [translated] by Eric John Dingwall, "arranged" by J.R. Brosslowsky, New York, The Medical Press, 1965. *History's Mistress: a New Interpretation of a Nineteenth-Century Ethnographic Classic*, edited and with an Introduction by Paula Weideger, Harmondsworth, Middlesex, Penguin Books; New York, Viking Penguin, 1985.

Pollig, Hermann, Susanne Schlichtenmayer, and Gertrud Baur-Burkarth (eds.). *Exotische Welten, Europäische Phantasien* [Exotic worlds, European fantasies], [Stuttgart], Institut für Auslandsbeziehungen, Württembergischer Kuntsverein, Edition Cantz, 1987.

Pollock, Griselda. "Territories of Desire: Reconsiderations of an African Childhood," in *Travellers' Tales: Narratives of Home and Displacement*, edited by George Robertson, Melinda Mash, Lisa Tickner, Jon Bird, Barry Curtis, and Tim Putnam, London and New York, Routledge, 1994, pp. 63–89.

Poovey, Mary. *Uneven Developments: The Ideological Work of Gender in Mid-Victorian England*, Chicago, The University of Chicago Press, 1988.

Pope, Alexander. *The Correspondence of Alexander Pope*, 5 vols., edited by George Sherburn, Oxford, The Clarendon Press of Oxford University Press, 1956.

Porter, Dennis. *Haunted Journeys: Desire and Transgression in European Travel Writing*, Princeton, Princeton University Press, 1991.

Porter, Roy. "Mixed Feelings; the Enlightenment and Sexuality in Eighteenth-Century Britain," in *Sexuality in Eighteenth-Century Britain*, edited by Paul-Gabriel Boucé, Manchester, Manchester University Press, Totowa, Barnes & Noble Books, 1982, pp. 1–27.

Porter, Roy. "The Exotic as Erotic: Captain Cook at Tahiti," in *Exoticism in the Enlightenment*, edited by G.S. [George Sebastian] Rousseau and Roy Porter, Manchester and New York, Manchester University Press, 1990, pp. 117–44.

Pratt, Mary Louise. *Imperial Eyes: Travel Writing and Transculturation*, London and New York, Routledge, 1992.

Praz, Mario. *The Romantic Agony*, translated by Angus Davidson, with a Foreword by Frank Kermode, Oxford, Oxford University Press, 1970.

Price, Sally. *Primitive Art in Civilized Places*, Chicago and London, The University of Chicago Press, 1989.

Pucci, Suzanne Rodin. "Letters from the Harem: Veiled Figures of Writing in Montesquieu's *Lettres persanes*," in *Writing the Female Voice: Essays on Epistolary Literature*, edited by Elizabeth C. Goldsmith, Boston, Northeastern University Press, 1989, pp. 114–34.

Pucci, Suzanne Rodin. "The Discrete Charms of the Exotic: Fictions of the Harem in Eighteenth-Century France," in *Exoticism in the Enlightenment*, edited by G.S. [George Sebastian] Rousseau and Roy Porter, Manchester and New York, Manchester University Press, 1990, pp. 145–74.

Purchas, Samuel. *Purchas his Pilgrimage, or Relations of the World and the Religions Observed in All Ages and Places Discovered, from the Creation unto this Present [. . .]*, London, Printed by William Stansby for Henrie Fetherstone, 1626.

Querard, J.-M. [Joseph-Marie]. *Les Supercheries littéraires dévoilées. Galerie des écrivains [. . .] pseudonymes facétieux ou bizarres* [Literary fakes exposed: gallery of authors . . . facetious or bizarre pseudonyms], 3 vols., Paris, G.P. Maisonneuve & Larose, 1964.

Rabasa, José. "Allegories of the *Atlas*," in *Europe and its Others: Proceedings of the Essex Conference on the Sociology of Literature, July 1984*, edited by Francis Barker, Peter Hulme, Margaret Iversen, and Diana Loxley, 2 vols., Colchester, University of Essex, 1985, Vol. 2, pp. 1–16.

Racine, Jean. *Bajazet, Œuvres de J. Racine* [Works of J. Racine], edited by Paul Mesnard. 8 vols., Paris, Librairie Hachette et Cie., 1885–88. Vol. 2, pp. 455–575. English translation: *Bajazet*, translated by Alan Hollinghurst, with an Introduction by Francis Wyndham, London, Chatto & Windus, 1991.

Radway, Janice A. *Reading the Romance: Women, Patriarchy, and Popular Literature*, Chapel Hill and London, The University of North Carolina Press, 1984.

Rafael, Vincente L. *Contracting Colonialism: Translation and Christian*

Conversion in Tagalog Society under Early Spanish Rule, Ithaca and London, Cornell University Press, 1988.

[Ralegh, Walter, Sir]. "The Discoverie of Guiana," in *The Discoverie of the Large, Rich and Bewtiful Empire of Guiana, with a Relation of the Great and Golden Citie of Manoa (which the Spaniards call El Dorado) [. . .] Performed in the Yeare 1595 by Sir W. Ralegh*, London, Robert Robinson, 1596.

Reade, Rolf S. [pseud. of Alfred Rose]. *Registrum Librorum Eroticorum* [Register of erotic books], 2 vols., London, Privately Printed for Subscribers, 1936.

Réage, Pauline [pseud. of Dominique Aury?]. *Histoire d'O* [Story of O], with a Preface by Jean Paulhan, Sceaux, Jean-Jacques Pauvert, 1954. English translation: *Story of O*, Paris, Olympia Press, 1954.

Reclus, Elie. *Curious Byways of Anthropology: Sexual, Savage and Esoteric Customs of Primitive Peoples*, New York, Robin Hood House, 1932.

Reichardt, Annie. *Girl-Life in the Harem: A True Account of Girl-Life in Oriental Climes*, London, John Ouseley, Limited, 1908.

Reitzenstein, Ferdinand [Emil], Freiherr von. *Das Weib bei den Naturvölkern: Eine Kulturgeschichte der primitiven Frau* [Woman among primitive peoples: a cultural history of primitive woman], Berlin, Verlag Neufeld & Henius, n.d. [ca. 1923].

Reynolds, George W.M. *The Loves of the Harem: A Tale of Constantinople*, London, Published for Mr. Reynolds by John Dicks, 1855.

Richard, Jean-Marc. *Dictionnaire des expressions paillardes et libertines de la littérature française* [Dictionary of the ribald and libertine expressions in French literature], Paris, Éditions Filipacchi, 1993.

Richards, Thomas. *The Imperial Archive: Knowledge and the Fantasy of Empire*, London and New York, Verso, 1993.

Ricoeur, Paul. *Time and Narrative*, translated by Kathleen McLaughlin and David Pellauer, 3 vols., Chicago and London, The University of Chicago Press, 1984.

Ridley, Hugh. *Images of Imperial Rule*, London and Canberra, Croom Helm; New York, St. Martin's Press, 1983.

Riza Bey. *Darkest Orient*, London, Arco Publications, Ltd., 1937.

Roberts, Diane. *The Myth of Aunt Jemima: Representations of Race and Region*, London and New York, Routledge, 1994.

Rodaway, Paul. *Sensuous Geographies: Body, Sense and Place*, London and New York, Routledge, 1994.

Rooy, Piet de. "Of Monkeys, Blacks, and Proles: Ernst Haeckel's Theory of Recapitulation," in *Imperial Monkey Business: Racial Supremacy in Social Darwinist Theory and Colonial Practice*, edited by Jan Breman, Amsterdam, VU University Press, 1990, pp. 7–34.

Rose, Gillian. *Feminism and Geography: The Limits of Geographical Knowledge*, Minneapolis, University of Minnesota Press, 1993.

Rosenberger, Joseph R. *Sex in the Near East*, San Diego, Greenleaf Classics, Inc., 1970.

Rothenberg, Tamar Y. "Voyeurs of Imperialism: *The National Geographic Magazine* before World War II," in *Geography and Empire*, edited by Anne Godlewska and Neil Smith, Oxford and Cambridge, MA, Blackwell Publishers, 1994, pp. 155–72.

Rouillard, Clarence Dana. *The Turk in French History, Thought, and Literature (1520–1660)*, Paris, Boivin & Cie., Éditeurs, n.d.

Rousseau, G.S. [George Sebastian] and Roy Porter (eds.). *Sexual Underworlds of the Enlightenment*, Chapel Hill, University of North Carolina Press, 1988.

Rousseau, G.S. [George Sebastian] and Roy Porter (eds.). *Exoticism in the Enlightenment*, Manchester and New York, Manchester University Press, 1990.

Rubinstein, Frankie. *A Dictionary of Shakespeare's Sexual Puns and their Significance*, London and Basingstoke, The Macmillan Press, Ltd., 1984.

Ryan, Simon. "Inscribing the Emptiness: Cartography, Exploration and the Construction of Australia," in *De-Scribing Empire: Post-Colonialism and Textuality*, edited by Chris Tiffin and Alan Lawson, London and New York, Routledge, 1994, pp. 152–68.

Rycaut, Paul [Sir]. *The Present State of the Ottoman Empire: Containing the Maxims of the Turkish Politie, the most material points of the Mahometan Religion, their Sects and Heresies, their Convents and Religious Votaries, their Military Discipline, with an exact Computation of their Forces both by Land and Sea*, London, John Starkey and Henry Brome, 1668.

Sade, [Count Donatien Alphonse François de]. *The 120 Days of Sodom, and Other Writings*, compiled and translated by Austryn Wainhouse and Richard Seaver, with Introductions by Simone de Beauvoir and Pierre Klossowski, New York, Grove Press, Inc., 1966, pp. 181–674.

Sade, [Count Donatien Alphonse François de]. *Les 120 journées de Sodome, ou l'école du libertinage* [The 120 days of Sodom, or the school of libertinism], in *Œuvres*, 1 vol. published to date, edited by Michel Delon, with an Introduction by Jean Deprun, [Paris], Gallimard, 1990. Vol. 1, pp. 13–383.

Said, Edward W. *Orientalism*, New York, Vintage Books, 1979.

Said, Edward W. *Culture and Imperialism*, New York, Alfred A. Knopf, 1993.

Salih, Tayeb. *Season of Migration to the North*, translated by Denys Johnson-Davies, London, Heinemann, 1969.

Sandys, George. *A Relation of a Journey begun An. Dom. 1610: Foure Bookes. Containing a Description of the Turkish Empire, of Aegypt, of the Holy Land, of the Remote Parts of Italy, and Islands Adjoyning*, London, W. Barrett, 1621.

Schaffer, Kay. "Colonizing Gender in Colonial Australia: The Eliza Fraser Story," in *Writing Women and Space: Colonial and Postcolonial Geographies*, edited by Alison Blunt and Gillian Rose, New York and London, The Guilford Press, 1994, pp. 101–20.

Scharfenberg, H. [Hermann] (ed.). *Persische Liebesgeschichten: Eine Sammlung erotischer Erzählungen aus dem alten Orient* [Persian love stories: a collection of erotic tales from the ancient Orient], München, Allgemeine Verlagsanstalt, 1924.

Schaub, Diana J. *Erotic Liberalism: Women and Revolution in Montesquieu's Persian Letters*, Lanham, Rowman & Littlefield Publishers, Inc., 1995.

Schick, İrvin Cemil. "Representing Middle Eastern Women: Feminism and Colonial Discourse," *Feminist Studies*, 16, 2 (1990), pp. 354–80.

[Schidlof, Berthold] B. Schidloff. "Sexual Life of South Sea Natives," in *Venus Oceanica: Anthropological Studies in the Sex Life of the South Sea Natives*, edited by R. [Ronald] Burton, New York, The Oceanica Research Press, 1935, pp. 33–318.

Schidrowitz, Leo (ed.). *Sittengeschichte des Hafens und der Reise: eine Beleuchtung des erotischen Lebens in der Hafenstadt, im Hotel, im Reisevehikel; die Sexualität des Kulturmenschen Während des Reisens und in fremdem Milieu* [Moral history of ports and travel: an elucidation of erotic life in the port city, in the hotel, in vehicles of transportation; the sexuality of civilized man during travel and in foreign settings], Vienna and Leipzig, Verlag für Kulturforschung, 1927.

Schiebinger, Londa. "Skeletons in the Closet: The First Illustrations of the Female Skeleton in Eighteenth-Century Anatomy," in *The Making of the Modern Body: Sexuality and Society in the Nineteenth Century*, edited by Catherine Gallagher and Thomas Laqueur, Berkeley, Los Angeles, and London, University of California Press, 1987, pp. 42–82.

Schiffer, Reinhold. "Bilder türkischer Frauen und Männer in Reiseberichten des 19. Jahrhunderts" [Images of Turkish women and men in nineteenth-century travelogues], in *I. Uluslararası Seyahatnamelerde Türk ve Batı İmajı Sempozyumu Belgeleri, 28.X–1.XI.1985*, Eskişehir, Anadolu Üniversitesi Yayınları, 1987, pp. 284–97.

Schweiger-Lerchenfeld, Amand, Freiherr von. *Die Frauen des Orients, in der Geschichte, in der Dichtung und im Leben* [The women of the Orient, in history, poetry, and life], Vienna and Leipzig, A. Hartleben's Verlag, 1904.

Schwoebel, Robert. *The Shadow of the Crescent: The Renaissance Image of the Turk (1453–1517)*, Nieuwkoop, B. de Graaf, 1967.

Sears, [Joseph] Hamblen (ed.). *Arabian Nights Love Tales*, New York, J.H. Sears & Company, Inc., 1926.

Segalen, Victor. *Les Immémoriaux* [The immemorial], Paris, Société du Mercure de France, 1907.

Segalen, Victor. *Gauguin dans son dernier décor et autres textes de Tahiti* [Gauguin in his last setting, and other texts of Tahiti], n.p., Éditions Fata Morgana, 1975.

Segalen, Victor. *Essai sur l'exotisme: une esthétique du divers* [Essay on exoticism: an aesthetics of the diverse], n.p., Éditions Fata Morgana, 1978.

Servantie, A. [Alain]. "Les médias modernes à grande diffusion, véhicules de stéréotypes politiques: bandes dessinées sur la Turquie" [Modern mass media, vehicles for political stereotypes: cartoon strips on Turkey], *C.E.M.O.T.I. Cahiers d'études sur la Méditerranée orientale et le monde turco-iranien*, 8 (1989), pp. 25–75.

Setton, Kenneth M. *Western Hostility to Islam and Prophecies of Turkish Doom*, Philadelphia, American Philosophical Society, 1992.

[Şeyhzâde] Sheykh-Zāda. *The History of the Forty Vezirs, or the Story of the Forty Morns and Eves*, translated and with an Introduction by E.J.W. [Elias John Wilkinson] Gibb, London, George Redway, 1886.

[Shakespeare, William]. *Othello*, edited by Norman Sanders, Cambridge, UK, Cambridge University Press, 1984.

Shammas, Anton. "Arab Male, Hebrew Female: The Lure of Metaphors," in *Reconstructing Gender in the Middle East: Tradition, Identity, and Power*, edited by Fatma Müge Göçek and Shiva Balaghi, New York, Columbia University Press, 1994, pp. 167–73.

Sharafuddin, Mohammed. *Islam and Romantic Orientalism: Literary Encounters with the Orient*, London and New York, I.B. Tauris Publishers, 1994.

Sharpe, Jenny. *Allegories of Empire: The Figure of Woman in the Colonial Text*, Minneapolis and London, University of Minnesota Press, 1993.

Shields, Rob. *Places on the Margin: Alternative Geographies of Modernity*, London and New York, Routledge, 1991.

Shipler, David K. *Arab and Jew: Wounded Spirits in a Promised Land*, New York, Times Books, 1986.

Shohat, Ella. "Gender in Hollywood's Orient," *Middle East Report*, 20 (1990), pp. 40–42. Revised version in Ella Shohat and Robert Stam, *Unthinking Eurocentrism: Multiculturalism and the Media*, London and New York, Routledge, 1994.

Shohat, Ella. "Imaging Terra Incognita: The Disciplinary Gaze of Empire," *Public Culture: Bulletin of the Center for Transnational Cultural Studies*, 3, 2 (1991a), pp. 41–70. Reprinted in Ella Shohat and Robert Stam, *Unthinking Eurocentrism: Multiculturalism and the Media*, London and New York, Routledge, 1994.

Shohat, Ella. "Gender and Culture of Empire: Toward a Feminist Ethnography of the Cinema," *Quarterly Review of Film and Video*, 13, 1–3 (1991b), pp. 45–84. Revised version in Ella Shohat and Robert Stam, *Unthinking Eurocentrism: Multiculturalism and the Media*, London and New York, Routledge, 1994.

Short, John Rennie. *Imagined Country: Environment, Culture, and Society*, London and New York, Routledge, 1991.

Showalter, Elaine. *Sexual Anarchy: Gender and Culture at the Fin de Siècle*, New York, Viking, 1990.

Shumway, David R. *Michel Foucault*, Boston, Twayne Publishers, 1989.

Sibley, David. "Outsiders in Society and Space," in *Inventing Places: Studies in Cultural Geography*, edited by Kay Anderson and Fay Gale, Melbourne, Longman Cheshire; n.p., Halstead Press, John Wiley & Sons, Inc., 1992, pp. 107–22.

Sibley, David. *Geographies of Exclusion: Society and Difference in the West*, London and New York, Routledge, 1995.

Silverman, Kaja. "White Skin, Brown Masks: The Double Mimesis, or with Lawrence in Arabia," *Differences: A Journal of Feminist Cultural Studies*, 1, 3 (1989), pp. 3–54.

Silverman, Kaja. *Male Subjectivity at the Margins*, London and New York, Routledge, 1992.

Simon, Reeva S. *The Middle East in Crime Fiction: Mysteries, Spy Novels and Thrillers from 1916 to the 1980s*, New York, Lilian Barber Press, Inc., 1989.

Sinha, Mrinalini. *Colonial Masculinity: The 'Manly Englishman' and the 'Effeminate Bengali' in the Late Nineteenth Century*, Manchester and New York, Manchester University Press, 1995.

Sivan, Emmanuel. "Edward Said and his Arab Reviewers," *Interpretations of Islam: Past and Present*, Princeton, The Darwin Press, 1985, pp. 133–54.

Skar, Sarah. "Andean Women and the Concept of Space/Time," in *Women and Space: Ground Rules and Social Maps*, edited by Shirley Ardener, New York, St. Martin's Press, 1981, pp. 35–49.

Sladen, Douglas. *Carthage and Tunis: The Old and New Gates of the Orient*, 2 vols., Philadelphia, George W. Jacobs & Co., 1906.

Slavy, Bob. *Le Harem océanien* [The harem in Oceania], Paris, Collection des Orties Blanches, [1935].

Smith-Rosenberg, Carroll. "Captured Subjects/Savage Others: Violently Engendering the New American," *Gender & History*, 5, 2 (1993), pp. 177–95.

Soja, Edward J. *Postmodern Geographies: The Reassertion of Space in Critical Social Theory*, London and New York, Verso, 1989.

Solomon-Godeau, Abigail. "Going Native," *Art in America*, 77, 7 (1989), pp. 118–29, 161.

Sonnini [de Manoncourt], C.S. [Charles Nicholas Sigisbert]. *Travels in*

Upper and Lower Egypt, Undertaken by Order of the Old Government of France, London, J. Debrett, 1800.

Spivak, Gayatri Chakravorty. "The Rani of Sirmur," in *Europe and its Others: Proceedings of the Essex Conference on the Sociology of Literature, July 1984*, edited by Francis Barker, Peter Hulme, Margaret Iversen, and Diana Loxley, 2 vols., Colchester, University of Essex, 1985. Vol. 1, pp. 128–51.

Spivak, Gayatri Chakravorty. "Three Women's Texts and a Critique of Imperialism," in *'Race,' Writing, and Difference*, edited by Henry Louis Gates, Jr., Chicago and London, The University of Chicago Press, 1986, pp. 262–80.

Spivak, Gayatri Chakravorty. "Can the Subaltern Speak?" in *Marxism and the Interpretation of Culture*, edited by Cary Nelson and Lawrence Grossberg, Urbana and Chicago, University of Illinois Press, 1988, pp. 271–313.

Spivak, Gayatri Chakravorty. "Poststructuralism, Marginality, Postcoloniality and Value," in *Literary Theory Today*, edited by Peter Collier and Helga Geyer Ryan, Ithaca, Cornell University Press, 1990, pp. 219–44.

Spry, William J.J. *Life on the Bosphorus: Doings in the City of the Sultan. Turkey, Past and Present, Including Chronicles of the Caliphs from Mahomet to Abdul Hamid II*, London, H.S. Nichols, 1895.

Spurr, David. *The Rhetoric of Empire: Colonial Discourse in Journalism, Travel Writing, and Imperial Administration*, Durham and London, Duke University Press, 1993.

Stallybrass, Peter and Allon White. *The Politics and Poetics of Transgression*, London, Methuen, 1986.

Staples, Robert. *Black Masculinity: The Black Male's Role in American Society*, San Francisco, The Black Scholar Press, 1982.

Stein, Howard F. and William G. Niederland (eds.). *Maps from the Mind: Readings in Psychogeography*, with a Foreword by Vamık D. Volkan, Norman and London, University of Oklahoma Press, 1989.

Stember, Charles Herbert. *Sexual Racism: The Emotional Barrier to an Integrated Society*, New York, Oxford; and Amsterdam, Elsevier, 1976.

Stern, Bernhard. *Medizin, Aberglaube und Geschlechtsleben in der Türkei: mit Berücksichtigung der moslemischen Nachbarländer und der ehemaligen Vasallenstaaten* [Medicine, superstition, and sex life in Turkey: covering the neighboring Muslim lands and the former tributary states], 2 vols. Berlin, Verlag von H. Barsdorf, 1903. Second volume published in English translation as *The Scented Garden: Anthropology of the Sex Life in the Levant,* translated by David Berger, New York, American Ethnological Press, 1934.

Stewart, Susan. *Crimes of Writing: Problems in the Containment of Representation,* New York and Oxford, Oxford University Press, 1991.

St. John, Bayle. *Village Life in Egypt; with Sketches of the Saïd,* 2 vols., Boston, Ticknor, Reed, and Fields, 1853.

St. Jorre, John de. "The Unmasking of O," *The New Yorker,* 1 August 1994, pp. 42–50.

Stocking, George W., Jr. *Victorian Anthropology,* New York, The Free Press; London, Collier Macmillan Publishers, 1987.

Stoler, Ann Laura. "Carnal Knowledge and Imperial Power: Gender, Race, and Morality in Colonial Asia," in *Gender at the Crossroads of Knowledge: Feminist Anthropology in the Postmodern Era,* edited by Micaela di Leonardo, Berkeley, Los Angeles, and Oxford, University of California Press, 1991, pp. 51–101.

Stoler, Ann Laura. *Race and the Education of Desire: Foucault's "History of Sexuality" and the Colonial Order of Things,* Durham and London, Duke University Press, 1995.

Stott, Rebecca. "The Dark Continent: Africa as Female Body in Haggard's Adventure Fiction," *Feminist Review,* 32 (1989), pp. 69–89.

Straayer, Chris. "The Seduction of Boundaries: Feminist Fluidity in Annie Sprinkle's Art/Education/Sex," in *Dirty Looks: Women, Pornography, Power,* edited by Pamela Church Gibson and Roma Gibson, with an Introduction by Carole J. Clover, London, BFI [British Film Institute] Publishing, 1993, pp. 156–75.

Stratton, Jon. *Writing Sites: A Genealogy of the Postmodern World,* Ann Arbor, The University of Michigan Press, 1990.

Stratz, C.H. [Carl Heinrich]. *Die Rassenschönheit des Weibes* [The racial beauty of women], Stuttgart, Verlag von Ferdinand Enke, 1911.

Street, Brian V. *The Savage in Literature: Representations of 'Primitive' Society in English Fiction, 1858–1920,* London and Boston, Routledge & Kegan Paul, 1975.

Strobel, Margaret. *European Women and the Second British Empire*, Bloomington, Indiana University Press, 1991.

[Sulaimān, Sharīf]. *Le Divan d'amour du Chérif Soliman* [The love poetry of the Sharīf Sulaimān], translated by Iskandar-al-Maghribi, Paris, Bibliothèque Internationale d'Édition [E. Sensot], 1911.

Suleri, Sara. *The Rhetoric of English India*, Chicago and London, The University of Chicago Press, 1992.

Sumner, Charles. *White Slavery in the Barbary States: A Lecture before the Boston Mercantile Library Association, Feb. 17, 1847*, Boston, William D. Ticknor and Company, 1847.

Sunder Rajan, Rajeswari. *Real and Imagined Women: Gender, Culture and Postcolonialism*, London and New York, Routledge, 1993.

Surieu, Robert. *Sarv é Naz: an Essay on Love and the Representation of Erotic Themes in Ancient Iran*, translated by James Hogarth, Geneva, Paris, and Munich, Nagel Publishers, 1967.

[as-Suyūṭī, Djalālu'd-dīn]. *The Book of Exposition [in the Science of Complete and Perfect Coition] (Kitab al-Izah fi'Ilm al-Nikah b-it-Tamam w-al-Kamal)* [*Kitābu'l-Iẓāḥ fī 'Ilmi'n-Nikāḥ bi't-Tamām wa'l-Kamāl*], translated and with a Foreword by an English Bohemian, Paris, London and New York, Maison d'Éditions Scientifiques [Charles Carrington], 1900.

[as-Suyūṭī, Djalālu'd-dīn] 'Abd al-Rahmane ibn Abi-Bakr al-Souyoûti. *Nuits de noces, ou comment humer le doux breuvage de la magie licite* [Wedding nights, or how to inhale the sweet liquor of licit magic], translated and with an Introduction by René R. Khawam, Paris, Éditions Albin Michel, 1972.

Szyliowicz, Irene L. *Pierre Loti and the Oriental Woman*, New York, St Martin's Press, 1988

Taha-Hussein, Moënis. *Le Romantisme français et l'Islam* [French romanticism and Islam], [Beirut], Dar al-Maaref, 1962.

Taussig, Michael. *Mimesis and Alterity: a Particular History of the Senses*, New York and London, Routledge, 1993.

Tavernier, J.-B. [Jean-Baptiste]. *Nouvelle relation de l'intérieur du Serrail du Grand Seigneur. Contenant plusieurs singularitez qui jusqu'icy n'ont point esté mises en lumière* [New relation of the interior of the seraglio of the sultan, containing numerous singularities which heretofore had not seen the light, translated as *The six voyages of John Baptista Tavernier*

[. . .] to which is added A new description of the Seraglio], Paris, Olivier de Varennes, 1675.

Thalasso, Adolphe (ed.). *Anthologie de l'amour asiatique* [Anthology of Asian love], Paris, Société du Mercure de France, 1907.

[Theille, Alfred de] M. le baron de St. Eldme. *Les Fastes de l'amour et de la volupté dans les cinq parties du monde. Description de sérails, harems, [. . .]* [The festivities of love and voluptuousness in the five parts of the world. Description of seraglios, harems, . . .], 2 vols., Paris, Les Marchands de Nouveautés, 1839.

Theweleit, Klaus. *Male Fantasies*, translated by Stephen Conway in collaboration with Erica Carter and Chris Turner, with a Foreword by Barbara Ehrenreich, 2 vols., Minneapolis, University of Minnesota Press, 1987.

Thomas, Nicholas. *Out of Time: History and Evolution in Anthropological Discourse*, Cambridge, UK, Cambridge University Press, 1989.

Thomas, William I. [Isaac]. "The Mind of Woman and the Lower Races," *Sex and Society: Studies in the Social Psychology of Sex*, Chicago, The University of Chicago Press; London, T. Fisher Unwin, 1907.

Thornton, Lynne. *Women As Portrayed in Orientalist Painting*, Paris, ACR Edition, 1985.

Tiffany, Sharon W. and Kathleen J. Adams. *The Wild Woman: An Inquiry into the Anthropology of an Idea*, Cambridge, MA, Schenkman Publishing Company, Inc., 1985.

Tiffin, Chris and Alan Lawson. *De-Scribing Empire: Post-Colonialism and Textuality*, London and New York, Routledge, 1994.

Tissot, S.A.D. [Samuel Auguste David]. *L'Onanisme; ou dissertation physique sur les maladies produites par la masturbation* [Onanism; or physical dissertation on the illnesses produced by masturbation], in *L'Onanisme; Dissertations physiques et morales,* [Lausanne], Antoine Chapuis, 1760.

Todorov, Tzvetan. *The Conquest of America: The Question of the Other*, translated by Richard Howard, New York, Harper & Row, Publishers, 1984a.

Todorov, Tzvetan. *Mikhail Bakhtin: The Dialogical Principle*, translated by Wlad Godzich, Minneapolis, University of Minnesota Press, 1984b.

Todorov, Tzvetan. *On Human Diversity: Nationalism, Racism, and Exoticism in French Thought*, translated by Catherine Porter, Cambridge, MA and London, Harvard University Press, 1993.

Tokson, Elliot. *Harem Games*, New York, Avon Books, 1984.

Tompkins, Edward Staats DeGrote. *Through David's Realm*, Troy, Nims & Knight, 1889.

Tompkins, Peter. *The Eunuch and the Virgin: A Study of Curious Customs*, New York, Clarkson N. Potter, Inc., 1962.

Torgovnick, Marianna. *Gone Primitive: Savage Intellects, Modern Lives*, Chicago and London, The University of Chicago Press, 1990.

Treves, Frederick, Sir. *The Land that is Desolate: An Account of a Tour in Palestine*, London, Smith, Elder & Co., 1912.

Trexler, Richard C. *Sex and Conquest: Gendered Violence, Political Order, and the European Conquest of the Americas*, Cambridge, UK, Polity Press, 1995.

Trinh T. Minh-ha. *Woman Native Other: Writing Postcoloniality and Feminism*, Bloomington, Indiana University Press, 1989.

Truong, Thanh-Dam. *Sex, Money, and Morality: Prostitution and Tourism in Southeast Asia*, London and Atlantic Highlands, Zed Books, 1990.

Tuan, Yi-Fu. *Topophilia: A Study of Environmental Perception, Attitudes, and Values*, Englewood Cliffs, Prentice-Hall, Inc., 1974.

Tuan, Yi-Fu. *Space and Place: The Perspective of Experience*, Minneapolis, University of Minnesota Press, 1977.

Tucker, Marcia. "Mechanisms of Exclusion and Relation: Identity," in *Discourses: Conversations in Postmodern Art and Culture*, edited by Russel Ferguson, William Olander, Marcia Tucker, and Karen Fiss, New York, The New Museum of Contemporary Art; Cambridge, MA and London, The MIT Press, 1990, pp. 91–2.

Uchard, Mario. *French and Oriental Love in a Harem*, New York, Falstaff Press, n.d. [ca. 1935].

[Usāmah ibn Munqidh]. *An Arab-Syrian Gentleman and Warrior in the Period of the Crusades: Memoirs of Usāmah ibn-Munqidh*, translated by Philip K. Hitti, London, I.B. Tauris & Co. Ltd., Publishers, 1987.

Valverde, Mariana. *Sex, Power and Pleasure*, Philadelphia, New Society Publishers, 1987.

Van Den Abbeele, Georges. *Travel as Metaphor: From Montaigne to Rousseau*, Minneapolis and Oxford, University of Minnesota Press, 1992.

[Vatsyāyana]. *The Kama Sutra of Vatsyayana: Love Precepts of the Brahmans*, Paris, Librairie "Astra," n.d.

[Vèze, Raoul] B. [Bagneux] de Villeneuve [pseud.] (ed.). *Le Livre d'amour de l'Orient* [The book of love of the Orient], 4 vols., Paris, Bibliothèque des Curieux, 1910–21.

Vierath, Willy. *Frauenliebe und Frauenleben im Orient* [Women's love and women's life in the Orient], Berlin-Schöneberg, Peter J. Destergaard Verlag, n.d. [ca. 1927].

Villiot, Jean de [pseud. of Georges Grassal]. *Black Lust*, translated by Lawrence Ecker, New York, The Panurge Press, 1931.

Voilquin, Suzanne. *Souvenirs d'une fille du peuple; ou la Saint-Simonienne en Egypte* [Memoirs of a girl of the people, or the Saint-Simonian in Egypt], Paris, François Maspero, 1978.

[Voltaire, François Marie Arouet de]. *Dictionnaire Philosophique* [Philosophical dictionary]. *Œuvres complètes de Voltaire: Nouvelle édition avec notices, préfaces, variantes, table analytique [. . .]*, 52 vols., [edited by Louis (Emile Dieudonné) Moland], following the text edited by [Adrien Jean Quentin] Beuchot, with an Introduction by [Marie Jean Antoine Nicolas Caritat, marquis de] Condorcet, Paris, Garnier Frères, Libraires-Éditeurs, 1877–85, Vols. 17–20.

Vovard, André. *Les Turqueries dans la littérature française: le cycle barbaresque* [Turkish motifs in French literature: the cycle of Barbary], [Toulouse], Privat, 1959.

Wagner, Peter. *Eros Revived: Erotica of the Enlightenment in England and America*, London, Secker & Warburg, 1988.

Walton, Alan Hull. *Aphrodisiacs: From Legend to Prescription. A Study of Aphrodisiacs throughout the Ages, with Sections on Suitable Food, Glandular Extracts, Hormone Stimulation and Rejuvenation*, with an Introduction by Herman Goodman, Westport, Associated Booksellers, 1958.

Ware, Vron. *Beyond the Pale: White Women, Racism and History*, London and New York, Verso, 1992.

Warner, Marina. *Monuments and Maidens: The Allegory of the Female Form*, London, Weidenfeld and Nicolson, 1985.

Weisshaupt, Winfried. *Europa sieht sich mit fremdem Blick: Werke nach dem Schema der "Lettres persanes" in der europäischen, insbesondere der deutschen Literatur des 18. Jahrhunderts* [Europe sees itself with a foreign gaze:

works following the schema of the *Lettres persanes* in European and particularly German literature of the 18th century], 2 vols. in 3, Frankfurt am Main, Bern, and Las Vegas, Peter Lang, 1979.

Weller, Emil [Ottokar]. *Die falschen und fingirten Druckorte: Repertorium der seit Erfindung der Buchdruckerkunst unter falscher Firma erschienenen deutschen, lateinischen und französischen Schriften* [The fake and bogus places of printing: listing of German, Latin, and French publications that appeared under fake imprints, since the invention of the art of book printing], 2 vols., Leipzig, Verlag von Wilhelm Engelmann, 1864.

Welty, Eudora. *Place in Fiction*, New York, House of Books, Ltd., 1957.

Wharton, Edith. *In Morocco*, New York, Charles Scribner's Sons, 1920.

Wheatley, Dennis. *The Eunuch of Stamboul*, London, Arrow Books, 1975.

Wiesner, Merry E. *Women and Gender in Early Modern Europe*, Cambridge, UK, Cambridge University Press, 1993.

Williamson, Judith. "Woman is an Island: Femininity and Colonization," in *Studies in Entertainment: Critical Approaches to Mass Culture*, edited by Tania Modleski, Bloomington and Indianapolis, Indiana University Press, 1986, pp. 99–118.

Wirth, Louis. *The Ghetto*, Chicago and London, The University of Chicago Press, 1969.

Wittkower, Rudolf. "Marvels of the East: A Study in the History of Monsters," *Journal of the Warburg and Courtauld Institutes*, 5 (1942), pp. 159–97.

Wolff, Janet. "On the Road Again: Metaphors of Travel in Cultural Criticism," *Cultural Studies*, 7, 2 (1993), pp. 224–39.

Wolfson, Susan J. "'A Problem Few Dare Imitate': Sardanapalus and 'Effeminate Character,'" *ELH*, 58, 4 (1991), pp. 867–902.

Wood, Dennis. *The Power of Maps*, with the collaboration of John Fels, New York and London, The Guilford Press, 1992a.

Wood, Raymund F. *Iskandar-Al-Maghribi and the Memoirs of Cherif Soliman: Genuine or Fabrication?* Encino, Privately Printed, 1992b.

Woodhull, Winifred. "Unveiling Algeria," *Genders*, 10 (1991), pp. 112–31.

Wright, John Kirtland. "*Terrae Incognitae*: The Place of the Imagination in Geography," *Human Nature in Geography: Fourteen Papers, 1925–1965*, Cambridge, MA, Harvard University Press, 1966, pp. 68–88.

Wurgaft, Lewis D. *The Imperial Imagination: Magic and Myth in Kipling's India*, Middletown, Wesleyan University Press, 1983.

Yeğenoğlu, Meyda. "Supplementing the Orientalist Lack: European Ladies in the Harem," *Inscriptions*, 6 (1992), pp. 45–80.

Young, Robert J.C. *Colonial Desire: Hybridity in Theory, Culture and Race*, London and New York, Routledge, 1995.

Zacks, Richard. *History Laid Bare: Love, Sex, and Perversity from the Ancient Etruscans to Warren G. Harding*, New York, HarperCollins Publishers, 1994.

Zamora, Margarita. "Abreast of Columbus: Gender and Discovery," *Cultural Critique*, 17 (1990–91), pp. 127–49.

Zerubavel, Eviatar. *Terra Cognita: The Mental Discovery of America*, New Brunswick, Rutgers University Press, 1992.

Zeyneb Hanoum. *A Turkish Woman's European Impressions*, edited and with an Introduction by Grace Ellison, London, Seeley, Service & Co. Ltd., 1913.

Zonana, Joyce. "The Sultan and the Slave: Feminist Orientalism and the Structure of *Jane Eyre*," in *Revising the Word and the World: Essays in Feminist Literary Criticism*, edited by VèVè A. Clark, Ruth-Ellen B. Joeres, and Madelon Sprengnether, Chicago and London, The University of Chicago Press, 1993, pp. 165–90.

Index